W9-DCC-477

Cabrini College Library

Radnor, Pa.

THE REVOLT OF
THE NETHERLANDS
(1555-1609)

By the Same Author

THE NETHERLANDS IN THE
SEVENTEENTH CENTURY I 1609-1648

THE NETHERLANDS IN THE
SEVENTEENTH CENTURY II 1648–1715

NAPOLEON FOR AND AGAINST

DEBATES WITH HISTORIANS

PIETER GEYL

The Revolt
of the
Netherlands

1555-1609

ERNEST BENN LIMITED
LONDON

149.2
Gey

DJ
156
.G485
1966

#732858

First published 1932 by Williams and Norgate Limited
Second Impression 1945

Published by Ernest Benn Limited
Bouverie House · Fleet Street · London · EC4
Second Edition 1958
Second (Corrected) Impression 1962

Third Impression 1966

© Pieter Geyl, 1958

Printed in Great Britain

CONTENTS

PAGE

PREFACE TO SECOND EDITION   13
PREFACE TO FIRST EDITION   15

INTRODUCTION

I

EARLY NETHERLANDS HISTORY   23

THE NATION AND THE DYNASTY

The seventeen Provinces, 23—By 1609 the disruption
along the line of the rivers had become an accomplished
fact, 24—The linguistic boundary, 25—The Dutch linguistic
area united by a common civilization, but disorganized
politically, 26—The Burgundian Dukes as agents of the
unifying process, 29—Foreign, gallicizing character of their
rule, 30—Clashes between the dynasty and the nation led
by the States-General, 31—Inability of the nation to build
a State without dynastic help, 33.

II

UNDER CHARLES V   35

a. CONTINUED STATE-BUILDING

Charles V inspired by extra-Netherlandish motives, 35—
Yet active in continuing the construction of a unified
Netherlands, 35—Interval of quiet after the conquest of
Gelderland, 1543, 36—Pragmatic sanction about the
succession, 1549, 38—Progressive centralization, 38—
Moderation of the Government, 39.

b. CIVILIZATION   41

The "new drapery" in the Flemish countryside, 41—
Antwerp heir to Brugge, 42—Foreigners in Antwerp
trade, 43—Holland merchant shipping and prosperity, 43
—General prosperity of the Netherlands and high level of
culture, 44—Impossibility of a harmonious civilization, 45
—The "Rhetoricians," 45—Humanism and Renaissance,
46—Architecture and Italianism, 47—Painting, 48—
Pieter Breughel, 49.

Cabrini College Library

41769

Radnor Pa.

PAGE

c. THE DISRUPTION OF CATHOLIC UNITY   50

Ecclesiastical abuses, 50—The Biblical Humanists, 51—
Erasmus; the national element in his figure, 51—Erasmus
at Leuven, 1517-1522, 52—Gradual reform upset by
Luther's action, 53—Biblical Humanism checked, 54—
The Inquisition, 55—Opinion profoundly affected, 56—
Anabaptism and Mennonism, 57—Rise of Calvinism, 58.

d. NATIONAL SENTIMENT   60

Tears at Charles V's farewell, 60—Suspiciousness towards
the ruler, 60—Chief cultural line of demarcation separates
East from West of Netherlands, 61—But is fading, 63—
Centres of cultural movement shifting, 63—Religious
movements cross provincial boundaries, 64—National
consciousness stirring, 64—In so far as it is based on the
State, it does not exclude the Walloons, 65.

THE STRUGGLE FOR INDEPENDENCE AND THE SPLIT

I

THE PRELUDE, 1555-1572   69

a. THE HIGH NOBILITY IN OPPOSITION

Philip continues the tradition of Charles V, 69—Trouble
with the States, 70—The inner-council and the magnates,
70—The new bishoprics, 71—Significance of the plan in
the absolutist and State-building programme, 72—Resistance, 74—The magnates versus Granvelle; his departure
(early 1564), 75—The magnates, 75—Supporters of a
national foreign policy, but at the same time of social and
particularist reaction, 77—Request for mitigation of the
Edicts, 78—Philip commands stricter execution, 78.

b. THE FIRST OUTBURST   79

Calvinism, 79—À Lasco and Utenhove, 80—London and
Emden, 80—Haemstede, 81—Guy de Bray, 82—The
Walloons and the oldest Calvinist organization in the
Netherlands, 82—Increasing hatred of religious persecu-
tion, 83—Commotion after Philip's negative reply, 84—

PAGE

Attitude of the magnates, 84—League of the (lower) Nobility, 85—Personalities and intentions, 85—Divisions among the magnates, 87—The League a manifestation of Netherlands unity, 88—Alarm of the Governess; the "Moderation," 89—"Hedge-sermons," 91—Orange at Antwerp; meeting at St. Truiden, 92—Breaking of the images, August–September, 1566, 92—The "Accord," 23 August, 1566, 94—The movement has lost its national character, 95—Only the Calvinists prepare for armed resistance, 95—Brederode the leader; Orange keeps in the background, 96—Disasters of Watrelos, Lannoy, December 1566, and Oosterweel, April 1567, 97—Orange and Brederode emigrate, 98.

c. THE TYRANNY OF ALVA   99

The triumph of the Governess, 99—Alva sent to replace her, 100—Egmont and Hoorne arrested, 101—The Blood Council, 102—Organized terrorism, 102—Alva's rigour with the towns, 103—The Wild Beggars, 104—Orange; plans and attempts, 104—Heiligerlee, May, Jemmingen, July 1568, 105—Orange across the Maas, October, 106—"Constant in adversity," 108—Alva undertakes the execution of the absolutist programme; the Tenth Penny, 108— Renewed ferment, 109—Orange and the Calvinists, 110— Attempts in 1570, 111—Strategic importance of the northern provinces, 112—The Sea Beggars, 113—Expectations of French assistance, 114—Partition scheme, 1571, 115—Sea Beggars capture The Brill, 1 April, 1572, 116— Extension of Orange's authority in the northern provinces, May–August, 116—Campaign in Brabant fails, August– September, 117.

II

HOLLAND AND ZEALAND IN REVOLT (1572–1576)   119

Subjection of the rebellious towns in the South and in the East, 119—Netherlandish powers of resistance concentrated in Holland and Zealand, 120—Prince's authority established at The Brill, Flushing, Veere, 122—Zierikzee, 3 August, 1572, Middelburg, February 1574, 123—Bossu after the capture of The Brill, 124—Enkhuizen, 27 May, 1572, Northern Quarter, June, 124—Oudewater, 19, Gouda, 21, Dordt, 23, Leyden, 23, Gorcum, 26 June, Haarlem,

8 CONTENTS

3 July; departure of the Spanish troops, 126—The Beggars and the townsfolk, 127—Annoyance over anti-Catholic excesses, 128—Lumey and Orange, 129—Orange's ideal: "the entire fatherland," 130—"Freedom of religions," July 1572; prohibition of the Catholic cult, spring 1573, 130—Protestantization, 131—Amsterdam on the Spanish side, 131—The Haarlem magistrates contemplate submission, 132—Siege of Haarlem, December 1572–July 1573, 133—The Alkmaar magistrates contemplate submission, 134—"At Alkmaar begins victory," October 1573, 135—Louis of Nassau defeated and killed at Mook, 15 April, 1574, 135—Requesens, November 1573–March 1576, 136—Siege and relief of Leyden, 26 May–3 October, 1574, 136—Reconstruction of society in Holland, 138—Peace negotiations of Breda, April–June 1575, 140—Spanish progress, summer–winter 1575–1576, 141—Death of Requesens, collapse of the Spanish administration, 142—The Reformed ascendancy in Holland, 143.

III

"The Entire Fatherland" in Revolt   145

a. Under the Pacification of Ghent

The Spanish mutineers, 145—Popular agitation at Brussels, 145—States-General convoked, September 1576; Aerschot, 146—War with the Spanish troops, 147—Difference between the events of 1576 and of 1572, 148—Pacification of Ghent, 8 November, 1576, 149—Don John of Austria; Eternal Edict, February 1577, 151—Orange incites the other provinces against Don John, 151—Position of Holland and Zealand, 152—Don John surprises the citadel of Namur, 24 July, 1577, 154—Orange and his adherents triumph, 154—Orange called to Brussels, September 1577, 155—Popular pressure on the States at Brussels and Ghent, 157—Constitution imposed on Matthew, 158—Weakness of the Central Government, 159—States' army beaten at Gembloux, 31 January, 1578, 160.

b. Religious Strife and Separate Unions   161

The Reformed dissatisfied with the Pacification, 161—Ghent and Flanders Calvinized, 162—Concern of Orange, 162—The Religious Peace, July 1578; proves no solution, 163—The "Malcontents" in Wallonia, 164—John

Casimir at Ghent, October 1578, 164—Orange loses control
over events, 165—John of Nassau, Stadtholder of Gelder-
land, 166—Holland scheme for a union with Gelderland,
167—John of Nassau presses Gelderland to Union and
Reformation, 168—Draft for the Union altered in a
Reformed sense, 169—Parma invades the Upper Quarter;
Union of Utrecht, 23 January, 1579, 169—Suppression of
Catholicism within the Union, 171—Orange must follow,
172—The Walloon provinces reconciled with the King,
May 1579, 173—Consequences of their secession, 174—
Situation fraught with danger, 175—Catholic discontent
in the North-East, 176—Secession of Rennenberg, March
1580, 177—The alienation of the Catholic majority weakens
the revolt, 178—The line of the ensuing split nevertheless
determined by military and geographical factors, 179.

                          IV
THE SPLIT   181

  a. PARMA'S CONQUESTS, 1580–1589

    Gloomy prospect, 181—Anjou Sovereign, 1581, 182—
    Disappointing campaign of 1581, 183—Allegiance to Philip
    renounced, 184—Progress of Calvinism in Flanders and
    elsewhere, 185—Mutual distrust of Anjou and the Nether-
    landers, 185—Attempts at a stronger central organization;
    the Council of State, 186—Actual dual organization the
    result of twofold strategical problem, 187—Exhaustion and
    impotence of the Government, 187—Ill-success of Anjou's
    government, 188—Unsuccessful *coup d'état*, February
    1583, 189—Resentment against Anjou and unpopularity
    of Orange's conciliatory policy, 190—Treason of Chimay,
    loss of Brugge, May 1584, 191—Wise moderation of
    Parma, 191—Deaths of Anjou, 10 June, and of Orange,
    10 July, 1584, 192—Orange's position and influence,
    193—The States-General persevere, 194—Scheme for
    offering the sovereignty to Henry III of France, 195—
    A Hollander's objections, 195—Loss of Ghent; Henry III
    declines, 196—Treaty with England, 20 August, 1585,
    196—Brussels and Mechlin captured; Nymwegen secedes,
    197—Siege of Antwerp, August 1584–August 1585, 198—
    Marnix's faintheartedness, 199—Emigration from Flan-
    ders and Brabant, 201—The revolt driven back to its last
    line of defence, 201—Parma's position one for further
    attack, 202.

PAGE

b. THE ESTABLISHMENT OF A NORTH NETHERLANDS STATE   203

Leicester made Governor, February 1586, 203—Parties within the rebellion, 203—The "Regents" of Holland and Calvinism, 204—The Libertinists; Coornhert, 205—Struggle between Church and State, 206—Between democracy and oligarchy, between Holland and the Generality, 208—The Flemish and Brabant refugees, 209—Democracy at Utrecht, 210—Edict against trading with the enemy, April 1586, 210—Threat of civil war, 211—Danger of English domination, 212—Deventer and Zutfen betrayed; the States of Holland take control in Leicester's absence, winter 1586–1587, 213—Leicester's return; unsuccessful *coup d'état*, September–October 1587, 214—His resignation, early 1588; order restored, 215—The oligarchic, erastian, decentralized Republic, 215—Preponderant position of Oldenbarnevelt and of Holland, 216.

c. THE CONQUESTS OF MAURICE   217

Favourable changes in the international constellation; the Armada, 217—Philip's interference in French affairs, 218—Maurice and William Louis, 219—The offensive; Breda, 1590; Zutfen, Deventer, Delfzyl, Hulst, Nymwegen, 1591, 220—Steenwyk, Koevorden, 1592, 222—Geertruidenberg, 1593; Groningen, 1594, 222—Governorship of the Archduke Ernest, 1594–1595, 223—Political impotence of the subjected provinces; Aerschot, 224—Triple Alliance, 1596, 225—Grol, Enschedé, Oldenzaal, 1597, 226—Peace of Vervins, 1598, 226—The Catholic clergy in the North, 227—Protestantization of the conquered districts, 228—Priests as ministers, 229—Counter-Reformation in the South, 231—Power the decisive factor in determining the religion of the populations in both North and South, 233.

d. STALEMATE   233

Economic prosperity of Holland and Zealand, 233—The Dunkirk privateers, 235—Expeditions against Spain, 235—East-Indian trade; Houtman accomplishes the first voyage to Java, 1595–1597, 236—Foundation of the United East India Company, 1602, 237—Share of the South Netherlandish immigrants, 238—Misery in the South; Spanish mutineers, 239—Cession of the Netherlands to Albert and Isabella, 1598, 239—Negotiations mooted; correspondence between the Northern and the Southern States, 240—The Southern States ask for a conference, 1600, 242—

Suspicions of the Northerners; plan for an invasion of
Flanders, 243—Maurice and the States, 243—Battle of
Nieuwpoort, June 1600, 244—Negotiations at Bergen-op-
Zoom, 245—Their failure, 246—Impotence of the Southern
States; dissolved by the Archdukes, 246—Siege of Ostend,
1601–1604, 248—Campaigns of Spinola, 1605 and 1606;
war fatigue on both sides, 249.

e. CONCLUSION OF THE TWELVE YEARS' TRUCE, 1606–1609   250

Negotiations at The Hague, 1607–1608, 250—The war
party and Maurice, 251—Motives; fear of Catholic inhabitants, 252—Little thought of a reconquest of the
South, 253—The scheme for a West India Company and
Usselinx, 253—Truce concluded, March 1609, 254—
Position of the Republic; closure of the Scheldt; advanced
posts towards the East, 255—Material and intellectual
decay of the South, 256—The split entailed political
dangers for the North as well, 257—Caused by foreign
force, it was a disaster to the Dutch race as a whole, 258.

V

REVOLUTIONS IN NETHERLANDS CIVILIZATION   260

Renaissance, Reformation, split, 260—Conflict between
Renaissance and Reformation; often unconscious, 261—
The Reformed ministers, 262.

a. BEFORE THE SPLIT   263

Painting, 263—Architecture; Vredeman de Vries, 263—
Literature, 264—Marnix, Coornhert, 265—Beggars' songs,
266—J. B. Houwaert, 267—Lucas de Heere and Jan
van der Noot; the new prosody, 268—Science and
scholarship: Dodoens, Mercator, Ortelius, 269—Plantin,
270—Lipsius and Kilianus, Latinism and the national
language, 271—Historians and grammarians, 272—Lead
of the South; disturbing influence of the war, 274.

b. AFTER THE SPLIT   274

Centre of civilization shifted northward, 274—Civilization
in Holland, however, neither exclusively North Netherlandish nor exclusively Protestant, 275—Painting at
Antwerp; beginnings of the Baroque, 276—Architecture

in the North; Southern influences, 277—Lieven de Key, Hendrik de Keyser, 278—Painting in the North; influence of the immigrants, 279—Resulting variety, 280—Classicism and Van Mander, 280—The boundaries of literature extended; voyages, chronicles, 281—The chroniclers: Bor, Van Meteren, Van Reyd, 282—National confidence; respect for the language, 283—Personalities in literature: Marnix, Coornhert, Van Mander, Spieghel, 284—Van Mander's group; Spieghel's group; the "Chamber of the Eglantine," 285—Leyden University and the Dutch language; Simon Stevin, 286—Renown of the Latinists; Lipsius, Scaliger, 287—Value of the centre of learning for national civilization, 288—Connection through religion; theological quarrels brewing; Arminius, 288—Lipsius' conflict with Coornhert, and his departure, 1591, 290—The academic world and the new nationalism; Douza, Van Hout, Scriverius, 290—Daniel Heinsius, 291—Old and new national sentiment, 292.

SOURCES OF THE QUOTATIONS   295

INDEX   299

LIST OF MAPS

I. THE NETHERLANDS IN 1555   *page* 22

II. THE NEW DIOCESES, 1561   73

III. HOLLAND AND ZEALAND IN 1572   121

IV. THE CONQUESTS OF PARMA, 1578–89   180

V. THE CONQUESTS OF MAURICE, 1590–1606   221

PREFACE TO SECOND EDITION

It is gratifying that twenty-five years after its first appearing in English a third edition of *The Revolt of the Netherlands* should be called for.

As this is to be a photographic reproduction, there is no possibility for anything in the nature of a revision such as one might feel obliged to attempt after so great a lapse of time. Frankly speaking, I do not regret this. The main lines of the story as I traced them in the original work still seem to me entirely convincing. The book is no doubt open to criticism on several points, but the view which inspires it, and which accounts for such importance as it may have, should stand the test in the form it took when I conceived this interpretation.

The historiographical background, a background of years of controversy, I discussed in 1949 in a lecture at Princeton University (repeated in 1952 at Smith College and at Pomona College), which is now published in my volume *Debates with Historians* (Wolters, Groningen; M. Nijhoff, The Hague; Batsford, London, and also Meridian Books, New York).

No systematic revision, therefore; but I must not neglect the opportunity to correct three passages.

One is that in which the coming existence of the linguistic boundary is described (p. 25/6). Much research has been done on that subject since I wrote, and although no complete consensus of opinion has been attained, it has become clear that the Frankish settlement was a longer process, also that it covered a larger area, than I suggested. A summary of recent views will be found in Ch. Verlinder, *Les Origines de la frontière Linguistique et la colonisation franque*, Brussels 1955, and Franz Petri *Zum Stand der Diskussion über die frankische Landnahme und die Entstehung der germanisch—romanischen Sprachgrenze*, Darmstadt, 1954.

Secondly, there is a slip on p. 70 (repeated in the index), where Granvelle is described as President of the Council of State. Through his relations with the Governors and with the King, he did, of course, play a most important part in that body, but Viglius acted as President.

Thirdly on p. 213, the statement that Vrancken, in his famous *Deduction* of 1587, " formulated the thesis of the absolute and independent sovereign right of the States of Holland ", a statement which was in accordance with the view most commonly presented in Dutch historical literature, I have since found to be untenable. In an article in *Bijdragen van de Geschiedenis der Nederlanden*, 1956, I pointed out that on the contrary he laid stress on the representative character of the States assembly. These thirty or forty gentlemen were not the sovereign, so he said, writing on behalf of the States themselves, they were the delegates of the nobility and of the town governments, which latter in their turn represented the commonalty. Now it is true that the commonalty took no part in electing these town governments, whose constitution was purely oligarchic, so that in course of time they were apt to behave as if they were completely sovereign. Yet this official declaration to the effect that their position, and that of the States, was not " independent " but representative remains an important fact. It was remembered all through the period of the Republic by the advocates of popular rights, and especially when two centuries after Vrancken wrote, an active and purposeful burgher democratic party heralded a change of regime.

PIETER GEYL

Harvard University
Cambridge, Mass.,
December, 1957

PREFACE TO FIRST EDITION

The present work is based on my *History of the Netherlandish Race* (*Geschiedenis van de Nederlandsche Stam*), the first volume of which was published by the "Wereldbibliotheek," Amsterdam, early in 1931.

  •   •   •   •   •

The revolt of the Netherlands is of all periods of Netherlands history the most popular in the English-speaking world. This is no doubt largely due to John Lothrop Motley, whose *Rise of the Dutch Republic* was at one time a favourite with the general reading public. Must not another book on a period to which he devoted seven volumes—four of *The United Netherlands*, 1584–1609, in addition to three of the *Rise of the Dutch Republic*, making in all some 3,400 pages—be considered somewhat superfluous? While disclaiming any ambition to supersede a work that will always remain a classic of historical narrative, I may perhaps be permitted to suggest that the difference in point of view between the nineteenth-century American and the twentieth-century Dutchman is considerable enough to warrant a fresh survey of the same events.

To Motley this upheaval was nothing but an illustration of the eternal struggle between right and wrong. To him Catholicism and Absolutism were Powers of Darkness, while Protestantism was one with Liberty, Democracy, and Light. The contest between the Netherlands and Spain is to him a contest between the principles of good and of evil, in which he feels compelled by the most sacred obligations of morality to join, and of course to join on the right side. The modern historian cannot see matters quite like that. It is not that to him no principles are involved in the great struggles of history, nor that his sympathies cannot be engaged on one of the opposing sides. But he knows that the other side, too, must have had its justification, and he will try to explain its position rather than overwhelm it with ridicule and invective. Speaking for myself, the point where I am conscious of the widest divergence from Motley in what I may perhaps call the philosophy of the subject is in the interpretation of Protestantism, which to me is not the radiant message of liberty and progress which it was to the New England Presbyterian; neither can I see in Catholicism merely the wicked system of mental sloth and persecution that it seemed to him. While, therefore, my sympathies are divided where the religious struggle is concerned, I can the more readily come to the conclusion that other issues were at least equally important with the religious, and that other factors had far more influence in determining the event of the contest. My nationality and the age I live in have caused me to devote particular attention to one great problem of which Motley did not even become aware.

Whoever attempts to trace in Motley's volumes the course of the break-up of Netherlands unity and to establish the causes of the failure of the rebellion in the South and of its success in the North, will emerge from his reading completely befogged. The only explanation that might occur to him would be that in Holland and Zealand Protestants were much more numerous than in the other provinces, and especially than in the South—a conclusion that would be quite wrong in fact. Yet Motley makes this statement in the most extreme form imaginable.[1] It is impossible to indicate in a few brief sentences what is involved for the interpretation of Netherlands history in this tremendous fact—which apparently remained hidden from Motley—that Protestants were only a minority in Holland and Zealand, and not less numerous in Flanders and Brabant. The truth is that Motley, while carrying on his impassioned polemics against Granvelle, Alva, Parma, and above all Philip II, and while enthusiastically putting the case for William the Silent's greatness as a champion of Protestantism, Liberty, and Democracy, was so little interested in the problems of Netherlands history that he never took the trouble to get up the necessary information about them.

It is a most significant fact that Motley ended his first book with the death of William the Silent.[2] The Prince was assassi-

[1] E.g. *Rise of the Dutch Republic*, iii. 4.
[2] The observation was made as early as 1862 by the great Dutch historian Fruin: *Verspreide Geschriften*, iii. 126. Motley's faulty composition was

nated at one of the most critical moments of the rebellion, when the fate of Ghent and Brabant was hanging in the balance. Yet not a word does Motley say about the situation in which his hero left the country, or on the issue of the great decisions that were then pending. Moreover, in his preface he commits himself to the statement that "the final separation of territory into independent and obedient provinces, into the Commonwealth of the United States and the Belgian provinces of Spain, was in reality effected by William the Silent." One hesitates to say which is the more amazing, the assertion that William the Silent was responsible for the loss of Flanders and Brabant, a disaster which he strove to avert with all his might, or the belief that the separation had already been consummated at the moment of the Prince's death. When in his sequel, *The United Netherlands*, Motley attempts a summing-up of the situation which he had left in the air at the conclusion of his first great work, he perpetrates a passage[1] full of the most startling confusions and inaccuracies of geography and chronology, which, moreover, proves once again his inability to rid his mind of the contemporary dual state system of Holland and Belgium. He "assumes, for general purposes," that Holland and Belgium had already sprung into existence at a moment when the permanent division along those exact lines could not possibly have been foreseen. He looks upon the emergence of the two modern countries as a foregone conclusion without even noticing how profoundly the situation he is describing differs from that which resulted from many more years of war. It is small wonder that this attitude of mind—which, let me add, has long been common among Dutch and Belgian historians as well—has prevented him from offering any explanation of what in reality was a long and complicated process.

Motley's work will survive the exposition of many more glaring errors and grievous shortcomings. Nor have I the slightest wish to attempt killing it. All I have wanted to make

nevertheless copied by the Rev. G. Edmundson in the *Cambridge Modern History*; his chapter on the first stage of the revolt is actually entitled "William the Silent." [1] I. 9.

clear by these observations is the reason for my belief that there ought to be room in English historical literature for a modern version of what must still be regarded as one of the most important events in modern European history.

.   .   .   .   .

Some explanation is required of my use of certain geographical names. The appellations current to describe the Low Countries, or parts of them, and their inhabitants, have fallen into a chaotic confusion which is a reflection of their chequered history, but which compels the historian to introduce some system of his own if he wants to convey clear impressions to the minds of his readers.

Netherlands: the entire seventeen provinces owing allegiance to Philip II on his accession (see Map I). Nowadays *Netherlands* is the official name of the North Netherlandish State; in this work the word is not used in that restricted sense.

Netherlandish: (*a*) appertaining to the whole of the Netherlands; (*b*) appertaining to the Germanic population of the Netherlands, and especially to their language. The linguistic boundary, north of which *Netherlandish* or *Dutch* and south of which French is spoken, is indicated by a line on each of the maps included in this volume. The use of the word *Netherlandish* in this restricted sense is common in the language itself, which the Northerner generally calls *Hollandsch* and the Southerner *Vlaamsch* (Flemish), but for which both have the official name of *Nederlandsch* (a word first used for the language about the middle of the sixteenth century, and in Flanders). When, however, a distinction is made between Netherlanders of Germanic and of Romance speech, there are obvious disadvantages attached to the use of the word *Netherlandish* to denote the Germanic part, and although I have not been able to do without it altogether, I have more commonly used *Dutch*, a word which presents problems of its own.

Dutch: appertaining to the Germanic population of the Netherlands. In modern English parlance *Dutch* means: appertaining to the population of the Northern Netherlands (commonly called Holland). In this work that use of the word is strictly avoided. There is complete historic justification for the application of the word to the wider area. Etymologically *Dutch* is the same word as *Duitsch* (*Deutsch*), which down to the seventeenth century was used by the Germanic Netherlanders themselves to indicate their own language; to-day in their parlance the word means German. (In the sixteenth century a distinction was beginning to be made between *Nederduitsch*—Dutch—and *Hoogduitsch*—German.) In any case *Duitsch* was never restricted to northern Netherlandish; neither was the dialectical variant *Dietsch* (see p. 28), which on the contrary is used to-day to denote more particularly the unity of race and language embracing Germanic Netherlanders of the North and of the South (Hollanders and Flemings, as modern usage has it). The word *Dutch* has been used in this work as an equivalent of *Dietsch*; and also commonly to indicate the language spoken by Hollanders and Flemings, which in that language itself would nowadays be called *Nederlandsch*.

Holland: the county on the shore of the North Sea, bounded by Zealand on the South, Gelderland, Utrecht, and the Zuider Zee on the East (see Map I). The modern usage by which the name is made to apply to the whole of the Northern Netherlands is strictly avoided in this work.

Hollander: inhabitant of the county of Holland.

Flanders: the county on the shore of the North Sea bounded by Zealand on the North, Brabant on the East, Walloon Flanders and Artois on the South (see Map I). The modern use of the name to indicate the whole of the Dutch-speaking part of Belgium is strictly avoided in this work.

Flemish: appertaining to the county of Flanders. *Flemish* (*Vlaamsch*) was commonly used by the inhabitants of the county to indicate their language, just as the Hollanders called their language *Hollandsch*. Foreigners, Italians, Frenchmen, Englishmen, often used the word in the sense of *Nederlandsch*, or *Dutch*, making, for instance, a Brabander or a Hollander speak *Flemish*. In modern times *Vlaamsch* is commonly used to describe the language, officially *Nederlandsch*, spoken in the whole of the Germanic part of Belgium. These uses are strictly avoided in this work.

Fleming: inhabitant of the county of Flanders.

•   •   •   •   •

I have found it impossible to conform to the English custom of calling all western continental towns by French names; it is utterly senseless to speak of *Bruges, Courtrai, Bois-le-Duc, Treves,* or *Aix-la-Chapelle.* Except, therefore, when there are true English names in current use, like Mechlin (instead of Mechelen), Antwerp (instead of Antwerpen), The Hague (instead of Den Haag), I have used the native names (Brugge, Kortryk, 's-Hertogenbosch, Trier, Aachen).

A list of these names for the Dutch-speaking area with the French translations in the second column is here inserted.

Aalst	*Alost*
Belle	*Bailleul*
Brugge	*Bruges*
Den Bosch or 's-Hertogenbosch	*Bois-le-Duc*
Dendermonde	*Termonde*
Grevelingen	*Gravelines*
Kortryk	*Courtrai*
(River) Leie	*Lys*
Leuven	*Louvain*
(River) Maas	*Meuse*
Meenen	*Menin*
St. Truiden.	*St. Trond*
St. Winoksbergen	*Berghes St. Winox*
Sluis	*l'Ecluse*
Tienen, Thienen	*Tirlemont*
Veurne	*Furnes*

References to the sources of the quotations from contemporary texts will be found at the back, as also a general note on sources and historical literature.

My thanks are due to Mr. S. T. Bindoff, B.A.(Lond.), and Mr. W. D. Robson-Scott, M.A.(Oxon.), for their kindness in reading through my manuscript and suggesting corrections of my English; also to my son, W. F. Geyl, for designing the maps.

P. G.

INTRODUCTION

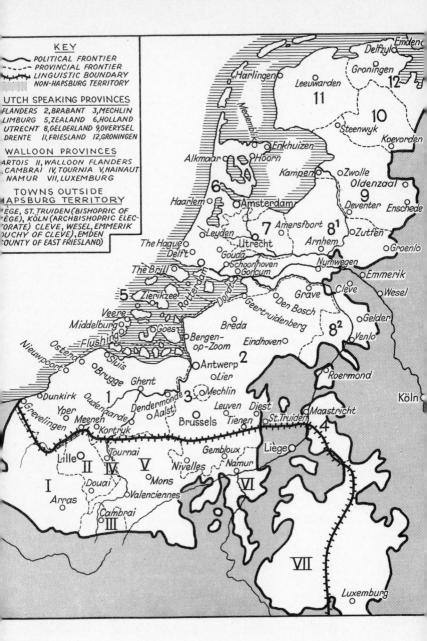

KEY
— POLITICAL FRONTIER
--- PROVINCIAL FRONTIER
⌁ LINGUISTIC BOUNDARY
▨ NON-HAPSBURG TERRITORY

UTCH SPEAKING PROVINCES
FLANDERS 2,BRABANT 3,MECHLIN
LIMBURG 5,ZEALAND 6,HOLLAND
UTRECHT 8,GELDERLAND 9,OVERYSEL
DRENTE II,FRIESLAND 12,GRONINGEN

WALLOON PROVINCES
ARTOIS II, WALLOON FLANDERS
CAMBRAI IV,TOURNAI V,HAINAUT
NAMUR VII, LUXEMBURG

TOWNS OUTSIDE
HAPSBURG TERRITORY
ÈGE, ST. TRUIDEN (BISHOPRIC OF
ÈGE), KÖLN (ARCHBISHOPRIC ELEC-
ORATE) CLEVE, WESEL, EMMERIK
OUCHY OF CLEVE), EMDEN
OUNTY OF EAST FRIESLAND)

MAP I THE NETHERLANDS IN 1555

I

EARLY NETHERLANDS HISTORY

When Charles V transferred the government of the Netherlands to his son Philip in 1555, delegates of seventeen provinces of varying size and importance composed the assembly of the States-General at Brussels, before which both the old ruler and the new appeared. In the course of Philip's reign practically the whole of this country rose in revolt, but only the seven northern provinces, situated beyond the great rivers that run out into the North Sea, succeeded in establishing their independence. An eighty years' war had to be waged before this independence was unreservedly recognized by Philip's second successor. In the later stages of this war the seven United Netherlands had taken by force of arms certain portions of the adjoining provinces, where in the meantime Spanish rule had been restored. During the lifetime of the Netherlands Republic these districts were administered as subject territory under the name of Generality Lands. To-day the seven provinces and the one-time Generality Lands south of the rivers constitute the Kingdom of the Netherlands, to which certain additional districts in the East, on the Maas, were joined in 1839. The provinces in which Philip II, with the resources at his disposal as King of Spain, succeeded in putting down the revolt, shorn of the acquisitions of the Dutch Republic and of the Dutch Kingdom in the North, of the conquests of Louis XIV in the South-West, of the larger part of Luxemburg in the South-East, but with the addition of the Bishopric of Liège, after centuries of subjection to successive foreign masters and after a short-lived reunion with the Northern Netherlands, form the Kingdom of Belgium as we know it to-day.

When the Twelve Years' Truce was concluded between the Dutch Republic and Spain in 1609, the issue had in its main lines been decided. It was certain that the North was to be free and Protestant, and that it was to be separated from the South, which returned to Catholicism and to submission under foreign rule. We shall therefore, in our account of the war from the beginning of Philip II's reign to the Twelve Years' interval, be reviewing the complete course of events in which some of the most fundamental problems of Netherlands history have their setting. What is the explanation of the partial success, as well as of the partial failure, of the revolt? In how far was the revolt a national one? In how far was its inspiration religious? Was the emergence of a Protestant North and a Catholic South in accordance with the aspirations of the populations concerned, or was it due to factors of a different nature? Was there, at the beginning of Philip's reign, a national consciousness embracing all the Netherlands, or was the specifically Northern consciousness, which acquired so undeniable a reality after the separation, really in being before it occurred? These are some of the questions that will have to be faced as our account of the events between 1555 and 1609 is developed.

But before ringing up the curtain on that great drama it will be necessary to examine the stage on which it was soon to be performed. We must know something of the peoples living in the Netherlands, their races and languages, their economic conditions, their religious outlook, their political and cultural traditions rooted in their medieval history. We must know something of the ruling dynasty, which had created a political unit of the seventeen provinces—in so far as they can be called a political unit. For the clash between the tendencies represented by the dynasty and the forces living in the people was more than the usual conflict between sixteenth-century monarchy—authoritarian, levelling, centralizing, modernizing—and the love of particular rights, the tenacity of vested interests, the conservative libertarianism characteristic of feudal society. What gives it a distinctive colour is that this dynasty was of alien origin and had lately become even more estranged from the Netherlands. The monarchy is to be regarded as an independent entity, superimposed upon the rich and varied life of the Netherlands community; and its age-old traditions need to be studied by themselves.

At the outset one great fact claims our attention. It is that in the seventeen Netherlands two races and two civilizations met. By far the larger part of the country was inhabited by a population of Low-Germanic origin and speech. In the southern fringe of provinces, however, in the so-called Walloon area—that is in Artois, Walloon Flanders (Lille, Orchies, and Douai), Tournai, Hainaut, Namur, as also in the southernmost district of Brabant (Nivelles) and in the western half of Luxemburg—French was spoken. Trace a line, starting from the North Sea shore in the neighbourhood of Grevelingen,[1] following the rivers Aa and Leie,[2] then, from a point several miles south of Kortryk,[3] continuing in an easterly direction and crossing the Maas[4] several miles south of Maastricht. That line is the linguistic boundary, north of which French was in the position of a foreign language. This, indeed, is still in the main the position to-day. For many centuries that boundary has hardly moved, so that it still cuts off the northern corner of France and divides Belgium in two almost equal halves. North of it only the towns in the Flemish district annexed by Louis XIV (as for instance, Dunkirk and Belle[5]) and Brussels have in varying degrees become gallicized.

The origin of this line of demarcation can be exactly indicated. It sprang into being at the time of the great Germanic migrations, in the sixth century, when the people of the Franks, coming from the East, out of the obscure depths of Germania, broke through the Rhine frontier of the crumbling Roman Empire. The country north of the rivers had already for a long time been inhabited by Germanic tribes, some of whom had entertained close relations with the Romans and had undergone their influence very deeply. South of the rivers, too, there were numerous Germanic settlements, although the substratum of the population was probably still Celtic. Incessant raids from

[1] Grevelingen: in French—*Gravelines*.
[2] Leie: in French—*Lys*.
[3] Kortryk: in French—*Courtrai*.
[4] Maas: in French—*Meuse*.
[5] Belle: in French—*Bailleul*.

the East had in any case so far devastated this region that large stretches were practically empty when the Franks, crossing the rivers Ysel, Rhine, Waal, and Maas, poured down into the valleys of the Scheldt and the Leie. In the course of not very many years they seem to have settled pretty densely most of the land down to the line which still divides the languages. Meantime their most renowned chiefs went on and subjected the Romanized country of Gaul south of that line, which, being more densely populated and more highly organized, succeeded in absorbing their numerous scattered settlements.

Two more Germanic tribes helped to compose the population of the Netherlands north of the linguistic boundary—the Frisians and the Saxons; but it was the Franks who, under the Merovingian Kings and their successors, the Carolingians, created the first political organization in which the whole region found a place, and it was their language that became the expression of its unity. The original area of Frankish settlement stretched over Flanders and Brabant (to use the names of a slightly later date which are still current) right across the rivers into Utrecht and the Veluwe up to the River Ysel. East of that river was Saxon country as far as Friesland and the Ommelands of Groningen, where on the shores of the North Sea the Frisians had their home. At the time of the great Frankish irruption, Holland and Zealand were already settled, but probably very thinly, by Frisians and Saxons. At a very early date, at any rate, that coastal region—with the exception of the small northern part of Holland which long retained the name of West-Friesland—became completely franconized, so that it was differentiated by its language from the northern Frisian as well as from the eastern Saxon areas, while being assimilated to the Frankish territory of Flanders, Brabant, western Gelderland, and Utrecht.

On the basis of linguistic unity there soon arose a common civilization, but political unity proved harder to achieve. In fact, the development of a Netherlands nation and a Netherlands state was from the start seriously impeded by the brilliant career which the leaders of the Frankish race made for themselves in Gaul. Their rise to greatness in that land of superior civilization divorced their interests from those of the bulk of their people, who had stayed behind to settle outlying regions—as they seemed to the dwellers on the Seine and the Loire—on the other side of the Ardennes and by the North Sea. In the large empire of the Merovingians and of the Carolingians after them, of which the centre of power lay among the inheritors of the Roman tradition, the backward and leaderless Netherlands could not attain to any individual status. Not even their unity was respected in the divisions which the successors of Charlemagne arranged amongst themselves. When the Middle Kingdom of Lotharius had come to the end of its brief career and the French Kingdom and the Holy Roman Empire of the German nation were left facing each other, their frontier in the North followed the Scheldt right across the Frankish area. Flanders, as the country between the Scheldt and the North Sea was now called, owed allegiance to the King of France; all the rest of the Germanic Netherlands, with a large slice of Walloon land, belonged to the German Empire. These distant parts proved fertile soil for feudal principalities, which became practically independent when the power of the French Kings, and afterwards that of the Emperors, declined. Soon the Netherlands were a chaos of petty states, each pursuing a territorial policy of its own and eternally at war amongst themselves. Flanders, while taking a strenuous part in the general *mêlée* of feudal anarchy, was from the middle of the twelfth century subjected to formidable attempts on the part of the French Kings to restore their authority over it. The French Kings were then building up a powerful state, and it was only the unexpected popular strength of the great Flemish towns, Brugge[1] and Ghent, that defeated their attempts on Flanders, and, in saving the Germanic character of the most exposed region, at the same time prevented the French Kings from replacing the imperial authority in the other Netherlands by their own. What the French monarchy failed to achieve, however, was later effected by a branch of their royal house, which derived its power from purely French possessions.

Long before the rise of Burgundian power united most of

[1] Brugge: in French—*Bruges*.

the feudal principalities of the originally Frankish area in a political structure, that area was the scene of a distinctive Netherlandish civilization. The great thirteenth-century poet Maerlant, for instance, covered practically the whole of it with his attention and his influence. Himself a Fleming, he composed a wider literary language, which he called *Dietsch*. He enjoyed the protection of the Count of Holland. He addressed some of his finest lyrical poems to ecclesiastics of Utrecht. His truest and ablest follower was a Brabander. At the same time, from this originally Frankish nucleus, political forces of various description stretched eastward, tending to withdraw the adjoining regions from participating in the political and cultural life of Germany. The East-Frankish country on the Maas was drawn into the orbit of Netherlands life by the union of the Duchy of Limburg with the Duchy of Brabant. The Saxon and Frisian country immediately to the north and east of the Frankish land had had special relations with it ever since the diocese of Utrecht had been formed under the immediate pressure of the Merovingian Kings. The town of Utrecht and the surrounding district and even Overysel and the town of Groningen long recognized the Bishop not merely as their spiritual but as their secular overlord, while at an early stage the episcopal see itself had fallen under the political influence of the Counts of Holland. Holland, too, tenaciously attempted to subdue Friesland, and long before—in the sixteenth century—actual political victory was achieved, Frisian language and civilization had begun to give way to Frankish influence, of which Holland was the agent. That some generations after Maerlant's death there existed a wider area of cultural affinity appears from nothing so strikingly as from the great religious movement of the Modern Devotion which, started towards the end of the fourteenth century by Geert Groote of Deventer, who was himself deeply influenced by Ruusbroec, the Brabant mystic, spread over all the Netherlands; the Brethren of the Common Life and their schools were a powerful factor in moulding the spiritual and intellectual outlook of the urban middle class, ever the most fertile of Netherlandish civilization. The Modern Devotion, in fact, also penetrated eastward into the Saxon regions of Westphalia, which never became incorporated with the Netherlands state such as the Burgundian and Habsburg rulers fashioned it. The truth is that there was not on that side any natural racial or linguistic boundary, and that the exact line which in the end came to separate the Netherlands from Germany was the result of political accident.

In the fourteenth century it was becoming clear that the days of extreme feudal confusion were counted. The only question was by whose agency would some sort of larger unity be achieved. Owing to the desertion of the Merovingian Kings, who had gone to seek world power in Gaul, there was not in the Netherlands any such old historic principle of union as was provided by the kingship in France or by the imperial idea in Germany. The four most powerful Netherlands princes, the Count of Flanders, the Duke of Brabant and Limburg, the Duke of Gelderland, the Count of Holland and Zealand (who was also Count of the Walloon country of Hainaut), balanced each other so nicely that it was quite impossible for any of them to raise himself to a position of supremacy. The great European rulers, however, all kept their eyes on that unstable region, whose wealthy towns, trade, and geographical position would inevitably bestow eminent power on its possessor. In spite of the efforts of German Emperors and Kings of England, it was the French family of the Dukes of Burgundy that won. They were descended from a King's younger son, and at first fully supported by the monarchy. In 1378 they acquired Flanders, and soon afterwards got a hold on Brabant. Holland, Zealand, and Hainaut fell to them before 1430, while with Luxemburg and other Walloon provinces they rounded off their Netherlands possessions.

If at first they had been able to use the French monarchy for their own purposes, soon, under Philip the Good, they came into open conflict with the country of their origin, and their design to found an independent state on the flank of France stood revealed. Charles the Bold pursued the policy of his father with a reckless ambition all his own. In the state as as it grew under him the Dutch-speaking Netherlands (though

B

still without the Saxon and Frisian provinces) were all united. Not only, however, was French the language of the dynasty and of the leading class of nobles and officials formed by it, but the Netherlandish country was linked up with a jumble of French and German lands with which no union on a sound national basis was conceivable. The inspiration of the Duke's feverish scheming was purely dynastic, and his ambitions were carrying him ever farther away from the Netherlands when he was overtaken by the disaster for which his great enemy, Louis XI, the King of France, had been waiting. The crisis into which Charles the Bold's death in 1477 threw the Burgundian state permanently altered its composition. More than half of the French possessions were detached from it, the Duchy of Burgundy among them; the County of Burgundy, Franche Comté, a French-speaking fief of the Empire, remained under Charles's daughter and heiress, but the possibility of bridging the wide gap separating it from the *pays de par deçà*—as the Northern possessions were called—grew very remote. The Burgundian state became essentially a Netherlands state. With the Dutch-speaking provinces a number of Walloon provinces remained united, but Flanders and Brabant, owing to their wealth and the economic importance of their great industrial and trading towns, were now the true centre of gravity once more.

This is not to say that the dynasty became nationalized in the Dutch-speaking part of the country. Charles's daughter, in the hour of her distress, had married the Emperor's son Maximilian of Habsburg; but German though he was, he readily adopted the Burgundian dynastic tradition, and spent the energy and resources of his wife's, and after her early death of his son's, subjects in senseless wars to recover the lost French possessions. It was to be no less true for the Habsburg period which he opened than for the Burgundian period which had come to a close that a principal factor of Netherlands history was the lack of national solidarity between rulers and ruled. Founded by foreigners, the Netherlands state continued to be ruled by foreigners. All along the princes, whose work for the building up of a Netherlands nationality looms so large

in the eyes of history, pursued other aims which had no connection with Netherlands interests whatever and which could
not but render the whole of their policy suspect in the eyes of
the people. In the revolts with which the great Dukes had had
to deal, especially from the unruly and formidable towns of
Flanders, the contrast between modern equalitarian administration and medieval urban exclusivism and particularism had
always been embittered by the difference of nationality. When
they wanted to ingratiate themselves with the men of Ghent
or of Brugge, the Dukes knew perfectly how to speak Dutch.
When they wreaked their vengeance, when they chastised and
humiliated, the language that made the Flemings tremble
was always French.

No doubt the Burgundians, like the Habsburgs after them,
did much to make the Netherlands people become politically
conscious of their nationality. An indispensable preliminary to
this development was that the resistance of provincial and
municipal particularism should be broken down, and that at
any rate was what their rule began if it did not complete it.
The bureaucracy which they created, instead of being swayed
by purely local interests, envisaged the country as a whole.
They raised up a high nobility which was similarly free from
provincial prejudices. Philip the Good's institution of the Order
of the Golden Fleece was a stroke of genius; it was remarkably
successful in giving a national outlook to the magnates who
were employed as Stadtholders of provinces or in the Prince's
Council. Philip, too, and Charles the Bold after him, had
accustomed the privileged classes—clergy, nobility, and urban
magistrates—of the various provinces to meeting each other
for the purpose of granting subsidies on a quota system: the
assembly of delegates from the various provincial States
(States being the name of the assembly of Estates in each
province) was called the States-General, and it was a most
potent means for developing a common political consciousness,
the effects of which were somewhat disconcerting to the
Dukes.

For they had done all this, not in order to develop the
Netherlands nation in accordance with its inherent qualities

and dumbly groping aspirations, but in order to make it more amenable to their own dynastic ambitions. The bureaucracy, the high nobility, the court, which the Dutch-speaking Nether-lands owed to them, were very largely French. And though they educated the Dutch-speaking Netherlands to the political union for which an unkind history had done nothing to prepare them, at the same time they connected them with a number of Walloon provinces, which, by strengthening the class and official position of the French language in the whole of the country, helped to corrupt their civilization. Moreover, if on the death of Charles the Bold most of the more distant provinces were lopped off, by the marriage of his daughter with the Habsburg Archduke a link was forged with even more remote interests, to which the rulers too frequently subordinated those of the Netherlands.

Small wonder, then, that the Netherlands union which they had helped to bring about turned against them on the first opportunity, and that they soon found the States-General, which they had instituted for the convenience of their financial administration, facing them in a hostile mood as the personifi-cation of the Netherlands people. Under Charles the Bold the political classes of the whole country had already realized their community of interests as against the grasping dynasticism of the ruler. But under him dissatisfaction was still countered by fear. On the accession of the helpless Maria, however, and again some years later, when after her early death Maximilian held the regency for their son Philip the Fair, there were violent attempts to subject monarchical rule to some sort of national control. It is true that these outbreaks of anti-dynastic opposi-tion were most effective in so far as they appeared in provincial forms, and in any case they were responsible for a recrudes-cence of the old particularist spirit. Nevertheless the idea of Netherlands unity had already obtained so much hold over men's minds that in no province, either in 1477 or from 1482 to 1490, was the continuance of the association with the others called into question, except—significant exception!—that the Flemings not only resented Maximilian's attempts to win back the French-speaking regions lost in 1477, but even, according to Commines, would fain have seen their ruler lose what still remained to him of Walloon subjects.

One thing, nevertheless, is made very clear in the critical times through which the Burgundian monarchy passed after Charles the Bold's death—namely, that to build up a firm political structure in opposition to the dynastic policy of the alien ruler was an undertaking that surpassed the forces of the Netherlands people. A groping towards national consciousness there was, and this was beginning to acquire a political significance. But the guidance of a dynasty which could appeal to the medieval feeling of loyalty was as indispensable in the case of the Netherlands as it was in that of any other European nation at that time, when most of the national states were being finally established. The tragedy of Netherlands history was that the dynasty called to this great task never lost its alien character and always pursued objects not only foreign but inimical to the cause of Netherlands nationality. Yet when the nation rose against its rulers, at once centrifugal tendencies appeared which, even though no conscious intention in that direction existed, jeopardized the newly established union of the provinces. In the struggle with Maximilian especially, Flanders, for all its ancient distrust of France, was inevitably driven to look for support in that quarter—a much more dangerous diversion in its case than in that of Gelderland, which also fraternized with the enemy of Habsburg, but which was situated at a safe distance from his territories. In suppressing the rebellion of Flanders, therefore, Maximilian, like the Burgundian dukes before him, unwittingly worked for the future of Netherlandish nationality, to which the reabsorption of Flanders by France would have been the gravest of blows.

For a time the dynasty and the nation seemed to have become really reconciled. When after a devastating war, in which the remnant of a Holland noblemen's party had made common cause with the urban opposition of Flanders, peace had been restored by Maximilian's German commander, Albert of Saxony, when Ghent had been made to feel the ruler's heavy hand as roughly as at any time in its stormy history, the whole collection of provinces, Dutch and Walloon, was in 1492 handed over undiminished to Philip the Fair, just growing into manhood. A sharp reaction manifested itself in favour of the monarchy, the restorer of order, the guardian of unity. Philip the Fair, free from the unpopularity that hung around his father as the foreign inspirer of Albert of Saxony's brutality, was hailed as a true native-born prince, the inaugurator of a happy period of peace.

Philip the Fair, it is true, was born and bred in the Dutch-speaking Netherlands, at Ghent and Mechlin. Yet not only was he surrounded by the Walloon nobility with which Philip the Good had filled the Order of the Golden Fleece and which had ever since grown in wealth and prestige, but he was the ruler who by his marriage to a daughter of Ferdinand of Arragon and Isabella of Castile prepared that unnatural connection of the Netherlands with Spain which was to lead to such disastrous results. He died young, before the destinies of his house had come to their full blossoming, but although his son Charles V, grown up at Ghent, was likewise regarded by the Netherlanders with affection as one belonging to themselves, he was nevertheless heir to that immense, multi-national empire, in which the Netherlands were no doubt one of the most valuable assets, but in which interests hostile to theirs too frequently directed policy.

UNDER CHARLES V

a. CONTINUED STATE-BUILDING

In two respects especially does it strike the observer how little
relation there was between the policy of the ruler and either
the mind or the interests of the nation. Charles V was faced
by the great religious upheaval that shook the ancient Catholic
unity of Europe and by which the Netherlands, as we shall
see, were profoundly affected. The severe repression with
which he met this crisis was far from being in accordance
with the temper of the Netherlands people. It was dictated
by what he thought was due to his position as the Holy Roman
Emperor, by the fanaticism of his Spanish advisers, by all
sorts of extra-Netherlandish considerations which made it
inevitable that he should throw in his fate with the South-
European Papal Church.

In the second place it is obvious that the wars he waged
with France throughout his reign were no more inspired by
Netherlands interests than had been the case with those of
his grandfather Maximilian, and as a matter of fact they were
no more popular. More than once the States became a little
restive under the repeated demands for more money that were
pressed upon them, and the war policy of the Government
always helped to keep alive in them that suspiciousness which
made them cling to their local privileges as the safeguards
against arbitrary power.

Yet here it must be admitted that this policy, even though
its inspiration was partly Spanish and partly German and all
the time dynastic, both directly and indirectly advanced the
formation of a potential Netherlandish state begun by Charles's
forebears. First of all Francis I was forced to renounce the
ancient suzerainty of his crown over Flanders. This, while it
prevented the Flemings from sheltering any longer behind the
Parliament of Paris against the encroachments of their for-

midable ruler's power, meant the elimination of a very old danger to Netherlands unity, which as recently as Maximilian's days had shown its actuality. At the same time it was really in pursuance of his feud with France that Charles extended Habsburg rule over those regions in the North-East whose continuously threatened independence had been temporarily reprieved when Charles the Bold's death threw the affairs of the monarchy into confusion. It is curious to observe that the States of those provinces which were most concerned owing to their contiguity, Brabant and Holland, never manifested much eagerness for the wars undertaken to subdue those regions. Yet Gelderland, Groningen, and Friesland, although largely non-Frankish, had always been in the closest contact with the Frankish Netherlands, and, once subdued, were destined to form an integral part of the Netherlandish nation. The state-building impulse was feeble in the Netherlanders, who had never been able to recognize themselves in their rulers. As for Charles, he was especially determined to have those provinces because, having been galvanized into action by the redoubtable Duke of Gelderland, Charles of Egmont, they now constituted a dangerous threat in his rear, the more dangerous through their alliance with his lifelong enemy Francis I. One by one they were conquered in a series of little wars, which were nevertheless exhausting and devastating, and which extended over a period of some twenty years, until in 1543 Gelderland itself was added as the seventeenth province under Habsburg rule. It was more than a century and a half since Flanders, more than a century since Brabant, Holland, and Zealand had fallen to the Burgundian Dukes.

The conquest of Gelderland was followed by an interval of quiet. Not that there was any inherent finality about it. East-Friesland and Cleve were both as deeply mixed up in the affairs of the provinces now conquered as these had been in the affairs of Holland and Brabant; they were indistinguishable from them in language and civilization; Cleve, moreover, was now enclosed on three sides by Habsburg territory. It might have been supposed that these regions would be the next to be swallowed, as soon as the latest acquisitions had been digested by the Habsburg system and appetite rose afresh. It was the revolt and the split which checked the eastward advance and caused the Burgundian Circle, such as Charles V created it in 1548, to wear in our eyes the appearance of a thing completed, of a thing expanded to its natural limits. Yet if the eastern frontier which Charles V traced has become the line of demarcation between the Netherlandish and German peoples, this is due to no inner necessity, but to the apparently arbitrary course of political events.

A breathing-space was badly needed, and that not only on account of the devastations which the war had caused in the new provinces and in Holland and Brabant. Force had been the decisive factor in the acquisition of all these new lands. In most cases, no doubt a few leading personages, or a few towns, had previously come to an understanding with the powerful Emperor, and always the contest had been concluded by treaties in which the provinces obtained recognition of their ancient constitutions in exchange for their acceptance of the new prince. Nevertheless time was required, after so protracted a resistance, before the leading classes of these several provinces could accustom themselves to Habsburg rule. No less troublesome were the inter-provincial feuds which the period of unrest had intensified—between Gelderland and Holland and Brabant—between Holland and Utrecht, between Groningen and Friesland.

It may seem surprising that in spite of all these weaknesses the achievement of the Habsburger has nevertheless proved to be so enduring. Yet there is nothing miraculous in this. Long ago the Burgundian Dukes had been greatly assisted in extending their authority over the southern and western Netherlands by the weakening of the particularist principle of the feudal age. The violence with which it had asserted itself once more in the North-East had at the same time exhausted it. Even the turbulent noblemen who had revelled in the guerilla warfare had enough of it for the time being. Submission to the powerful ruler seemed to be the only safeguard against a renewal of the intolerable anarchy which had ruined the country. Thus it was without much difficulty that

Charles in 1549 carried a most important measure which was calculated to consolidate Habsburg rule in the Netherlands even more than the formation of the Burgundian Circle. In all provinces the States assemblies and towns swore fealty to their future prince, his son Philip, who had come over from Spain, while at the same time they ratified a uniform regulation of the succession, a Pragmatic Sanction as it was called, notwithstanding such ancient privileges and customs as might conflict therewith. This was intended to obviate the danger lest differences of opinion should arise at any time as to the succession, or that any provinces, owing to divergent law in this matter, should become separated from the others. The Governess, Maria of Hungary, had previously sought the opinion of the Great Council of Mechlin upon the question whether the Emperor were competent to regulate the succession for his descendants in this way. The Council returned a characteristic reply:

We do not entertain any doubt but that His Majesty may arrange this affair. The measure not only is in accordance with law and reason, but it is founded on the important and inestimable advantage which by preventing dissensions and wars (by which otherwise they might be visited) it will bring to these provinces and subjects.

This utterance deserves to be called characteristic because in it are indicated the principles which inspired the entire policy of the Burgundian-Habsburg rulers in the Netherlands. Against the ancient privileges of provinces and towns, classes and groups—against tradition, in fact—they appealed to law and reason, to the common weal. Under Charles V and Philip II the monarchy was no less eager to reform than it had been under Philip the Good and Charles the Bold, and it still found its principal assistants in lawyers and officials who assailed the usages handed down from former generations with rulings derived from Roman Law and common sense.

In each new province organs of the prince's authority were established, after the usual pattern: Court of Justice, Chamber of Accounts, Stadtholder. Moreover, the central administration was organized anew. In 1531 a famous "Ordinance," expressing the tendency towards specialization which had long manifested itself in the Prince's Council, created three Councils in order to assist the Governess. The Secret Council, which dealt with matters of justice, and the Council of Finance were composed mainly of "long-robed men," while the magnates sat on the Council of State, which was consulted on matters of general policy.

These magnates were at the same time employed as Stadtholders in the several provinces. Moreover, the Order of the Golden Fleece, to which most of them belonged, still possessed the right of counselling the prince on matters of state. The high nobility thus occupied an important position in the Burgundian-Habsburg polity, and this position was one of general, not merely of provincial or local, significance. Even in the capacity of Stadtholders, for all the independence with which they were allowed to act, they still represented central authority, and as a rule a nobleman did not fill the Stadtholder's office in his native province or in the province where the bulk of his estates was to be found. The policy initiated by Philip the Good with so firm a hand had been continued, and the high nobility had acquired a Burgundian outlook. There was, however, this difference, that Burgundian without Burgundy, lost in 1477, had developed into Netherlandish (albeit with a preponderance of the Walloon element), while at the same time Burgundian interpreted in this guise was no longer synonymous with the dynasty, which had become Habsburg, Imperial, Spanish. Under Charles V this difference still remained hidden, and the nobility served him with entire conviction. Under his successor the contrast was soon to come to light. In any case, apart from the relations with the ruler, the high nobility was a unifying factor in the Netherlands community, although it was at the same time a centre of gallicization.

This whole centralizing effort met with little but opposition from the old political organs of towns and provinces, but indeed the Government, at least under Charles V, walked warily on the whole. A violent incident such as that of the Ghent rebellion of 1539, for which the incorrigible town was mercilessly punished, remained exceptional. Most of the town governments, in all of which the prince had caused the oligarchic system to prevail, entertained good relations with the central authority and its representatives. The privileges of towns and provinces were respected. From the side of the Government, it is true, there was no end of pushing and pressing, to which the subjects often gave way, but when they did hold firm, the Government yielded: it never resorted to downright coercion. This holds good even for the cruel persecution for religion's sake, although as we shall see it led to many clashes. But the fact is that in consequence of the opposition it encountered it was far from being carried out as systematically as the Government would have wished.

His wars with France were doubtless responsible for much in this wise moderation of Charles V. His representatives were everlastingly pestering the States with requests for money. As his reign grew older finance became ever more his predominant care, and there was already so much grumbling about heavy charges that it was necessary to humour the States on other points. In addition to this the Emperor was always fearful lest quarrels with his Netherlands provinces would open the door to French interference. (The people of Ghent had been so unwise as to select for their revolt a moment when Charles V and Francis I were fraternizing.) Whatever the motives, as a matter of fact the Habsburg state in the Netherlands was very far removed from the "French slavery" which before their annexation in 1527 had been a bogey to the magistrates of Utrecht.

We must now face the question as to what was the attitude of the people, or of the various sections of the people, towards the monarchy, how firmly knit was that state of the seventeen provinces, and what were the feelings of nationality which inspired the inhabitants. But first it will be necessary to glance at the cultural movement of the period, and especially to consider the most striking event, the disruption of the age-old Catholic unity which brutal oppression could not heal but only cover up.

b. CIVILIZATION

In spite of civil wars, floods, and plagues, in spite of the painful embarrassment into which large social groups were brought by the devaluation of money—a consequence of the discovery of America—the first half of the sixteenth century was a period of amazing economic development for the Netherlands. Not all the provinces, certainly, had an equal share in this. The North-East resumed a modest and gradual progress only after the conquest, which secured peace. In Flanders the old centres of prosperity had sadly decayed. The silting-up of the Zwin could be checked no longer, and Brugge was a mere shadow of what it had been. The industry of Ghent and Yper had now definitely fallen behind in their competition with the English. The three great towns still possessed much ancient wealth, but their guilds had lost all hold on economic life and struggled in vain against unemployment. But in the country and in the small towns which were now protected by the prince's authority against the tyranny which the three used to exercise in medieval times, a new industry had sprung up which, free from the limitations and restraints of the medieval guild system, and using the cheaper Spanish wool, found markets where the English manufacturers could not follow. The area of this "new drapery" extended from the coast near Dunkirk and Veurne[1] down into Walloon Flanders: St. Winok's Bergen,[2] Hondschoote, Armentières were centres. Moreover, a linen industry began to flourish along the Leie, using Flemish flax for its raw material, and especially in the neighbourhood of Oudenaarde thousands were employed in tapestry weaving, first raised into an art in the Walloon town of Arras and now also practised in Brabant towns, especially Leuven[3] and Brussels. Flanders therefore remained an important industrial region, even though an economic revolution was taking place there which caused a great deal of misery. The new rural proletariat, moreover, scattered as it was, and outside the organization of the guilds, had much less chance

---

[1] Veurne: in French—*Furnes.*   [2] St. Winok's Bergen: in French—*Bergues.*
[3] Leuven: in French—*Louvain.*

of protecting itself against the increasingly powerful capitalists.

About the middle of the sixteenth century Flanders still raised more than any other province under the system of quotas as introduced by Philip the Good; its share was about one-third of the total amount raised by what was called "the patrimonial provinces"—that is, the seventeen without the recently conquered north-eastern ones. Brabant—without Mechlin—paid a little less than Flanders; Holland half of what was paid by Brabant, Zealand one-fourth of what was paid by Holland. It will be noticed that the Dutch-speaking provinces in the aggregate raised by far the larger half of the total: the share of the Walloon provinces was not more than about one-fifth, or, if the north-eastern provinces are counted in, considerably less. Within the Dutch-speaking provinces, although Flanders still occupied the first place, the principal centres of economic development were to be looked for elsewhere—at Antwerp, and in Holland and Zealand.

Antwerp had become the heir to Brugge, the pivot of the great European movement of exchange of northern for southern produce, at the same time the port for the Flemish and Brabant textiles and for the Liège and Hainaut metals. One consequence of the Portuguese discovery of the sea route to India and of the Spanish discovery of America was to increase the importance of this European trade of exchange between North and South: Lisbon became the staple port of the Indian spices; Sevilla of the gold and the other products of America. Both Portuguese and Spaniards made Antwerp their headquarters for the distribution towards the North. The German and Italian bankers established offices there. The town grew rapidly, although even by the middle of the sixteenth century it was not a large town if measured with modern standards: the number of its inhabitants is estimated at 100,000. But in the Europe of its own time it made an imposing appearance; in European commerce the place it occupied was unique.

A weakness, however, in the position of Antwerp was the fact that this great trading movement, which gave employment of many kinds to the industrious natives and fostered their prosperity, yet went mainly through the medium of colonies of foreigners. Apart from the French who, without being properly organized as a colony, were to be found there in large numbers, there were at Antwerp colonies of Scandinavians and Germans, Italians, Spaniards, English, and Portuguese (and of them all the Spaniards were most numerous). Add the Walloons, of whom many settled in the town, and it will become clear how important was the non-Dutch element in the Antwerp trading world. Guicciardini, the Florentine, who lived at Antwerp, and in 1567 published his famous *Descrittione di tutti i Paesi Bassi*, notes that French is taught at several schools, and gives it as his opinion that before long that language would be generally spoken at Antwerp. This is the superficial judgment of a foreigner. Even in the business world French was still far from occupying a dominating position. In the administration and in the law courts, in public and intellectual life the town remained as Dutch as it had ever been. The weakness which I indicated was a purely economic one. Although bound as time went on with ever more numerous ties to the labour, the skill, and the capital of the native citizens, trade yet remained as it were a visitor to Antwerp. Especially as there was still another peculiarity about the position.

Just as Brugge had been in her time, so was Antwerp a port without a merchant fleet of her own. The vessels with which she maintained the intercourse with northern and southern Europe either belonged to those distant countries or had their owners in the ports of Holland and Zealand. Those ports were therefore not merely Antwerp's competitors. They were this in so far as they gave the most immediate access to the northern Netherlands and disputed the German hinterland to Antwerp. For certain goods some became the staple ports for wide areas, such as Amsterdam for wheat from the Baltic, Dordt for Rhine wine. But at the same time their merchant fleets served the Antwerp trade of exchange and themselves benefited by Antwerp's prosperity.

The steady growth of the trade of Holland and Zealand is one of the most noticeable phenomena in the economic history of the first half of the sixteenth century. Amsterdam was still far from equalling Antwerp, but it was already an important trading town, and in the Baltic trade its position was a dominating one. Capital flowed into the Holland towns, rousing them to unprecedented activity. The country-side, too, benefited, and cattle breeding and dairy farming still formed the basis of the Holland economic system. Guicciardini grew enthusiastic over Holland. While still possessing a reputation for boorish backwardness, in reality the province, according to him, was a model of ordered civilization. The organization of the dykes and the waterways filled the Italian observer with admiration, and even more so did the appointment of dwelling houses.

To enter their houses and to examine the abundance of furniture and all kinds of utensils, all equally neat and well kept, causes great pleasure and even greater astonishment, for, indeed, there is not perhaps in the whole world anything to equal it. This is what I have heard said by the quartermasters of the Emperor Charles V, who had been over most of Europe with His Majesty; and as everyone knows, they, who in all towns enter the houses, are better able to judge of this than anyone else.

In fact, in spite of local differences it may be said of the whole of the Netherlands in the days of Charles V and Philip II that here was a prosperous and highly cultured people. In 1473 the first printing-presses were founded at Aalst[1] and Leuven. In the next twenty years the number had steadily grown in Flanders and Brabant, but even more in the northern provinces. The country-side was still dominated by nobility and clergy, who were more exclusively the proprietors of the soil, and enjoyed a higher prestige and exercised a greater political influence in some provinces than in others. This was so (leaving out the Walloon area) in all the inland provinces, both north and south. Yet even there the urban middle class, enterprising, well educated, keen on their privileges and liberties, played an important part in economic, intellectual, and political life. Looking at the Netherlands as a whole they appear

---

[1] Aalst: in French—*Alost*.

a veritable land of towns; both in their economics and in their civilization the third estate dominated.

However admirable were some of the features of that civilization, a harmonious development had for some time been beyond its reach. The middle-class basis and conditions were not in themselves the greatest difficulty. But this middle-class society was contained in a monarchical state, and, what was worse, that monarchy was foreign, and, without intending to do so, inevitably alienated from the people the nobility whom it honoured and the officials whom it employed. From the court at Brussels, from the Great Council of Justice at Mechlin, there radiated much stronger forces of gallicization than from the foreign merchants at Antwerp. This is not merely a question of linguistic purity. Whole spheres of intellectual life were closed to Dutch civilization, and, bound to the towns which were themselves kept in tutelage, it could not but begin to wear a certain appearance of localism and particularism. Literature, whose medieval inspiration was running dry, could not in those circumstances easily find the fresh sources that it needed. The Chambers of Rhetoric were almost the sole guardians of Dutch poetry.

These were originally religious institutions which under the Burgundian Dukes had spread from the North of France over the whole of the Dutch-speaking Netherlands owing allegiance to them (that is to say, they were to be found in large numbers in Holland and Zealand as in Flanders and Brabant, but not in the eastern provinces north of the rivers). The part they played in the public and intellectual life of a town was now a large one. On festive occasions they produced a play; when princely visitors were to be welcomed they contributed greetings in verse for which biblical and classical antiquity were plundered. Their "Land Jubilees" became ever more splendid; these were competitions where Chambers from widely distant towns met together and prizes were assigned to the best poems or plays; they were especially frequent in the Flemish and Brabant towns, though Holland and Zealand later on had their share of these festivities. The honour of a town was involved in the appearance of its Chamber on these occasions and the expenses were borne by the municipal exchequer. No more brilliant "Land Jubilee" was ever seen than that held at Antwerp in 1561. An English spectator, obviously impressed, describes the gorgeous entry of the fourteen visiting Chambers from Flemish and Brabant towns, the festive mood which interrupted business for a few days, and the rich banquets. But although the Chambers of Rhetoric bore witness to the ostentatious prosperity of the burgher class, and even to their intellectual and artistic interest, true poetry was not produced by them. A really high standard could not possibly be maintained in the circle of those excellent and merry citizens. Only some verses of Anna Bijns, an Antwerp school teacher, who wrote after the manner of the Rhetoricians, probably without belonging to a Chamber herself, are still alive with the passion with which she defended the Catholic church against the schismatics of her day.

The poetry of the Rhetoricians was an offshoot of the medieval spirit whose inspiration, as I said, was exhausted. We are soon bored by ingenious tricks such as double rhymes and chain rhymes, which had to do service for poetic beauty, by the hollow emphasis, by the cheap pretentiousness of words taken from the French with which the Rhetoricians' language was flooded in Holland no less than in the South. Yet it is possible to see in all this a reflection, albeit a pale one, of the vehement striving after renovation which inspired the cultural life of all Europe at that time. Everywhere there was a searching after new truths and new forms, everywhere the individual detached himself from the community and demanded freedom and space. Dreams were dreamt of a world order in which man would master his fate by means of reason. The Middle Ages had cherished an innocent admiration for Antiquity without being conscious of the profound differences which distinguished its civilizations from their own. Now the restless thinkers and scholars and artists recognized in it their own ideals. Humanism flourished exceedingly in the Netherlands. It is true that it expressed itself only by means of Latin, but its influence made itself felt on the whole of intellectual life. Nevertheless this European movement contained in itself a grave danger. It would not do to impute the disharmony characteristic of sixteenth-century Netherlands civilization solely to the peculiar political circumstances in which the life of the Netherlands race was set. In all countries Renaissance and Humanism, in the exuberance of their joy at new discoveries, were brushing aside hopeful cultural traditions, too frequently replacing them by no more than a slavish love of imitation. This was certainly not the essence of the new European spirit. In the noblest minds the contemplation of the wise and beautiful world of Greece and Rome encouraged a loving cultivation of native possibilities. Now and again some Dutch writer, too, possessed enough independence to read the lesson of antiquity aright, and to understand that pride in borrowed feathers was no true wisdom. In 1553, for instance, Jan van de Werve, a well-born citizen of Antwerp, published a *Tresoor der Duitsche tale*, in which he made a spirited attack on the abuse of Romance words:

Help me, I ask you, to raise up our mother language, which now lies concealed in the earth like gold, so that we may prove how needless it is for us to beg for assistance of other languages.

It should not be overlooked that the man who wrote these words belonged to a higher social class than that which set the tone in the Chambers of Rhetoric. Such utterances in any case long remain somewhat scarce and timid, in comparison with France, where Du Bellay had written his *Défense et illustration de la langue française* in 1548. It is only in a later period, as we shall see, that the true Renaissance spirit together with the desire for intellectual independence assert themselves in Dutch literature.

Architecture and painting were no more able to keep themselves free from the overwhelming southern influence. The architectural forms of the Italian Renaissance had long been known, as may be seen from the pictures of Van Eyck and Memlinc. But the practice of architecture depended too much on the skill of the artisans as it was handed down from one generation to another to follow suit at once. Now, however, sculptors and decorators began to play with the new Italian-antique

motives. The burgher class wanted to see their prosperity osten-
tatiously expressed in civic buildings, as did the nobility in their
palaces, and the artists revelled as whole-heartedly in the rich
ornamentation of the Renaissance as did the Rhetoricians in
their foreign words and mythological allusions. But if the
enjoyment was of the same character, far greater was the
mastery with which architects and sculptors fashioned pilasters
and architraves, gryphons and medallions, plants shooting
upward from vases. A number of most attractive works came
into existence, as the oaken roodscreen at Enkhuizen, the
porch of the Mint and the choirstalls in the great church at
Dordt, the House of the Salmon at Mechlin. Looking at these
products of the Netherlands Renaissance one is often tempted
to think oneself transported into an earlier period of the great
movement in Italy. And yet this is not always the impression
received. In the famous mantelpiece of the Free District Court
room at Brugge, even more than in that of the Town Court
room at Kampen, these forms adopted from abroad express
a peculiarly Netherlandish quality of feeling, heavier and more
exuberant than that of the more subtle Southerners with their
unfaltering sense of measure. In the general planning of
buildings, moreover, the native traditions offered tenacious
resistance. Not only did the pointed arch long remain pre-
valent, but even at a time when the names of Vitruvius and
his Italian prophets, Alberti and Serlio, were mentioned with
respect—about 1540 Pieter Coecke, of Aalst, published Dutch
translations of their writings—buildings which in details conformed to their precepts yet preserved, with their high roofs,
gables and towers, an entirely unclassical and un-Italian
character. A peculiarly Netherlandish Renaissance style was
thus developed, especially in the South; the Chancery at
Brugge (about 1530) is an early example of this.

Meanwhile, the painter's art was suffering from the evil of
imitation much more severely. By the middle of the sixteenth
century the national tradition was being most woefully over-
grown by the Italian fashion. Yet the native genius for this
art was far from being exhausted. Until 1530 Antwerp possessed in the cultured Quinten Matsys, the friend of humanists,

a noble representative of that generous love of beauty so characteristic of the age. Gossart of Mabuse (Maubeuge), a Walloon who worked at Antwerp for some time—the town attracted artists from all parts—the first who went to Italy in person and preached the undiluted doctrine of Italianism, was himself a figure of undeniable talent. At the same time there were in Holland Lucas van Leyden and Jan van Scorel, the latter working mostly at Utrecht, both men who underwent the Italian influence and yet preserved an individuality of their own. After them, however, a stiff academic spirit grew dominant. An Italian journey became indispensable if a painter wanted to be taken seriously, and an insufferably artificial style compelled universal admiration. The artistic world bowed down before men like Michiel Coxie and Frans Floris, who worked at Mechlin and at Antwerp respectively, and whose art breathes the same spirit as the increasingly conventional and stilted poetry of the Rhetoricians; they were also, as Karel van Mander was soon to relate, equally fond of a pot of beer in their leisure hours. In the North the situation was no better. Instead of having conquered freedom for a more courageous individualism, this generation allowed itself to be swept off its feet by another mighty wave of southern civilization.

And yet this same period witnessed the miracle of Pieter Breughel. Born in a North-Brabant village he worked at Antwerp and Brussels after having been to Italy like everybody else, but in the choice of his subjects as well as in spirit and technique hardly any painter before him was more thoroughly Netherlandish than he; it is true that he owed something in this respect to the Amsterdam master Pieter Aertssen, who had worked at Antwerp for some time. Breughel paints the Brabant peasant and the Brabant landscape with unsurpassed directness. At the same time his work is impregnated with a sense of the tragic which raises it high above mere realism.

Was it the tension caused by Reformation and religious persecution—a tension of which neither the academic painters nor the Rhetoricians seemed to be aware—that was responsible for the tremor one detects in Breughel's art? Here was another factor, and the most potent of all, to disturb the harmony of sixteenth-century Netherlandish civilization.

c. THE DISRUPTION OF CATHOLIC UNITY

In the spirit of the time there lurked a danger. In their eager search for truth and reason men were brought to smash irreparably the forms in which State and Church had settled down, and, when they were checked midway, there resulted the great disruption which the Reformation betokened for the whole of Europe north of the Alps and the Pyrenees. The Church was undeniably in a condition of decadence which the best minds observed with pain. The Papacy offered a sorry spectacle. In the Netherlands as elsewhere, too many priests were worldly and indifferent, thinking only of money and benefices. The country vicars were hardly less rude than the villagers, and almost without exception were living openly in concubinage. The monasteries had lost sight of their spiritual task. As a result of the economic power which it owed to its ever increasing landed property, the Church was in continual conflict with the urban communities and with the Government itself. Scholastic theology hampered the intellectual movement which at one time it had supported. The faith that was preached to the multitude had a mechanical quality and practices were permitted—especially the trade of indulgences —which revolted really religious souls. Reformation was sorely needed. But reformation had been sorely needed many times and had been effected without a break with the past. Was it inevitable that now, because men's minds were full of new longings and expectations, reformation must spell demolition?

In the first decades of the sixteenth century that was certainly not the opinion of those who in the Netherlands were most keenly interested in those problems. A new generation of humanists had grown up, trained in the schools of the Brethren of the Common Life, clerics, rectors of Latin Schools, men for whom learning and piety had to go hand in hand, and who held that reformation of abuses would follow from enlightenment as a matter of course. The mystical spirit of Ruusbroec and Geert Groote worked in them less strongly than the spirit of research and investigation of Wessel Gansfort. Not only therefore did they bitterly criticize the clergy, but they often arrived at unorthodox conclusions. Especially the symbolical interpretation of the communion was frequently foreshadowed by Netherlands thinkers. But the medieval Church left considerable latitude to individual opinions on doctrine, and the Biblical Humanists, as the Netherlands school is often called to distinguish it from the paganistic humanists of Italy, did not dream of secession. On the contrary, their mood was one of hopefulness. Their influence on the educated middle class was indeed great, and it is quite justifiable to speak of a national movement, which nevertheless, since it used Latin almost exclusively, flowed out imperceptibly in every direction into great European currents. This use of Latin at the same time determined the somewhat aristocratic character of the movement. We may quote it as an instance of the fact, which the history of medieval civilization demonstrates again and again, that it was in the sphere of religion that the Netherlands under foreign rule were capable of the most original and valuable intellectual manifestations. It should be noted that in scholarship and through Latin the barriers between the nation and the governing classes were eliminated. Erasmus, the most representative figure amongst the Biblical Humanists, a man whose mind had its roots deep in Netherlands traditions of civilization, and who at the same time enjoyed a European fame such as had not yet fallen to the lot of any Netherlander—Erasmus had his friends amongst princes and noblemen, prelates and high officials, and it was on such that he counted for the carrying-out of his schemes of reform.

Superficially Erasmus of Rotterdam gives one the impression of a complete cosmopolitan. He was overjoyed when he was able to go to Paris in 1495 (just before he completed his thirtieth year). The quickened interest in true Latinity, behind which Greek was beckoning with an even fairer promise, created out of enthusiasts of all countries a republic of scholars in which Erasmus felt completely at home, the more so as he was so generally honoured as its first citizen. Nearly the whole remainder of his life was spent abroad. A couple of years as a dependant in a nobleman's castle near Veere; twice a period of a few years at the University of Leuven; for the rest, after France it was England, then Italy, again England, Germany, and Switzerland. After 1522 Erasmus, who died in 1536, did not see his country again. (By *patria* at first he understood only the County of Holland, but later Flanders and Brabant were also comprised in the term). His most famous works were written and printed abroad. His most intimate friends in the prime of his life were the great English humanists. His letters, in which he discussed problems of scholarship and theology and the affairs of the world with irresistible wit and zest—they were really a high form of journalism, and, going from hand to hand, and soon printed, contributed powerfully to the propagation of his ideas—these letters were addressed to correspondents of all nations.

Yet nothing is plainer than that the opinions of the religious leader—and Erasmus was that no less than he was a scholar, especially during the later period of his life—sprang from a Netherlands tradition, that of Geert Groote, largely as it had been developed by Wessel Gansfort. Subtle disputations about dogma, cold-hearted denunciations on the grounds of theological opinions, were to Erasmus intensely hateful, no less than the excesses of popular religion, which he branded as superstitions. For him Christianity consisted in christian love and christian life. That temper—it can hardly be called a theological system—of which reasonableness, humanity, tolerance were the characteristic features, nowhere penetrated so profoundly as in the Netherlands, where it found the soil prepared, and where, moreover, Erasmus's personal influence counted for more than anywhere else. Here, too, Erasmus came to face the great practical task of his life—a task which he was unable to fulfil, but the enterprise alone ennobles his career. In 1517 he came to Leuven in order to bring about the triumph in his own country of "good letters" and pure piety.

Leuven was a stronghold of traditional theology. Erasmus,

whose fame was at its zenith, was received with distinction, but not without suspicion. He felt himself borne along on the current of the time. A Leuven citizen, Hieronymus van Busleyden, a member of the Great Council of Mechlin, had bequeathed to the University a fund for the establishment of a *Collegium Trilingue*: for the study of Hebrew, Greek, and Latin, the three languages of the Bible and the Fathers. Nothing could have been more congenial to Erasmus, and he exerted himself as much as possible to make a success of the college, whose chairs were occupied by his disciples. Erasmus believed whole-heartedly in academic truth. Restore in its purity the knowledge of the Bible and the Fathers, dispel the dark cloud of scholasticism, and the reign of heartfelt and simple Christianity, such as he understood it, would begin. To him mankind seemed to possess in its reason a key to its own perfection, and to earthly and heavenly happiness. It was a noble dream, but it was rudely shattered by the flood-tide of religious passion set in movement about that very time by Luther in Germany.

Luther was incapable of waiting for the gradual penetration of the influence of "good letters." When after his first indignant protest Emperor and Pope wanted to force him to submission, they drove him to the discovery that the immediate contact with God in which he found his strength had no need of the Church and its means of grace. Taking his stand on that ground he hurled his defiance into the world, and the century in ferment responded with jubilation to the promise of deliverance. Erasmus, although agreeing with Luther on many points, dreaded the consequences of his vehement onesidedness too much to join in the chorus, but he disapproved none the less of the violence with which the zealots on the other side attacked the daring monk, even before his final condemnation, as if on purpose to drive him on. This was not enough to preserve for Erasmus the sympathies of the many who denounced as half-heartedness all hanging back where Luther rushed forward. At the same time the division which had now come about in Germany caused all conservative forces in the Netherlands as well to adopt a harsher attitude, so that in their eyes, too, the exponent of a reasonable reformation, and the entire cause of "good letters," became suspect. This was a heavy blow, for it was on the persuasion of the powerful that Erasmus had built his hopes, and indeed they had begun to give him their attention. But now they pressed him from all sides to take part in the struggle against Luther. Leuven, leaning on a Government whose determination to maintain orthodoxy was decided by quite other than Netherlandish considerations, came forward as a champion against the heretic. But Erasmus held fast to his conviction that only ruin could result from strife. Rather than abandon his independence, he left Leuven in the autumn of 1521 and retired to Switzerland. His attitude in those years compels the deepest respect. Against Luther as well as against the obscurantists who blamed "good letters" for all the trouble, against fanatics on both sides, he continued to proclaim undaunted the rights of reason and criticism, but also of respect for tradition. The age listened to him no more. In the grip of a furious gale of hatred and misunderstanding it hurried past him, into disasters and disruptions without end.

In Germany Lutheranism was spreading, and in a number of states organizing itself under the protection of the princes; finally, in 1555, even obtaining imperial recognition. The King of England broke away from the Papacy and the English people was by degrees protestantized. At the same time in the Netherlands the ruler, without regarding the opinion of his subjects, obstinately attempted to root out all heretical sentiments by means of force. It was impossible to eradicate Biblical Humanism from men's minds, but the opportunity for its adherents to lead a conservative reformation had gone for ever. As late as 1529 Laevinus Ammonius (Lieven van der Maude), a Carthusian monk of Ghent, addressed to Erasmus at Basel a pressing invitation to come and settle down at Ghent.

All the members of the Council of Flanders (he wrote) are heartily devoted to you; a large number of the monks have abandoned their superstitious practices and have returned to true piety.

But in the following year the writer was expelled by a new prior. Others who could be charged with more decidedly heretical opinions had already made their submission, as for instance Grapheus, the secretary of Antwerp. Some, on the other hand, went over to Protestantism, and had to seek a refuge in Germany; such were Gnapheus, a Hollander, author of a little book of edification in the vernacular that was soon placed on the index (*The Consolation and Mirror of the Sick*), and two Flemings, Berthulfus and Rex, who both had served Erasmus as secretary. The Inquisition, meanwhile, found quite a different kind of people to deal with.

An Episcopal Inquisition had long existed in all countries; but in the Netherlands, where the organization of the dioceses was thoroughly antiquated, this was considered to be entirely insufficient. In 1522, therefore, Charles V, who wanted to make of his hereditary lands an example of what such things should be, organized an Inquisition of his own, and although this had soon to make room for a papal establishment, the monarch arrogated to himself complete control over the clerical heresy-hunters. No doubt he defended orthodoxy for the sake of God's honour, but no less for the strengthening of his own power, which unorthodox opinions seemed to threaten. Side by side with the Inquisition properly so called, which in the face of resistance based on privileges it proved impossible to introduce into certain provinces—Groningen, Gelderland, Brabant—courts of law and sheriffs carried on religious persecution on the strength of the edicts issued by Charles in the plenitude of his sovereign power, and which were binding on all the secular authorities in his Netherlands provinces. From the very first these edicts pronounced draconic punishments on all who were even remotely connected with heresy; every new one was more severe than the last, until in 1550 the limit of frightfulness was reached with the "edict of blood," in which all loopholes were stopped and death was enacted for all trespasses.

It was a monstrous policy, and, if it had been carried out to the letter, it would have placed all Netherlands towns under the continual smoke of the faggots. But the execution could not but meet with endless difficulties in a country where both officials and magistrates were impregnated with the spirit of Erasmus, while, moreover, the latter wanted to protect their citizens against so arbitrary a procedure for the sake of the privileges and of free commercial intercourse. In vain the Government tried to undermine society itself by promising to informers a share in the spoils of forfeitures. In the opinion of those who designed the system, religious persecution in the Netherlands never worked anything but defectively.

Nevertheless, after the first deaths by fire—the victims were two Antwerp Augustinian monks, burnt at Brussels in 1523—the number of the martyrs kept steadily growing, and soon the terror of the persecutions began to cause emigration. Particularly the edict of 1550 made a profound impression. The magistracy of Antwerp, fearing that it would frighten away trade, offered tenacious opposition, but in vain. And yet this horror, imposed by the wish of a practically foreign ruler, achieved no more than that the opinions which it was intended to kill were driven underground. Men who could have given a lead kept quiet or left the country, but the spectacle of the martyrs' sufferings and courage made many thousands of simple souls take the new heresy into their hearts. In the parlour and the market place, in the workshop and in the meetings of the Rhetoricians, passionate discussions went on about the problems of faith. Souls that were inaccessible to the learning of the humanists now thirsted after the new doctrine.

Meanwhile the lead given by Netherlands thinkers did not lose all effect, and while during those early years all heresy in the Netherlands was described as Lutheranism, and, indeed, had been roused by Luther, it nevertheless had a character of its own. On the whole—and this was far from being Lutheran —it had a Sacramentarian tendency, that is to say, the communion used to be interpreted symbolically. In any case men's minds were profoundly affected. Antwerp, with its German colony and trading relations, was an active centre for the distribution of the heresy.

What disputations there are amongst people!
The world is full of error, where shall we flee!
It has come to this, by Luther's poison,
That all that may stir to sin is praised,
While all that may purge the soul is blamed.
Where have we come to! May God take pity on us.

Thus lamented Anna Bijns: "for this sort"—the heretics—
"is fast growing among Dutch and Walloons." Indeed, at the
"Land Jubilee" held at Ghent in 1539, where nineteen Chambers, mostly from Flanders and Brabant, met, a question had
been proposed for the playwrights: "Which is the greatest
comfort to a dying man?", and practically all the moralities
breathed an unorthodox spirit, so that the book in which they
were collected and published at once fell under the Imperial
ban.

But at that time another form of heresy had already sprung
up which even outsiders were able to distinguish from Lutheranism. Anabaptism was persecuted with uncommon bitterness, in which social hatred reinforced religious intolerance.
It, too, came from Germany, where religious excitement had
given rise to all kinds of social movements. It was a creed for
extremists, for simple-minded people with no share of the
world's goods. The Anabaptists renounced society as light-
heartedly as they did the Church, they admitted no other code
of law but the bible, no other tie but faith and love. The
economic difficulties of the period favoured the spread of this
new gospel. In their ecstatic bliss the converts expected the
approaching end of the world. Soon it was the purest religious
mania. The strength of the movement lay in Holland, but it
was at Munster that in 1534 Jan Mathijsen of Haarlem founded
the new Jerusalem, whither the faithful were summoned if
they would avoid eternal damnation. Thousands set out from
Holland, but were intercepted and caught by the troops of
the Government. As long as the fantastic Reign of God lasted
at Munster—Jan Mathijsen had been killed and an even
wilder fanatic, Jan Beukelszoon of Leyden, had proclaimed
himself king—unrest continued in the whole of the northern
Netherlands. With the fall of Munster in the summer of

1535 their high expectations everywhere collapsed. The community, however, survived, but only by reacting sharply against the excesses which had made it notorious. A new leader arose in the Frisian preacher, Menno Simons, an ex-priest, who mostly kept himself in safety in East Friesland (an independent County), but not without risking many expeditions in order to teach and organize "the allies" groaning under Habsburg rule. His influence caused the Baptists or Mennonists to develop into a quiet unworldly sect, with little inclination towards dogma, but greatly concerned about morality, averse from matters of state, all wrapt up in their personal search for the narrow path of God and in the endless quarrels and schisms which resulted from their markedly individualistic belief. In the forties and fifties Protestantism, which did not cease to expand underneath the Catholic surface, was mainly Baptist, and the southern provinces, especially Antwerp and Flanders, now came under the influence of that doctrine as much as the North. In the whole of that period the Baptists supplied the bulk of the martyrs burnt or drowned for the sake of religion. However harmless they had become, the terror of Munster still attached to their name. Soon—for the first time in 1562—the confessions and last letters of the martyrs were collected and printed by the care of their leaders. *The Lord's Sacrifice* (as the book was called) contains moving confessions of those pious and simple souls, small citizens and artisans all of them, men and women from Amsterdam and Rotterdam, from Leeuwarden, Antwerp, and Ghent. In the firm conviction that it is for the honour of God, they steel their hearts to suffer a bitter death; they comfort and admonish their relatives, and refrain from judging their judges and executioners. Theirs was a faith which taught how to bear persecution with dignity, and I should almost say with grace, but which on account of its gentleness as well as of its individualism was unfit for the task of rousing a people to resistance.

That task fell to Calvinism, which began to penetrate in the fifties and sixties from Geneva into the whole of the Netherlands, and also from France into the Walloon region, and thence into the Dutch-speaking provinces. If the Baptists' faith has been little more than an episode in Netherlands history, making room for Calvinism almost without a struggle as soon as the critical times of Philip II began, it was no doubt mainly due to the political sense of Calvinism being more strongly developed. When matters came to a crisis between the nation and the monarchy, Mennonism with its lower middle class appeal could not possibly stand up against this fighting creed, which understood organization and discipline, and which had armed itself with a philosophy for state and society.

The thing that most forcibly strikes the unprejudiced observer to-day in this development of the religious conditions in the Low Countries is the lack of liberty in their spiritual life. For a generation and more the fire is kept smouldering in the depths before it can break out in flames. There is an appearance of constraint about the whole of that period. A harmonious development on national lines was out of the question. Such a development might have been possible, even after the cataclysm in Germany, under the leadership of the humanists and their supporters amongst the officials and the magistrates. When, however, under the influence of German events, the Government, that is to say Charles V and his Imperial and Spanish councillors, wedded the cause of reaction and repression, the schism in the nation's life inevitably extended into this sphere as well. The exchange of thought on the burning questions of the day between the people and its natural leaders was hampered; promising lines of development were cut off. Only the emigrants, living together in large numbers in London, Emden, Frankfort, were able to organize themselves freely. On the whole, unless acquiescing in the orthodoxy that was prescribed and severely maintained, people could look for salvation only in foreign ideas of reform. In the upshot it seems as if the ironic fates of history willed Charles V to prevent the Netherlands people from finding its own way in religious matters for no other purpose than that after his death it should be the less able to offer resistance to French Calvinism.

d. NATIONAL SENTIMENT

To consider at last the question which we left unanswered before—what was the attitude of the people, or of its various component parts, towards the monarchy and towards the state, what was the nature of the sentiments of national consciousness entertained by the inhabitants?

In spite of diverse discontents—over the heavy expenditure necessitated by the endless wars, over the religious persecutions, etc.—Charles V's person was still able to rouse the feelings of attachment to the dynasty which had become traditional in the "patrimonial provinces." It was only in the Netherlands, where forty years ago he had shouldered his heavy task, that he abdicated with public solemnity. The scene is well known. At Brussels, in October 1555, the old Emperor, old before his time as a result of his incessant cares and labours, crippled by gout, appeared before the assembled States of his seventeen Netherlands provinces. Leaning on the shoulder of young William of Orange and surrounded by all the knights of the Golden Fleece, he protested before God that it was not ambition, but a sense of duty by which he had been guided in the exercise of his more than human power. He was aware of his insufficiency. It was not out of fear for responsibility, but because his health was broken and his son had attained the vigour of his manhood, that he now laid down his authority over these countries in the latter's hands.

And here he brake into a weeping (so we are told by an English witness of the scene), whereunto, besides the dolefulness of the matter, I think he was moche provoked by seeing the whole company to doo the lyke before; there being in myne opynion not one man in the whole assemblie, stranger or other, that dewring the tyme of a good piece of his oracion poured not oute abondantly teares, some more, some less.

Yet, notwithstanding these tears at his farewell, the States of the Netherlands provinces under Charles V as well as under his predecessors had always eyed the ruler's authority with that suspiciousness which is natural towards a foreign power. Their constant fear was lest they should be dragged into a dynastic foreign policy. This suspiciousness was a real obstacle to the development of a national state. Always, behind the Government's tireless admonitions to get closer together in order to be the better able to render mutual assistance in case of foreign danger, the subjects suspected that the intention was to extort more money and to encroach on provincial autonomy. In 1534 and 1535, for instance, a project for a closer confederation of the provinces was submitted to the States-General on behalf of the Governess. In case of war all were to contribute to expenditure according to a fixed scale. But great opposition arose. Holland was willing to co-operate with Brabant and the new north-eastern provinces against Gelderland (then still independent under Charles of Egmont), but it refused to let itself be mobilized against France; while Flanders, which since the acquisition of Tournai and Lille was fairly protected against its ancient enemy France, would have nothing to do with the scheme at all. The idea of a standing army to be supported on the fixed contributions of all provinces roused general aversion. In the later years of the reign, when the finances got more and more into confusion, the endless wars meant only one thing to the public, and that was expenditure.

It was the misfortune of Netherlands history that the national forces living in the people found it so difficult to co-operate with the state-building forces directed by the monarchy. But what about these national forces themselves, as we see them at work in the sixteenth century? Now, as before, a lack of harmony seems characteristic of Netherlands civilization. The main cleavage was along social lines, although there also were geographical diversities in the area of Dutch speech, the importance of which in this period, however, tended to grow less.

The chief of these geographical lines of demarcation ran from north to south, and separated the eastern from the western part of the area which is to-day considered to be homogeneously Dutch. Holland and Zealand, which were in any case by their Frankish local dialect related much more closely to Flanders and Brabant than to Gelderland and the

C

North-East, had moreover been connected with these southern
provinces in one and the same political structure a century
before the others. They now formed with Flanders and Brabant
a real cultural unit, which received most of its more significant
influences from the Romance South. The eastern region, on
the other hand, during the period of strenuous resistance to
the advancing Burgundian-Habsburg power, seemed to have
directed its attention eastward more consciously than before.
The gentry of Gelderland intermarried with those of Cleve[1]
and Gulich[2]; the burghers of Groningen mixed themselves up
in the affairs of East Friesland; in the houses and schools of
the Brethren of the Common Life no discrimination was made
between natives and Westphalians. An eastern literary language
was in the process of formation during those years, in competition with that of Flanders–Brabant–Holland. It was used
in the Gelderland chancery and in the town hall of Groningen,
by the writers of chronicles and of works of edification. It
accentuated the unity with the region adjoining on the east,
for until vanquished by Luther's southern High German it
was current over a wide area of Germany. These conditions
were still largely fluid. The religious movements, for instance,
as we saw above, crossed these boundaries without difficulty.
Even before the conquest Dutch cultural influences radiated
from Antwerp eastward together with the town's trade. In the
churches of Calcar and Xanten, which never came under
Habsburg and are German to-day, one can still admire the
beautiful sixteenth-century wood-carvings from Antwerp. The
University at Leuven attracted into the circle of Dutch civi-
lisation "Overlanders" (as the Easterners were called), before
they had accepted the same ruler. As for Friesland, the Frisian
language had now definitely failed to rise to the position of
a language of civilization, and not only the administration, but
even provincial historiography and religious movements used
a language that was in all essentials Dutch. Holland as well
as Groningen influence had helped to bring this about. Menno
Simons, for instance, wrote a form of Dutch which has no
doubt an eastern colouring, but which nevertheless is nearer

[1] Cleve: in French—*Cleves*.   [2] Gulich: in French—*Juliers*.

the Holland–Brabant–Flemish language than is the language of the Groningen chronicler Sicke Benninghe or of Charles of Gelderland's chancery.

After the annexation at all events there was no question any longer of the eastern provinces attempting to maintain their cultural independence as against the western and southern region. It is conceivable that they might have done so, although less deliberately than these things are done in our days, had they continued to resist Habsburg authority. But, as we saw, they submitted readily to it, and since then the State, by promoting economic and intellectual intercourse, and by bringing Overlanders and Netherlanders together on the same political stage (where so intensely gripping a drama was soon to be performed), effected almost automatically the cultural amalgamation of the new provinces with the old. There remained differences, but there was no longer any danger that they would become the basis for divergent national development.

As to the West and South, one may notice certain changes in the parts played by the various provinces in the cultural movement. Even more than in the fifteenth century Flanders has fallen behind Brabant. Brabant, with Brussels, Leuven and Antwerp—the capital, the university town, and the commercial metropolis of the Netherlands—has become the central region of intellectual life. Antwerp is a place of exchange of ideas for the whole of the Dutch-speaking country, just as it is a place of exchange of goods for Europe. The increasing importance of Holland is making itself felt especially in its contributions to humanism and to painting; in Dutch literature the North is still following the lead of the South. But in all those spheres, how striking is the close intellectual relationship! The Chambers of Rhetoric in Holland and Zealand— —the only northern provinces in which they flourished— imitated the example of the South in their organization and activities, and their archives were stocked with the products of the rhyming zeal animating the Flemish and Brabant brethren. There were intimate relations between the printers, and that is to say the publishers, of North and South. The

Holland painters learnt from those of Brabant, and inversely, as mentioned above, Breughel owed a great deal to the Amsterdammer Pieter Aertsen. These are no more than a few instances taken at random. The development of Erasmus, for whom Leuven came to have such importance, who found as much admiration and support among Flemings and Brabanders as among Hollanders, and who in the end felt himself, as we saw, to be no longer a Hollander but a Netherlander—that development is typical.

A fact deserving especial attention is that the religious development, sketched above, did not anywhere intensify provincial differences. Undoubtedly, a closer examination reveals many-featured variety rather than flat uniformity. But it is a shifting variety. In the reactions of particular regions to the religious problem, the observer finds no constant differences which would suggest the existence of deep-seated internal causes, certainly none which would seem to announce in any way the sharp separation into a northern Protestant and a southern Catholic block which was to result from the fast approaching crisis. In Flanders and Brabant the cultured and politically privileged burgher class was no less Erasmian than it was in Holland. The Baptists, having worked off their ecstatic and revolutionary period in Holland, afterwards spread their influence in the South as well. Calvinism, as we shall see, nowhere found so ready access as it did in Flanders and Brabant, and if in the long run it was driven from the South and subjected the North, it was the result of foreign interference.

Once more, therefore, the facts of the history of civilization reveal the Netherlands as a unit, with as much variety as every cultural area needs for a healthy and vigorous life, but with the north-eastern region attached somewhat more loosely to the closely knit and dominating combination of Flanders, Brabant and Holland. A unit in fact, but whose consciousness was still feeble and obscure. Intellectuals, poets, royal officials, high nobles, these no doubt thought more and more beyond their particular provinces. It is in this period that the language and the country acquire a name of their own. Instead of *Duitsch*, which embraced, of course, German as well—although, as we saw, Maerlant used the dialectical variant *Dietsch* in the more restricted sense—*Nederlandsch* was coming into use. At the same time *Nederlanden*, or even *Nederland* in the singular, was still largely a literary, not an official nor a popular word. A little later *Nederlanders* (*Belgae* in Latin) abroad began to organize apart from the wider Germanic nation—thus, for instance, students at Italian universities. But in this there was still a great deal of uncertainty. When under the influence of the classics the sixteenth century began to idealize the "fatherland"—the word was translated out of the Latin about this time—it automatically based the conception on the State, merging it with that loyalty towards the dynastic which had been dear to the Middle Ages, and which still had power over men's minds. That is to say that in the Netherlands the Walloon provinces were included.

It goes without saying that this was less easily done in intellectual intercourse. Walloon painters (like Gossart, whom we mentioned above, or the landscape painter Patinir) worked at Antwerp. Walloons took an active share in the propagation of Calvinism all over the Dutch land. But other religious movements, as we have seen, did not so easily cross the linguistic boundary, and at any rate it was naturally a different matter where literature was concerned. It is significant of the importance of the Dutch-speaking provinces that they could claim the name of the country for their language. Men were nevertheless entirely familiar with the notion of the country being inhabited by two groups, the Dutch-speaking and the Walloons. The Protestant refugees abroad as a matter of course organized their churches in two divisions—thus at Emden, London, Frankfort, Köln. But these arrangements were simply demanded by practical considerations. National sentiment did not rule out the Walloons. In Flanders especially, as the chroniclers bear witness, there existed an old popular hatred against the Walloons, but at this moment it seemed to slumber. The worst linguistic abuses which had characterized the régime of Charles the Bold were avoided by the Habsburg rulers. The quiet infiltration of French was causing no uneasiness.

But the test of all this was only to come when the conflict with the monarchy broke out, and national feeling suddenly had to stand on its own feet. For the makers of the Beggars' songs "Netherland" was the country of the Seventeen Provinces: the new North-East as well as the Walloon area were comprehended in the patriotic enthusiasm of the first stage. How this conception fared in the reality of the terrible struggle is a question that will be closely examined in the course of this work.

THE STRUGGLE FOR INDEPENDENCE
AND THE SPLIT

I

THE PRELUDE, 1555–1572

a. THE HIGH NOBILITY IN OPPOSITION

Just as in the case of Philip the Good and Charles the Bold, so it is usual to make a contrast between Charles V, wise, moderate, and popular, and Philip II, short-sighted, unbending, and detested, and to extend this contrast, with as little right in the one case as in the other, to the principles of their systems of government. Undoubtedly the son lacked those particular qualities which had rendered his father's rule acceptable, and there was moreover that one insurmountable obstacle—he was a foreigner. Brought up in Spain, he could not even speak French, let alone Dutch, and this had been made painfully apparent to his subjects assembled at the solemn gathering at Brussels where the transference of the government had taken place: on that occasion the Bishop of Arras, Granvelle, had had to speak for their new ruler. As soon as the war with France (which Philip inherited along with the sovereignty) was finished, he took the road back to Spain, and the Netherlands saw him no more.

And yet, in the main, Philip simply pursued the policy of Charles, and the forces which so speedily broke out in opposition to him had been gathering under his predecessor. It was, indeed, a heavily mortgaged estate that Charles V bequeathed to him. Discontent was everywhere rife. At the same time the finances were in such confusion that the monarch was wholly dependent on the co-operation of the States, at least while the war with France lasted. At first, therefore, Philip attempted to win over the nobility. A number of the most important were nominated to the Order of the Golden Fleece (now no longer an exclusively Netherlandish institution), and were granted stadtholderships and seats on the Council of State. It was a bitter disappointment to him when these nobles, on whose help his father, though he gave them less power, had always been able to reckon, remained none the less intractable. It was like a return to the days of Maximilian when the nobility in 1556 censured the war with France, alleging that it was waged not in the interests of the Netherlands, but to give Spain a firm foothold in Italy. And soon they were stiffening the States in demands which seemed to the King to attack his power and his honour.

First, in 1558, there was the affair of the nine years' subsidy, which the States would only grant if they were allowed to raise it through their own commissioners. Then, just before Philip's departure, there was the stipulation made by the States-General at Ghent that, now that there was peace, the three thousand Spanish troops, who had got themselves detested wherever they were stationed, should leave the country. This dispute, which mortally offended Philip, stirred up popular feeling to an astonishing degree, and after lengthy attempts at evasion the King had to give way. It was the first mutter of the approaching storm. But this was not how Philip read the signs of the times. By the peace with Henry II of France the two rulers had agreed that they should wage a more vigorous campaign against heresy in their respective dominions, and, apart from this, Philip believed that more amicable relations between Habsburg and Valois would put him in a better position to carry out the complete absolutist programme. But in his absence the high nobility entered almost immediately into systematic opposition.

The King had left behind him as Regent or Governess his half-sister Margaret of Parma, but his real confidant was Granvelle, whom he had made President of the Council of State and who corresponded directly with him. Together with the Presidents of the other two Councils, Viglius, a Frisian jurist, and Berlaymont, a Walloon noble with many children and a short purse, Granvelle formed an inner council of officials, who knew no law but the King's will, and who awaited directions from Madrid for the policy of the country. And a long wait it sometimes was! Philip was slow in coming to a decision and could leave nothing to others. The loss of all initiative, which this dependence on a distant and dilatory master involved, seriously weakened the Brussels Government in the crisis which was now near at hand, and the absurdity of the situation was sometimes vividly illustrated by their helpless hankering after orders from Madrid. And over against this group of servants, by means of whom the monarch gave expression to his will, there now stood the high nobility of the country, glittering with honours, but with sadly restricted power.

Philip, wise by experience, intended the Council of State to be no more than an ornament of the Crown, while the popularity and splendour of the Knights of the Fleece must be used to cover whatever was done by the absolute monarch and the servants he had raised from nothing. But at a time when political questions began to kindle such passions and the trend of the monarchical policy to excite such opposition, it is little wonder that the great nobles failed to be attracted by the rôle assigned them. They wanted to make the Council of State a powerful body and take part in the government, but always they found their president, Granvelle, opposing this ambition and admonishing them in the King's name to be tractable.

In these first years after Philip's departure one thing in particular provoked a formidable commotion, much worse than that over the Spanish troops, uniting all the different elements of opposition present in the Netherlands into an impassioned chorus of complaint and protest. This was the establishment of new bishoprics, which obtained the papal sanction in 1559; in 1561 a second bull worked out the details. It was a striking instance of what the monarchy could do in the way of state building, and exhibits Philip as a diligent worker in the tradition of his house.

The ecclesiastical divisions in the Netherlands, which had come into being with the earliest expansion of Christendom, corresponded little indeed to the later political organization or even to the linguistic conditions. What Philip aimed at in the first place (and here he was reviving an old scheme of Charles V) was the elimination of foreign ecclesiastical authority. Secondly, he wanted to see an increase in the number of bishops so that they might the more effectively combat the growth of heresy. At the same time the right of nomination was taken from the chapters and given to the crown, in order that the bishops might be the faithful servants of the secular power. A provision which gave great offence to the nobility stipulated that bishops should be skilled theologians, so that the episcopal chair should no longer be a resting-place for the sons of great lords. The plan also struck at the independence of the wealthy abbots, who, particularly in the States of Brabant, joined lustily in all opposition to the Government: the new bishops were to be endowed out of the revenues of historic abbeys like those of Afflighem, of Tongerloo, of Marienweerd, while they were to usurp even the abbatial title and sit in the States, where the Government would be able to rely upon them.

It is not to be wondered at that there arose a storm of opposition to a plan which involved such a strengthening of the King's authority at a moment when his designs were viewed with distrust on all sides. Indeed, quite apart from the special circumstances, this concordat, for so the arrangement deserves to be called, implied such a complete subjection of the Church to the State, that liberty, which in the Middle Ages had benefited by the antagonism between these two powers, was seriously threatened. The same tendency had already appeared in the organization of the Inquisition. In both cases for that matter, the Habsburger was only following in the footsteps of the French monarchy, which half a century before had already secured papal recognition of its authority over the Church. Elsewhere, in the German states and in England, it was the Reformation which helped to put the seal on absolutism by investing the ruler with supremacy over the Church. Putting aside for the moment such considerations (though it is easy to understand that they were all-important to contemporaries), we can see how greatly this much-maligned measure would have contributed to the consolidation and rounding off of the Netherlands state, had not its future been ruined by the rupture between King and people. Even so this measure did at least free the churches of Brabant and Flanders from their long dependence on Walloon sees.

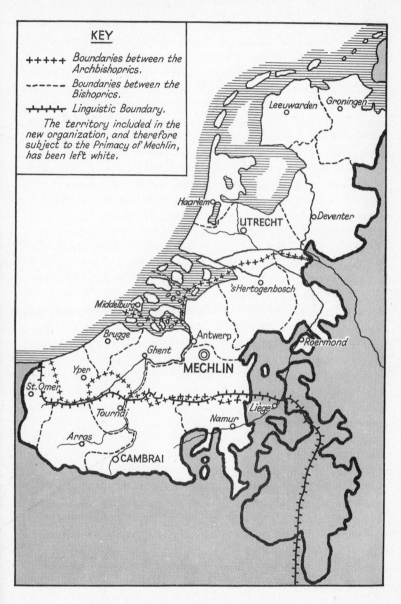

KEY

+ + + + +　Boundaries between the
　　　　　　　Archbishoprics.

- - - - -　Boundaries between the
　　　　　　　Bishoprics.

+†+†+†+　Linguistic Boundary.

　The territory included in the
new organization, and therefore
subject to the Primacy of Mechlin,
has been left white.

Leeuwarden　Groningen

Haarlem

UTRECHT　　Deventer

'sHertogenbosch

Middelburg

Brugge　　Antwerp　　Roermond

Yper　Ghent

MECHLIN

St.Omer

Tournai　　Namur　Liège

Arras

CAMBRAI

MAP II THE NEW DIOCESES, 1561

Nearly the whole of Habsburg territory in the Netherlands
—the Bishopric of Liège remained outside the reform—was
taken out of the ecclesiastical provinces of Rheims and Cologne,
and erected into three independent provinces. Cambrai,
Mechlin, and Utrecht became Archbishoprics; the Archbishop
of Mechlin was to be Primate over the whole Netherlands
Church. Of the three provinces under the authority of these
archbishops that of Cambrai comprised the Walloon area, with
four other sees: Arras, Tournai, St. Omer, and Namur; that
of Mechlin, the area as far northward as the great rivers, with
Yper, Brugge, Ghent, Antwerp, 's Hertogenbosch[1] and Roermond; finally, that of Utrecht, the whole of the remaining
territory, with Middelburg, Haarlem, Deventer, Groningen,
and Leeuwarden. The demarcation of the two southernmost
groups of Bishoprics did not conform exactly to the linguistic
boundary, but the sees of the central strip were now all located
in Dutch-speaking towns, and there was the expressed intention of organizing "the churches which use the French tongue"
separately. All together it was a very great measure; its bold
logic and symmetry and its vigorous attack on historic development and ancient rights were thoroughly characteristic of the
spirit of the monarchy and its rationalistic lawyer servants.

Resistance was violent. All classes—the nobility, the clergy,
and the towns—made a great outcry about the violation of their
rights. Abbots and Knights of the Fleece fraternized. The
pensionaries, the legal officers of the towns, industriously ferreted
into old documents and drew up lengthy remonstrances. The
bishops had to be inducted into most of the sees almost by
force. Those in the new eastern provinces—Leeuwarden,
Groningen, Deventer, and Roermond—could, indeed, only be
occupied at the time of Alva, when everything lay crushed
under the heel of the oppressor. Antwerp, where business
interests were greatly disturbed at the prospect of a bishop
residing within the city walls, even sent a couple of envoys
to the King in Spain and obtained a suspension. The reception of the measure showed how inflammable was the state
of public opinion in the whole of the Netherlands. What

---

[1] 's Hertogenbosch or Den Bosch: in French—*Bois-le-Duc.*

excited the multitude was the fear of keener religious persecution, but the real danger which the Government so blindly
prepared for itself lay in the injury it did to the private interests
of the privileged classes, thereby stimulating their already
awakened spirit of opposition.

Although Granvelle had had nothing to do with the preparation of the reform, he profited more than anyone by it;
he became the first Archbishop of Mechlin and Primate of
the Netherlands Church, at the same time receiving the Cardinal's hat. Moreover, upon him fell the task both of defending
and executing the measure. Thus the affair helped not a little
towards making his name hated, and it was a natural tactical
instinct which caused the malcontent lords to raise the cry
"Away with Granvelle," whereby they could, without openly
attacking the King, give expression to their demand for a
complete change in the system of government. Under the
leadership of the Prince of Orange and the Count of Egmont
they formed a league against the Cardinal; the lower nobility
also began to participate noisily in the movement. The members of the Council of State sent one of their number, Montigny, to the King; Orange, Egmont, and Hoorn addressed a
written request to him, and, when this remained unanswered,
created a popular sensation by withdrawing from the Council
of State until their wish should be fulfilled. Finally, after much
wavering, Philip gave in, albeit with a bad grace. In the beginning of 1564 Granvelle was ordered to leave the country.
Margaret of Parma, to the profound alarm of Viglius and
Berlaymont, undertook to govern with the Council of State.

These great lords, to whom the Netherlands cause now
seemed to be entrusted, were princes both by rank and position, the equals not only of the powerful feudal nobles by
whom the monarchy in France was still surrounded, but of
the greatest of the German princes; and with both of these
they were linked by numerous marriages. For Orange, the
eldest son of a Count of Nassau, the position in the Netherlands to which he succeeded as a child had appeared to be
so great a good fortune that his parents had handed him over
to be educated as a Catholic and set apart the countship for

his younger brother John; in 1561 Orange married a daughter of Maurice, the Elector of Saxony, the man who had proved so fatal to Charles V, and this marriage was an event of international importance. Egmont's wife was a Duchess of Bavaria. For Aremberg first a Princess of Cleve, then a Vaudemont of Lorraine was thought of for a bride.

The magnates owed their rise and position to the Burgundian-Habsburg monarchy, so that each one's broad lands lay spread over several provinces. Orange's Netherlands possessions had their centre in Brabant at Breda, but he also owned land in Holland and Zealand, of which provinces he was Stadtholder. Egmont's house sprang originally from Holland; one branch had occupied the ducal chair of Gelderland. But Egmont's father, a faithful follower of Charles V, had married a Walloon heiress who brought him estates in Luxemburg and Flanders, and Egmont, Stadtholder of Flanders, could no longer be considered a Hollander. Orange was not the only one of German origin; there was Mansfeldt also. For the rest, the great nobles mostly belonged to Walloon families, even if they owned lands in Brabant, Limburg, or Gelderland, and were known by the Dutch names of these estates. Aerschot was a Croy, son of Philip the Good's favourite Chièvres; Aremberg, Stadtholder of Groningen, Friesland, and Overysel, a Ligne; Meghen, Stadtholder of Gelderland, a Brimeu; Hoorn a Montmorency; Hoogstraten a Lalaing; Bergen a Glimes. These men kept a truly princely state. Aerschot's son, Chimay, when a student at Leuven, lived in a palace with a governor and a tutor, besides twelve pages. At his marriage there were present representatives of the Pope, the Emperor, the King of France, a number of German and Italian princes, and the States of Brabant, Flanders, and Hainaut. From their youth onwards these men were employed in the service of the monarch for the most important military, diplomatic, and political missions. The question that confronts us is whether the national cause was safe with them.

Their zeal in guarding against the subordination of Netherlands foreign policy to Philip's Spanish ideas cannot be doubted. Themselves Catholics without much fervent conviction, they detested the policy which would make of the Netherlands an outpost of a system of Catholic aggression in northern Europe. Philip and Granvelle watched with profound distrust the evidences of Orange's friendliness with his relatives in Germany; but for that matter the nobles as a whole looked at events abroad with very different feelings from the King. They rejoiced, for instance, at every success of the Huguenot nobility in France, where, to Philip's consternation, serious religious strife had broken out after the death of Henry II. In other words, anything which might hinder the establishment of Philip's despotism in the Netherlands was welcome to the nobility; but how weak nevertheless was the leadership they could offer! From the beginning they were divided by jealousies and dissensions. Aerschot held aloof and exercised some influence over Aremberg and Meghen. It was quickly apparent, too, that the victory of the Council of State was not solely the victory of the national principle, but that it was as much the victory of privilege. The monarchy had endeavoured to make great and small alike subject to the law; happy in the consciousness of power regained the nobility now trampled the law underfoot. Particularism, too, raised its head. Gelderland, for instance, immediately attempted to get the "foreigners"—that is, the natives of other provinces—removed from the Court which since 1543 had represented royal authority at Arnhem.

But the worst part of it was that while it lay in the power of the nobility after Granvelle's departure to prevent many things and to create much mischief and confusion, for constructive purposes their victory was only apparent. Far away the silent Philip still remained the arbiter of Netherlands destiny. Armed with the power derived from his other dominions, he could still forbid, and, if need be, command. So, if the nobles were not prepared to carry their opposition to extremes, the development of affairs in the Netherlands was bound to escape from their control. The people still looked confidently to them. But while the exuberance and light-hearted insolence which marked the proceedings of the nobles at times give the impression that they were only playing at politics, the people were in deadly earnest. The new creed of Calvinism was gaining more and more ground, and hatred of the Inquisition became a consuming passion.

To their credit be it said that the nobles were not blind to the feelings which agitated the people. They had too large a share in the Erasmian culture of the country to be able to give the religious persecutions whole-hearted support. The decisions of the Council of Trent, which was just then devoting itself to the task of formulating a stricter Catholic creed and of tightening up the organization of the Church to fit it for the struggle, were repugnant to them, and Philip's command to promulgate these decisions unconditionally appeared impolitic even to the most loyal Catholics among them. But Orange in particular realized that the religious question could no longer be shirked. In full assembly of the Council of State on New Year's Eve, 1564, on the occasion of the drawing up of instructions for Egmont, who had once again to go and discuss the situation with Philip, he made a speech of which Viglius, who was mortally alarmed by it, has left us a short report:

The King errs if he thinks that the Netherlands, surrounded as they are by countries where religious freedom is permitted, can indefinitely support these sanguinary Edicts. However strongly I am attached to the Catholic religion, I cannot approve of princes attempting to rule the consciences of their subjects and wanting to rob them of the liberty of faith.

It needed Egmont's vanity to be deceived by the vague promises which he brought back from Spain. In November 1565 the Governess received the King's final answer in the famous letters from Segovia. Now no one could delude himself any longer. Against the growing unrest Philip recognized only one weapon—sterner repression. Peremptory orders were addressed to all authorities to carry out the Edicts and to assist their execution. Great was the resulting excitement of the people, who had expected much from the intervention of the magnates. A profound impression was created by their refusal to share the responsibility for the government any longer. Orange, Egmont, and Hoorn withdrew once again from the Council of

State, while Bergen and Meghen requested to be relieved of their Stadtholderships. The Governess, the monarch's reluctant agent, was thus brought face to face with the popular movement.

b. THE FIRST OUTBURST

We have already noticed that what Protestantism in the Netherlands lacked was organization and political sense. Lutheranism, which had risen in Germany only by reason of its alliance with the princes, was helpless wherever the Government remained loyal to the old religion. Anabaptism was a creed for long-suffering lower middle-class people. The National Reformers, as the Sacramentalists have been called, remained too individualistic to construct anything. From Geneva there now began to spread over Europe the influence of Calvin.

In the *Institutes*, the first edition of which appeared in 1536, when he was still only twenty-seven, Calvin had elaborated a complete system of Protestant theology. By its logical strength it made a deep impression on an age which in every sphere was bringing reason to bear against long-established traditions. To the Church, appealing to her ancient rights, Calvin opposed the authority of Holy Scripture, which to his mind contained complete and absolute truth for all circumstances and for all ages. Mighty indeed was the driving-power which he gave thereby to a new and individualistic religious life, but at the same time he set narrow limits to its functioning, and entrusted their maintenance to the ministers, who were empowered to fix binding articles of faith. At Geneva, from 1540 onwards, Calvin was able to test his ideas on a living social organism, and to erect a state which should fulfil what was in his conception the highest purpose of the State, namely, the glorification of God. The Church must include the whole body of citizens, and be under the constant supervision of the consistory, ministers, elders, and deacons, the guardians of orthodoxy and of the moral life of the community. Society and State were alike subject to its rule, and freedom of thought was as little tolerated there as in the strictest Catholic countries.

The first Netherlanders to follow the example of Calvin did so outside the Habsburg Netherlands, outside the reach of oppression. At Emden in East Friesland there grew up in the 'forties what may be called the Mother Church, after whose example the Reformed communities "under the cross"—that is to say, hiding from the persecution—were generally modelled. It was a Polish nobleman, Johannes à Lasco, who under the protection of the Countess reformed the national Church of East Friesland after his own fashion, but on the whole in accordance with the Calvinistic ideal, and a number of Netherlands refugees sought shelter there, and were made familiar with the Calvinistic ideas of discipline and co-operation. À Lasco introduced the consistory, the council of elders and deacons under the minister, and the *coetus*, or assembly of ministers, and drew up a catechism. When, as a result of Charles V's victory over the Schmalkaldic League, Germany was re-Catholicized, à Lasco emigrated to London, where a Netherlands Church was established on the same lines for exiles from Flanders, Brabant, and Holland. Here, in the church of the Austin Friars, which still belongs to the same community, now become exclusively North Netherlandish, were sung the first Dutch psalms as rhymed by Utenhove of Ghent. Here also à Lasco drew up in Latin the first comprehensive declaration of faith, which Utenhove likewise translated into Dutch. In his capacity of elder, Utenhove was one of the leaders of the community. He was a man of good family, his father having been president of the Court of Flanders. The ministers were Micronius, also of Ghent, and Delenus, who probably came from Alkmaar.

I do not think [wrote Utenhove] that hitherto our Netherlands nation ever had a community in which the word of God was preached in such purity, the sacraments performed with such sincerity, and Christian punishments so zealously and faithfully administered as in this our community.

According to Reformed ideas he was right. This first bloom, however, was of short duration. In 1553 there began under Mary a Catholic reaction in England, and à Lasco, along with a number of followers, among whom were Utenhove and Micronius, returned to Emden, "the shelter of God's Church," which now, after the final defeat of Charles V, became more than ever a beacon for the whole of Netherland Protestantism.

Many were the preachers who, in the years that followed, went forth from Emden to minister to the Protestant communities in towns throughout the area of Dutch speech, and who introduced the needful uniformity and organization. The advice of Emden was sought on difficult points of Church discipline or doctrine, as, for instance, the consistory of Antwerp did in 1558 when it had a dispute with its minister Haemstede. A remarkable man this Haemstede. A Zealander of good family, he acquired great influence with the well-to-do citizens at Antwerp. He was the author of the famous *Book of Martyrs* which was published at Antwerp in 1559, and of which many later editions were brought out elsewhere. On one occasion, on the day of the procession of the Holy Sacrament in 1558, he was bold enough to speak before the multitude in the streets, in the sight of the priests passing by. Shortly afterwards he emigrated to London, where he was expelled from the community as a heretic, because he persisted in calling the Baptists his brethren. It is hardly an inspiring spectacle to see the victims of persecution themselves casting out that spirit of tolerance and anti-confessionalism which was a heritage of the Netherlands people, and which could substantiate the justice of their cause in the struggle against Spanish oppression. But do men for their struggles trust to justice alone? Against the might of the enemy the confusion attendant on well-meaning individualism would have been powerless, and, just as Catholicism had done at Trent, so Protestantism had to arm itself with order and unity of belief. No more efficient weapons can be imagined than those of stern Calvinism.

In so far as it came by way of Emden and London, the influence of Calvin operated in the Dutch-speaking Netherlands mainly by means of Dutch speech. But about 1560 a rising wave swept over from France. The peace of 1559 not only freed the Government, as Philip had hoped it would, from the burden of guarding the southern frontier. It re-opened the traffic of Antwerp and Wallonia with France, where Calvinism was just beginning to organize itself on a firm basis. A synod had secretly been held at Paris and a confession of faith drawn up for the French Church. Many were the communities, each with its minister and consistory, scattered throughout the country. Naturally this example made a deep impression on the Walloons. In 1561 Guy de Bray, one of their most zealous ministers, who laboured at Tournai and from there as far as Mons and Lille, drew up a confession of faith for the Netherlands Church modelled on the French confession. The Walloon underwent French influence, but for the realization of his ideas he could not but look northward: the State must furnish the foundation for it, the State which with its persecution set the rising faith its greatest problem. Just as Calvin himself, in his preface to the *Institutes*, had addressed Francis I directly, so de Bray wrote a letter to Philip II, which he caused to be thrown by night, along with the confession of faith, inside the ramparts of the Castle of Tournai. It was childish to think that the monarch, deceived by the enemies of the Reformers, would be led to conclude from the statement of their beliefs that they were peace-loving citizens whose lives he could spare without danger. But what is most striking in this document is the self-assurance with which this man stands before the King and says that "his people" can no longer endure the religious persecution.

De Bray's *Confession*, which was speedily translated into Dutch, acquired much authority among the Reformed communities. In numerous towns there now existed secret organizations on the usual model, and the bonds between them were tightened by means of frequent synods. It would seem that before 1566 the Calvinistic organization proper, with consistories and synodal assemblies, did not extend to the North. Spreading outwards from the Walloon country through the industrial region of Flanders, it had established itself in most of the towns of any importance in Flanders and Brabant, and finally made its headquarters at Antwerp. That Antwerp acquired such importance for the movement was in a measure due to the existence there of a Walloon community alongside the native one. The Walloon ministers of Antwerp (since 1565 there was a Frenchman, Franciscus Junius, amongst them), together with the lawyer Gilles le Clerq of Tournai, the trusted agent of the Antwerp Walloon consistory, did much to promote the co-operation between the Walloon and Dutch-speaking consistories, and, when the time was ripe, the alliance of both with the malcontent nobility. The organized communities comprised for the most part artisans and small citizens; the circles of the Rhetoricians probably furnished a goodly number. No doubt many wealthy merchants were also touched by Calvinism—I have mentioned the influence of Haemstede—but they had more to fear from the Edicts, and had to keep in the background. And, as in France, there were converts from among the ranks of the nobility who sometimes introduced Reformed preachers on their estates.

All told, however, the convinced Calvinists still formed but a tiny fraction of the Netherlands people, and by their side existed yet other sects: the Baptists, who, however, were to some extent absorbed by the new Church; and the Lutherans, especially strong at Antwerp, who were more successful in maintaining their individual existence. But meanwhile public opinion assumed an ever more critical attitude towards priests and monks, religious persecution more and more became an object of hatred. The terrible scenes witnessed at the stake aroused a loathing no longer to be controlled. Sometimes there was resistance, and executioners and sheriffs went in danger of their lives: as, for example, in 1564 at the execution of Fabritius (De Smet), a former Carmelite of Brugge, who had ministered to the Reformed community at Antwerp. At his examination before the magistrates Fabritius had roundly admitted his offences.

"So it is not we put you to death," said the Sheriff, "but the King's decree." Whereupon Fabritius made answer: "Look well to it, then, that this decree answer for you and protect you at the great and awful day of the last Judgment." After these words they condemned him to death in accordance with the edict and decree of His Royal Majesty, but with such pallid countenances that one might easily trace therein the misery, oppression, and terror of their consciences.

The judges themselves did not believe in the harsh law which they had to administer. What more natural than that the whole people had watched with anxious expectation the efforts of the nobility to obtain the relaxation of the Edicts, and that the disappointment at the close of 1565 caused a violent commotion? On all sides the Brussels Government was overwhelmed with protests from the authorities in towns and provinces. Flanders, under the leadership of Brugge, was up in arms against the hated inquisitor Titelman. In the north-eastern provinces, where it had as yet proved impossible to establish the new bishoprics, although Protestantism had made much less progress there than in the South, the several provincial States made an agreement amongst themselves to offer united resistance. In Brabant wild rumours went abroad of designs to introduce the Inquisition (as distinct from the persecution arising out of the Edicts) there also, and the chief towns, however meticulously loyal the behaviour of their magistrates had so far been, bestirred themselves in anticipation. But out of the masses there rose sounds of fury and revolt. Notes were thrown in the palace of Egmont at Brussels urging him to join the ranks of Calvinism, and holding out the dominion over the Netherlands as his reward. Lampoons were circulated, branding Philip as a perjurer who violated the privileges, and to whom, following the old law of the "Joyous Entry," no further allegiance was due. In Antwerp people were reminded of the ancient ties with the Empire, where the Religious Peace had put a check on persecution.

The driving-force behind all this agitation was hatred of the Inquisition, but whatever discontent there was at the un-national appearance and tendencies of the Government and at its reforming zeal, together with all the social unrest and economic distress, combined with this feeling to swell the excitement to the proportions of a mighty national movement. Mighty it was, but uncertain of its goal. It cried out for leadership. The Calvinists, who alone knew what they wanted, could not openly furnish this. The people looked up to the magnates to be "chieftains unto them."

What did these magnates mean to do? They had taken care

that the King's refusal to give ear to their demands should be noised abroad, and by applying for their relief from office they had at the same time made clear their intention that he alone should bear the responsibility. The violent agitation of public opinion was not unpleasing to them. But what next? Egmont was certainly far from any idea of securing for himself the dominion over the Netherlands. Sulk as he might, he knew less than anyone what he wanted. Orange looked at events with a cooler and a clearer mind, but he, too, for the present, kept himself in the background. The front of the stage was now occupied by nobles of the second rank, confidants and servants of the malcontent magnates, partly encouraged by them, partly bent upon pushing them on.

Already in the summer of 1565 parleys had taken place at Spa between a few noblemen of decidedly Protestant persuasion: Louis of Nassau, a brother of Orange, who as a Prince of the Empire could be a Lutheran with impunity; Nicholas de Hames, Herald-at-Arms of the Order of the Golden Fleece; and Marnix, lord of Tholouse, a Brabant noble, who with his brother Marnix of St. Aldegonde had imbibed Calvinism from the fountain-head at Geneva; Gilles le Clerq was also there representing the contact with the consistories.

The possibilities of a league of the lower nobility were discussed. After the arrival of the letters from Segovia, at a moment when Brussels was the scene of magnificent festivities in celebration of the marriage of Alexander of Parma, son of the Governess, to which the nobles flocked from all sides, there met in the palace of the Count of Culemborch the constituent assembly of the famous Compromise or League of the Nobility. Besides Culemborch, who was a native of Gelderland, and Louis of Nassau, the most notable personalities among the assembly were the Count van den Bergh, a brother-in-law of Orange and also a "Geldersman," and the Hollander Hendrik van Brederode, all intimately related to the magnates and of the same social standing, but, not being Stadtholders, or members of the Order of the Fleece or the Council of State, less closely connected with the Government. In addition there were present several of the smaller nobility, such as the

Marnixes and de Hames, Leefdael, Blois van Neerijen, and Bakkerseele, the last three all belonging to the household of Egmont.

All were Protestants or favourably disposed to the new creed, but they resolved to enlist as many supporters as possible throughout the various provinces, and so it was essential not to deter Catholic noblemen. From the beginning the goal they set before themselves was to bring pressure to bear on the Government to obtain the relaxation, if possible the withdrawal, of the Edicts. From the first moment, however, the leading spirits among them were prepared to use force, and all the time they kept their eyes fixed on Germany, where Louis of Nassau could act as their mediator. There was even some hope of Orange himself. Had he not some time before already examined the possibility of prevailing on the Calvinists to accept the Confession of Augsburg, so that it would be easier to co-operate with the Lutheran princes of Germany, some of whom were bitterly opposed to Calvinism? As far as character went, there were marked differences between the various leaders of this new movement. Firm conviction and idealism characterized the Marnixes and de Hames; Bakkerseele was an ambitious intriguer. Brederode, who at Vianen recognized no master above him (as little as Culemborch did in his town), was the perfect example of the blustering, bellicose, mutinous noble, scion of a long line of fighters who had played their parts in the Hookish wars of the previous century. A survival of the Middle Ages, but yet at the same time how modern! Every revolutionary epoch is familiar with his kind.

Meanwhile, in all secrecy, members were recruited. It should not be thought for a moment that the four or five hundred who joined meant harm to the Catholic religion. The Edicts were hated by Catholics and Protestants alike. Moreover, in the tense atmosphere of that year, the appearance of conspiracy appealed strongly to all turbulent elements, to all who execrated the bureaucratic State and the Brussels centralization. This explains why the Compromise made recruits particularly in the North, and nowhere so many as in Friesland.

The Walloon provinces were but scantily represented. Meanwhile, the leaders, in consultation with Orange, determined their line of action. Marnix of Tholouse and Louis of Nassau drew up a petition which was to be presented to the Governess at Brussels in April 1566. With a reference to the ferment among the people, which threatened to break out into rebellion, the request was put forward that the King abolish the Inquisition and the Edicts, and in concert with the States-General take new measures to deal with the religious question; the nobles demanded a suspension of the persecution until the King's answer should be received. The members of the League were urged to attend in as large numbers as possible the presentation of this petition at Brussels.

But before venturing upon this public step, the leaders sought to reach an understanding with the group of magnates who had pursued a common line of action since the struggle with Granvelle. A conference at Hoogstraten served to show, however, that fatal differences of opinion predominated in this group, while Aerschot, as we know, stood apart, and Mansfeldt, too, had virtually withdrawn. Orange advocated an open avowal of the League and support of the petition, but to Egmont and Meghen this seemed to be taking up too antagonistic an attitude towards the Government. In the upshot the great lords decided that the League must bear its own responsibility, but agreed to represent its demands to the Governess in as favourable a light as possible. In other words, when it came to the point, Egmont and Meghen dared not use their position as Stadtholder and Councillor of State against the Government; on the contrary, they felt that this position bound them indissolubly to the monarchy.

Nevertheless, the sudden disclosure of the existence of the League and the announcement that a petition would be presented at first threw the Governess into a panic. The appearance at Brussels in the first days of April 1566 of some four hundred nobles from almost every province of the Netherlands, their solemn procession to the palace of the Governess, the presentation of the petition by Brederode, Berlaymont's derisive remark about the impudence of these "beggars" (*gueux*), cheerfully transformed by the Leaguers into a title of honour, the banquet where they sat with the chains and wooden cups on their breast—all this constitutes a great event in Netherlands history. Never before had the political unity of the Netherlands nation manifested itself in such dramatic manner. What strikes us most in the description of that vivid and colourful scene, as it was played out in the characteristic setting of old Brussels, studded with the palaces of the nobility, is the use of the French tongue. French was the language of Margaret and her courtiers, as well as of the petition which was being presented to her; and although the overwhelming majority of the nobles themselves were of Dutch speech, for them too French was, so to say, the official language, in which the leaders corresponded amongst themselves, and in which were couched all the watchwords and the entire terminology of the movement. And yet a great noble like Brederode, whose library at Vianen is known to have contained little but French books, was still so far from expressing himself easily in this tongue that in the verbal discussions with Margaret a Walloon noble had to come to the help of his leader. But for the moment nobody took exception to these linguistic conditions. *Gueux* was roughly "Dutched" into *geus*, and "*Vive le Geus!*" shouted the mob at Brussels and Antwerp, at Breda, at Delft, and at Amsterdam, to express their gratitude to the nobles. In these nobles they saw themselves and all the provinces, "the whole of these Netherlands," united against the Spanish king. That was in this movement something new, and something of the greatest importance.

All former rebellions or movements of revolt, even when they were so widespread as that which followed the death of Charles the Bold (when, moreover, the north-eastern provinces still lay outside the State), had borne a distinctly local or provincial character. The States-General, it is true, had more than once, by the very nature of the problems with which the policy of the monarch had confronted them, been inspired with a national consciousness and been driven into a national attitude, but never on former occasions had the people participated so generally and with such enthusiasm as they did

at this time, when the folk of Holland and Friesland, Gelderland, Brabant and Flanders followed with tense interest the
complications between the Governess and the magnates and
the nobility, when Orange and Egmont, Brederode and Culemborch had become figures of truly national dimensions.

This is not to say that the movement expressed itself everywhere with the same dramatic intensity. On the contrary,
although it certainly drew from all parts the forces that sus-
tained it, Brabant was the heart of the Netherlands, and
political life pulsated there at its strongest. Brussels was a
focal point because Court and Government resided there;
Antwerp because of its own national importance. It is noteworthy, too, that the voice of the people, which spoke with
more power and greater political sense there than anywhere
else, always made mention of the Netherlands, and, carrying
the conflict outside the limits of the old Duchy of Brabant,
proclaimed Antwerp as the champion of the seventeen provinces. Netherlands and Netherlandish are now no longer mere
literary terms; they have acquired political meaning. The
innumerable pamphlets and manifestoes, soon to be followed
by the ballads, even though they start from the "Joyous Entry"
of Brabant and speak of Antwerp's special privileges, nevertheless extend their view over the whole Netherlands. Nothing
is more natural. The State had become too unmistakably the
framework of the great political events. No single province
could claim the magnates as its own. The religious movement
ignored provincial boundaries, and the League of Nobles
covered the whole land. National consciousness, prepared for
many a year, but now pushed on by the energy of the rising
revolutionary movement, broke through with elemental force.

On the first tidings of what was in store for her, the Governess implored the great lords to return to her council, and
even before the petition was presented she had deliberated
with them and with the high officials, and decided to yield
on the most pressing point. All the agents and organs of the
Government in the seventeen provinces were instructed to
proceed with caution in the execution of the Edicts. This
amounted to a suspension, and in the meantime the matter

was to be submitted to the King. The nobles celebrated their triumph in boisterous fashion. Orange and even Egmont, who was now veering round once more, appeared at the banquet in the palace of Culemborch, and it was a moment of wild enthusiasm.

But again everything hung on Philip's decision. Two of the great nobles, Bergen and Montigny, were sent to Spain, with the consent of the Governess, to expedite the King's answer—an unfortunate step which was destined seriously to weaken the old union of the magnates in the crisis at hand. Bergen's energy, in particular, could ill be dispensed with at this juncture. Meanwhile the officials and the Knights of the Fleece prepared for the Governess a scheme to mitigate the Edicts, a "Moderation," which might form the basis of a positive religious policy. No one in the Central Government supposed that liberty of conscience, let alone freedom of worship and organization for the heretical sects, was a possible solution, and even Orange dared only very cautiously to hint at this. The scheme of Moderation was known already before the end of April, and it was of such a nature that the people called it the "Murderation." The League was now put to a test in which the sharp cleavage existing between the aims of the Protestant-minded majority among the leaders and the still loyally Catholic majority among the rank and file was soon revealed.

For the Moderation went right against the development of public opinion, which had naturally drawn not a little encouragement from the sensational activities of the nobility at Brussels. All who inclined towards Protestantism considered the Edicts abolished; the refugees, among them many ministers, flocked back from all the neighbouring countries. In May the roads and fields of the textile-manufacturing district of West Flanders began to be the scene of public preaching, a scandal which could never be justified by the promises of the Governess. But it spread like a contagion. While the Governess issued a fresh Edict against the preachers, the consistory of Antwerp resolved to have public worship there also. It was as though a signal had been given. In every province preachers and thirsters after the new gospel emerged from their hiding-places, and that summer saw "hedge-sermons" delivered in the environs of countless Netherlands towns.

Already (this was in mid-July) the Calvinists observed a certain order in their services. The women sat in the middle inside a circle marked out with stakes and cords; their servants and soldiers, who kept guard, formed fighting-order after the sermon, and then they fired stray shots and now and then would shout, "*vive le geus!*" At Ghent the assemblies outside the town were commonly twenty thousand strong, and were attended by people from other places where there was no preaching. And if there should happen to be two successive holy-days, then they stayed the night there, so that they should not have to come back, and cooked their food in the fields. So it was throughout almost all Flanders, Holland, and Zealand.

In this energetic and passionate movement the Calvinists, with their uncompromising theology and with their genius for organization, inevitably became the leaders. Up till now the majority of the Reformers, especially in the North, had not yet joined their ranks. At Antwerp, too, besides the Lutherans, we meet with a figure such as the pastor of the suburb Kiel, who preached after the new fashion without wanting to break away from the Church. Such a middle-position, however, became more and more untenable as popular excitement waxed higher and higher. People wanted to sing the psalms; a new version, based on the French of Marot, had just been published by a West Flemish minister, Dathenus of Kassel. People wanted to listen to the most fiery preachers, such as Moded of Zwolle, who in July had drawn great crowds at Ghent and Brussels, and who came to Antwerp in August.

The Governess looked on in desperation at this breaking down of all barriers. It is true that she had quickly discovered the discord among the great nobility, and there were men about her already advising strong measures. In the States of the Walloon provinces, where nobility and clergy held a ruling position, great annoyance had been expressed at the audacity of the League. Meghen brought some troops into the neigh-bourhood of Antwerp, and appeared to be contemplating an attack on the town. Thereupon Brederode, with a hundred and fifty followers, all clad in "Beggars' grey," made his way into it; the inhabitants received him with tumultuous enthusiasm as a liberator. It looked as if Antwerp were becoming the starting-point of civil war. However deep her mistrust of him, Margaret was compelled to send Orange (who among his many honorary offices numbered that of Burgrave of Antwerp) to guard the town for the Government. For him Brederode was willing to vacate the place, in him the burghers felt confidence. With the strong support of the burgomaster Van Straelen and the pensionary Wesembeke, he now established order there.

But he was as impotent as anyone to check the march of events. The leaders of the League of Nobles, disquieted by the delay in the King's decision, summoned a new assembly for the middle of July at St. Truiden.[1] Although a goodly number of Catholic confederates held aloof, while others, infuriated at the insolence of the Calvinists, vehemently reproached Louis of Nassau and Brederode; although Orange urgently warned his brother that by encouraging the Calvinists he would ruin everything—nevertheless the nobles and the representatives of the consistories resolved upon close co-operation. The leaders foresaw that it would come to fighting. The Lutheran princes must be won over and troops raised in Germany. The consistories must provide the money, the nobles, claiming the right of resistance as belonging to their rank and competent to wield the sword, must lead the revolt. But the Calvinist community did not let itself be restricted to the passive rôle prescribed for it in these plans. The holding of meetings outside churches did not give sufficient vent to their long-suppressed feelings. They longed for action, and in the breaking of the images they found it.

The movement started on the linguistic frontier, in the area where the new cloth manufacture had created an industrial proletariat, particularly amenable to the propagation of a new creed, and whose religious ecstasy was nearly allied to social unrest. A transport of rage suddenly possessed the multitude. Crowds surged into the churches to destroy all the most

[1] St. Truiden: in French—*St. Trond*.

treasured symbols and ornaments of the old religion. This wave of frenzy swept from village to village, Dutch-speaking or Walloon, throughout that industrialized country, and then turned and engulfed town after town. The first outburst, at Poperinghe, took place on August 14th. On the 18th the storm struck Oudenarde, whence it reached Antwerp on the 20th, Ghent on the 22nd; that same day it swept to Amsterdam (where the mob was roused by the sight of fragments of statuary which two merchants brought from Antwerp); thence to Leyden and Delft; on the 25th to Utrecht, and in the following weeks into Friesland and Groningen. In the Walloon country the movement was less widespread, but at Valenciennes it displayed peculiar energy and raised the extreme Calvinist party, led by two ministers, Guy de Bray and Pérégrin de la Grange, into virtual power. Elsewhere, too, the ministers or the consistories had sometimes directed the operations of the iconoclasts. For the most part, however, these excesses caused surprise and discomfiture to the leaders whose fanatical phraseology had roused the temper of the mob to the right pitch. In any case it was a truly Calvinistic work, fierce and honest, restrained by no respect for art or beauty, striving to purge the land for God's elect from the devilish ornaments of idolatry, and to pull down at one blow a past of a thousand years. Nor did the deed once done lack dour approbation from the side of the intellectual leaders of Calvinism.

It is a small matter, or revenge, thus to have destroyed the images, which are only a species of idolatry, since the ecclesiastics have done us a thousand times more hurt and hindrance through their persecutions which broke those statues which God Himself had made and for which He once shed His precious blood, namely, our dearest friends, fathers and mothers, sisters and brothers.

Thus wrote a man of Ghent, and Marnix of St. Aldegonde in a French pamphlet argued to the same effect.

Meanwhile, almost everywhere the authorities had looked on at this savage scene as though paralysed with fright. The clergy hid themselves. In several places, such as Ghent, Yper,

D

and Antwerp, the churches were in the hands of the Calvinists, and Catholic worship was interrupted. On August 23rd the Governess, who felt as if her world came crumbling to pieces before her very eyes, gave her assent to an "Accord" with the leaders of the Compromise, whereby preaching was permitted in all parts where it was already practised, provided that the people laid down their arms and did not interfere with the old religion. Actually it was the Government that had the best of this arrangement, as it gained time to reassert itself, and would alone have armed forces at its disposal—for even the Compromise was dissolved by this agreement—if differences should arise over the execution of the Accord. But in reality the sudden predominance of Calvinism did not rest on sound foundations. In the Walloon provinces, outside Valenciennes and Tournai, a vehement Catholic temper asserted itself under the protection of powerful Stadtholders. But in the Dutch-speaking provinces, too, the town-magistrates were everywhere as much offended as they were terrified by the outburst.

The exercise of the new or Reformed religion (wrote the pensionary of Leyden, Paulus Buys) has led many people to resort to idleness, to forget the duty of submission to authority, and to bring justice into disrepute.

The Stadtholders, charged with the carrying out of the Accord, did their best to stir the intimidated majority out of their frightened passivity; thus did Egmont in Flanders, and even Orange at Antwerp, though the latter was now distrusted by the Catholics. In his hands the Accord became at Antwerp a formal religious peace between the three persuasions, Catholic, Calvinist, and Lutheran; and, with his eye on Germany, he was particularly careful to encourage this last.

Meanwhile, the Governess had recovered from her fright. She had found in Mansfeldt an intrepid counsellor, while some time ago Philip had sent her money, so that she was in a position to raise troops. And now it was quickly apparent to what an extent the fierce emergence of the Calvinistic element had robbed the movement against the Government of that attraction which it had hitherto exercised over the national

instincts of the Netherlandish community. As soon as the
Governess bravely came forward as the protectress of Church
and Society, she was again accepted as the natural leader of
the nation, and many who had taken part in or sympathized
with the movement of opposition now, frightened, disillusioned,
or indignant, rallied round her.

So when it came to a trial of strength, it was in the most
unfavourable circumstances. And a trial had to come, for the
situation created by the Accord of August 23rd could not last.
Margaret roundly condemned the interpretation Orange had
given the Accord at Antwerp, and she had not a good word
to say even for the agreements concluded by Egmont for
carrying it into execution in the Flemish towns. And then
there was still the King; indeed, in the long run, there was only
the King. No one but a past-master in self-deception, like
Egmont, could believe that the King would ever put up with
even the most conservative interpretation of the Accord. Very
soon there came rumours of the King's anger, of his plans
to punish the Netherlanders—and in particular the great
nobles, whom he regarded as the authors of the disturbances—
and of military preparations. Orange wanted to attempt armed
resistance, and held that a national revolution was still possible
if Egmont and Hoorn would stand by him. Egmont even now
retained the confidence of many Catholics, and might be able
to heal the rupture in the national movement caused by the
image-breaking. But Egmont obstinately refused co-operation.
He persisted in his delusion that the Government would be
moved to call the States-General together, although it should
have been obvious that Philip would know better than to
provide the opposition with such a rallying-point, which had
already proved so dangerous in the time of Maximilian, and
of which he himself had had most disagreeable experience.
Egmont's vacillations had a demoralizing effect. Although it
was plain that the policy of the Governess aimed at the annul-
ment of the Accord, it proved absolutely impossible to recon-
stitute the Compromise that had been so rashly dissolved. On
the contrary, every day erstwhile members came to Brussels
to avow their repentance. On the other hand the Catholic

nobility of the Walloon provinces began to manifest an ever
more bellicose attitude in support of the Government.

There remained, of course, a party which could not submit.
These were the Calvinists, for whom it was a question of life
or death. But they stood alone in opposition to a Government
now growing daily stronger. At a synod held at Antwerp and
attended by representatives not only of Flanders, Brabant, and
the Walloon region, but of Friesland as well, it was determined
on December 1st that in the Netherlands a group of vassals
had the right, in conjunction with a part of the population,
to offer armed resistance to the monarch if he laid hands on
the privileges—old Netherlandish doctrine which could now
be fortified with Calvin, since he invested the "lower authorities" with the right of resistance. A "group of vassals" could
indeed be reckoned on. Brederode, who had removed the
statues and introduced the Reformation in his own town of
Vianen, was found ready to assume the command of the troops
which were to be raised in Germany with the money supplied
by the Calvinist congregations.

Orange had been asked first. He certainly had no longer
any illusions about the intentions of the Government. At
Antwerp and in his Stadtholderships, whither he betook himself in the autumn, he did what he could, ostensibly on the
basis of the Accord, to strengthen the position of the Calvinists.
He sent reassuring (and false) reports to Brussels on the subject
of Brederode's activities at Vianen. With the arrangement he
made at Utrecht for Calvinistic worship the States and Court
of this province would have nothing to do, so anti-Catholic
did it appear to them, while at Amsterdam Orange had to
push through the arrangement against the will of the staunchly
Catholic town government. But openly identify himself with
the Calvinists he would not. He felt too strongly that the
national tide was running against them; moreover, he feared
that to do so would be to prejudice his connections in Germany,
and that was after all where the troops must come from.

The results of the collection of money among the Calvinists
were bitterly disappointing. Moreover, the leaders could not
control the movement. When in December the Governess went

right against the Accord, at the same time pronouncing Valenciennes to be in a state of rebellion and despatching a force under the Lord of Noircarmes to lay siege to it, bands of men sprang to arms as if of their own accord throughout Artois and Walloon Flanders, and in the traditionally unruly coast-land of Flanders. The "wondrous year" 1566 was not yet come to an end, when they were annihilated by Rassenghien, Stadtholder of Tournai, at Watrelos, and by Noircarmes at Lannoy. The remnant fled to Antwerp and took service with the troops which Brederode, from his headquarters at Vianen, was now having recruited.

While the Court party rejoiced over the success of the first encounter, while Egmont slid still farther away from his one-time friends and in Flanders began forcibly to destroy the arrangement, which he had himself carried into effect on the basis of the Accord, Brederode's party girded itself for a desperate effort. In February 1567 the Lord of Bombergen marched from Antwerp and threw himself into Den Bosch. But the chief attack was launched on Zealand. Orange was now looking on from Antwerp once more, still further alienated from the Government at Brussels, to which he had refused to take a special new oath of allegiance demanded of all Stadtholders, high officials, nobles, and officers (Egmont had taken it). It was thought that Orange's covert assistance would be valuable to an enterprise in a province of which he was Stadtholder; once they had conquered this territory, so well defensible from a strategic point of view, the rebels would be able to defy the Government. The leadership of the expedition was entrusted to Marnix of Tholouse. The attempt on Flushing in the beginning of March 1567 miscarried, however, and the troops, disembarked at Terneuzen, wandered about in the neighbourhood of Antwerp. Without a doubt Tholouse had hopes of mastering Antwerp, which after having been the spiritual centre of the movement for so long would then have become the strategic centre as well. But Orange was not to be hustled out of his middle course. With the help of the Catholics and Lutherans, who together formed the great majority of the citizens, and who declined at any price to be

drawn into the incalculable hazards of a rebellion, he kept the
gates of the city shut. Tholouse and his men were thus still
in the open country—at Oosterweel—when the troops of the
Governess appeared on the scene; they included some companies of Egmont's and were led by the Lord of Beauvoir.
At danger to his life Orange held the excited Calvinists of
Antwerp in check, while their brethren were cut to pieces at
Oosterweel. Tholouse was killed. The next day Valenciennes
surrendered to Noircarmes; De Bray and De la Grange,
bitterly denouncing Orange as a traitor, were hanged.

The ill-tidings reached Brederode at Amsterdam, where he
had forced his way in and was living on terms of armed peace
with the Catholic-minded magistrates. There was no longer
any hope for the cause of the rebellion. In the East the Stadtholders—Aremberg in Friesland, Groningen and Overysel,
Meghen in Gelderland—had suppressed the preachings and
occupied towns which thought of resistance. Orange's position
had become untenable. In April he left Antwerp and the
country; for the present he went to Dillenburg. For Brederode,
too, nothing remained but flight; he went to Cleve. A number
of his noblemen fell into the hands of the Stadtholder of
Friesland on their retreat across the Zuider Zee. Thousands
of others, nobles and citizens, who were Calvinists or in some
way compromised in the commotions, followed their leaders
into exile.

It was not only from Margaret and the men who carried
out her policy that they fled. The Governess was indeed
mistress of the country, and Mansfeldt and Aerschot, Meghen,
Aremberg, and Noircarmes were triumphant, while the wretched
Egmont added a wavering voice to the chorus of rejoicing. But
in Italy, meanwhile, there had been gathered together from
Naples and Sicily, Milan and Sardinia, four regiments of
chosen Spanish infantry, together with 1,200 cavalry, who in
the beginning of June 1567 set out, over the Alps, through
the Franche-Comté and Lorraine, towards the Netherlands,
where they arrived in August. Their commander was one of
Philip's most noted military captains and statesmen, the Duke
of Alva, the man who in the Spanish Council had always

advocated the policy of rigour against the unruly Netherlands and whom Philip, immediately on receipt of the crushing news of the image-breaking, had appointed to carry out his vengeance.

c. THE TYRANNY OF ALVA

The resistance to the non-national tendencies of Philip's rule, to the Spanish troops, to the excessive centralization and to the religious persecution, had proceeded from the politically privileged classes. The national movement had found expression in the activities of the Knights of the Fleece, the lower nobility, the town governments, and of the States assemblies, in which all these could co-operate. Calvinism had at first added a warlike element to the movement, but before long it brought about a split in the nation, and through the image-breaking it scared in particular the politically privileged, the politically active. Thus the Brussels Government had been able to subdue the country with the help of the native nobility (among the most considerable and energetic of whom the Walloons, it is true, were much over-represented), and with the sympathies of a great part of the citizens, particularly of the town governments.

The prospects in the summer of 1567 were therefore as favourable as possible to the distant monarch. Never had there been so much readiness to accept the government of his representative as a national Government. The old watchwords of opposition seemed for the moment forgotten. In the reaction from the violent events of the past year the people of standing and the local authorities vied with each other in their show of loyalty. All the most intractable elements of the opposition had emigrated and filled the German border-towns—Emden, Wesel, and Köln—with their misery and their bickerings. It is easy to understand that many were in a bitter mood.

> We are by all deserted, and forlorn;
> In truth a just reward, which doth requite
> Our talk of Orange's power and Breero's might.
> Right worthy are we now of all men's scorn.

Thus one of the "Beggars' songs" which expressed the varying moods of the party of resistance in those years. Brederode, meanwhile, was diligent enough and travelled round in northern Germany to raise men and money. But the money would not come, and he had soon to disband the troops he succeeded in collecting. Orange sat tight in the ancestral castle at Dillenburg, greatly distrusted by the many who could not forgive him his anti-Calvinistic activities at Antwerp. All told, Margaret of Parma could be very well satisfied, and she was not a little proud of her achievement.

But nothing was farther from Philip's mind than the idea of accepting it as the basis for his policy. Margaret had always governed with the nobility and come under the influence first of one group then of another. Finally, although no doubt circumstances were not a little in her favour, she had taken excellent advantage of the dissensions among the nobles; but Philip detested in his soul the very idea of allowing any part of the nation a say on its affairs. To him it seemed that now was the moment to make the royal authority in the Netherlands completely independent. Alva came not only to visit the evil-doers with merciless retribution and wipe out the last vestiges of sedition and heresy, but to destroy the ancient privileges of the country, the root of all the evil, and to raise up on the site thus cleared and levelled the straight, symmetrical edifice of absolutism, the ideal of the new age. In course of time this attempt was to rouse all the forces of national resistance once more out of their seeming death-slumber, and at the same time to give the exiles, and the radical party in general, a fresh chance to seize the leadership they had lost.

On August 22, 1567, Alva rode into Brussels. Margaret, greatly concerned about her position and deeply offended, had for a moment thought of resisting, although in the country where eight years earlier the withdrawal of the Spanish troops had been so vehemently demanded no voice was lifted against their return. Alva assured the Governess that he only came to assist her, a piece of dissimulation which was necessary in order that the Count of Hoorne, who was away in Germany, should not be deterred from coming back. Hoorne came back on September 7th. On the 9th he and Egmont, together with Bakkerseele and Van Straelen, were unexpectedly made prisoners by the arbitrary command of the Duke. As soon as the news of the successful *coup* reached Spain (but what a pity that neither Orange nor Hoogstraten had let themselves be enticed from their hiding-places!), Hoorne's brother, Montigny, whom the King had thus far held fast by means of the most flattering pretences, was taken into safe custody; Bergen had died some time before.

To understand the tremendous impression caused by the arrest of Egmont and Hoorne, it is necessary to recall what a position the great nobles possessed in the Habsburg-Burgundian State, how much the people looked up to them, and how solemnly the personal safety of the Knights of the Fleece was guaranteed by the privileges of the order. But according to the political theory preached by Alva nothing could hold out against the crime of lese-majesty, and on the same theory all the opposition offered to the King during the last few years could be brought under that head. Who then could consider himself safe? There was still a small group of Knights of the Fleece at Brussels; Aerschot, Berlaymont, Aremberg, Meghen, and Mansfeldt. Of these the three last had once participated in the campaign against the Cardinal. They trembled and bowed their heads. The protests and admonitions of the German princes who belonged to the Order were unsupported by action. Margaret, deeply mortified, could only mingle her tears with those of the Countess of Egmont, and at the end of the year took her departure, accompanied by Mansfeldt, leaving Alva both in name and in practice the ruler of the country. The other great officers of the Netherlands, however greatly dismayed at heart, continued to function. It was not so much that their co-operation served to conceal the brutal fact of foreign domination as that their knowledge of the country and people was of value to Alva, and this was true particularly of Viglius, who, reserving recrimination and lamentation for his confidential correspondence, continued to serve.

The Duke's first and chief act of government after the

arrests of the 9th of September was the institution of a special court to punish those guilty of the commotions of the year before. Viglius assisted in composing that body, the very purpose of which was to hack its way through all opposing privileges. These arbitrary proceedings became even more insulting when foreigners—Spaniards—were appointed to membership, and, confident of the Governor's favour, soon assumed a tone of authority. The Chancellor of Gelderland and the Presidents of the Courts of Flanders and Artois thus met at the council board Del Rio and De Vargas, the latter of whom had incurred a dishonouring sentence in Spain. He was nevertheless a man after Alva's heart, who in his letters to the King keeps on praising his zeal, which forms so brilliant a contrast to the hesitations and the juridical scrupulousness displayed by the natives. Among the members of the Blood Council this De Vargas, who knew no French and used to bully his colleagues as well as his victims in bad Latin, acquired a notoriety of his own. The phrase which he threw at the frightened delegates of the University of Leuven come to protest against the abduction of Orange's eldest son—*non curamus privilegios vestros*—is still remembered.

At first, since Alva's governing consisted entirely of the organization and execution of a reign of terror, the Blood Council was in effect the highest organ of government. The Duke was not only its president, but his signature was required to make decisions valid, and the opinion of a minority sufficed. Neither by law nor equity was Alva guided in planning his policy, but solely by the interest of the State which, as he and Philip saw it, demanded that men should be intimidated. This is what he himself wrote to the King in January 1568, when the public, downcast as was their mood, were beginning already to whisper of "a general pardon":

A great deal remains to be done first. The towns must be punished for their rebelliousness with the loss of their privileges; a goodly sum must be squeezed out of private persons; a permanent tax obtained from the States of the country. It would therefore be unsuitable to proclaim a pardon at this juncture. Everyone must be made to live in constant fear of the roof breaking down over his head. Thus will the towns comply with what will be ordained for them, private persons will offer high ransoms, and the States will not dare to refuse what is proposed to them in the King's name.

Morning and night, therefore, he laboured, with Berlaymont, Noircarmes, and Viglius in the Council, drafting the sentences of the emigrant lords, whose estates were seized as well as those of the late Marquess of Bergen; drawing up rules to create new categories of culprits; studying the reports of the commissaries sent out into the provinces. In the meantime Egmont and Hoorne were examined. As to the prisoners of a lesser rank, if it was thought that they were able to implicate the magnates, they were lifted on to and off the rack for months. On one day in March 1568 five hundred new arrests were made all over the Netherlands. It was not long before the executions began, and in the meantime it was Alva's chief concern to stop the emigrations, which started afresh after every act of terror, and obtain the forfeiture of the victims' possessions, notwithstanding the privileges, and at the expense even of their creditors. Most of the signatories of the Compromise, in so far as they had not fled, were left unmolested after submission.

Against the towns, on the other hand, Alva proceeded with extreme rigour. As early as October 1567 he had gone to Antwerp in person, compelling the magistrates, frightened by Van Straelen's fate, to raise a tribute, out of which a castle was built. Indictments were now drawn up against practically all the principal towns, charging them with the crimes of commission or of omission of which their magistrates had been guilty during the troubles. A number of pensionaries—salaried legal advisers of town governments—were successively arrested: Joost Borluut, pensionary of Ghent; Vorroux, pensionary of the States of Namur; Van den Eynde, pensionary of the States of Holland; Jan van der Cammen and Pieter Wasteel, pensionaries of Mechlin; Roeland de Rijcke, pensionary of Leuven. In the end only Vorroux was found guilty, but Van der Cammen and Van den Eynde did not survive their captivity. Dirk Volkertszoon Coornhert, too, secretary to the magistrates of Haarlem, was carried off to The Hague, "pinioned, manacled, and handcuffed like the meanest criminal," and was imprisoned for some time at the Gevangenpoort.

Never was nation subjected to a reign of terror with more calculated deliberation or more systematic persistence. The "Iron Duke's" imperturbable severity had a paralysing effect. The Netherlands people had offered no resistance to the entry of the ten thousand Spanish troops. They now let themselves be maltreated by the man who commanded their halberds and musquets. Only in West Flanders stirred rebellion, strengthened in January 1568 by the return from England of some fifteen hundred refugees. Bands led by rude chieftains roamed over the country, plundering the vicarages and murdering or torturing the priests. It needed only a few regular troops to put down that movement, although for a long time to come Wild Beggars (as they were called) continued to hide here and there in the woods and marshes of that distant region. No good could come of such ferocious outbursts of popular despair. If the country was to be saved, it must be by a great leader and by means of external assistance.

That great leader could be no man but Orange, even though Alva's tyranny had not yet pushed the religious question into the background to such an extent that it was possible for anyone man to possess the confidence of the whole nation. The Calvinists found much to object to in Orange, but they could not do without him, especially when Brederode, the only man they might have tried to raise up in his stead, died unexpectedly in February 1568. As for the Prince, the circumstances in which he now found himself inevitably drove him on towards the Protestant camp. In January 1568 he had been summoned before the Blood Council—together with Count Louis, Hoogstraten, Brederode, Culemborch, and Van den Bergh—a summons which was the sure forerunner of condemnation and forfeiture of goods. He now lived as a Lutheran with his Lutheran relatives in Germany. Were he to raise the banner of revolt, the Calvinist exiles would naturally flock to it from all sides. He could not but appear to the Catholic people of the Netherlands as the champion of Protestantism. But the way things had gone, it was inevitable that Protestants

should man the front ranks in the struggle with foreign domination. Orange at least never lost sight of the great fact that
the nation was still largely Catholic, nor did he ever conceive
the aim of the great movement to be the overthrow of this
Catholicism. What he constantly strove for was the union of
all against the Spanish oppressor, and in the free Netherlands
of which he dreamt there was to be freedom for Catholics
no less than for Protestants. Amongst all the leaders in exile
Orange was the one who held to this view most firmly. Nor
was any of them a European figure in the way he was. None
could make such an impression as he did when he protested
in the face of all Europe against the summons of the Blood
Council and Alva's usurpation—as he termed it—of authority.
None was so true a statesman, able to survey Europe in order
to make use of any political opportunity that might offer itself.

Truth to tell, the readiness to help of the Lutheran princes,
to humour whom he had always kept the Calvinists at arm's
length, fell very far short of his expectations, and as no great
sums were obtained from Antwerp and the exiles either, he
was left to scrape together what money he could with the
assistance of his brothers. The County of Nassau was involved
in heavy debts. The friendship of some leading princes was
nevertheless valuable in that it enabled Orange to make full
use of the anarchy prevailing in much-divided western Germany, where nobody disturbed him when he levied troops and
prepared attacks on the neighbouring Habsburg state. Soldiers
were plentiful and to be had cheap that summer as a result
of the peace ending the French civil war, in which numbers
of German mercenaries had served.

Numerous attempts were planned by Orange and his asso-
ciates in 1568. All were based on the expectation of some
co-operation on the part of the Netherlands people. Several
proved instant failures, but at the end of April the impetuous
Louis, at the head of a small band, invaded the Ommelands
of Groningen from East-Friesland. Only in the town of
Groningen was there a garrison, and that a weak one, so the
Stadtholder, Aremberg, had to wait for Spanish reinforcements
from the South. When at last he was able to advance against

the Beggars, their numbers had been swollen considerably by local sympathizers, and at Heiligerlee he and his Spaniards were defeated. Aremberg himself was killed. Alva showed himself equal to the emergency. He marched north in person in order to wipe out the impression of the event. But before leaving he staged a number of executions so as to strike terror into the hearts of the provinces from which he had for a brief period to withdraw so many troops. On the 1st of June eighteen noblemen were beheaded on the Sablon square at Brussels; some of them belonged to the party which had fallen into Aremberg's hands on the Zuider Zee more than a year before; amongst the others was Van Straelen; all had been sentenced by the Blood Council months ago. The next day a few more heads fell. Then, on the 5th of June, the execution of Egmont and Hoorne took place on the Great Market Square in Brussels. It was not without justification that the Beggars' song imputed Egmont's fate to his "inconstancy." However that may be, Alva's severity achieved its object. He was able to take his army to Groningen-land with an easy mind.

And yet, suppose that Orange had been ready to attempt his invasion of the heart of the Netherlands and had marched into Brabant at this moment! But Orange was not ready, lack of money was holding him back, and Alva was given time to restore affairs in the North. He pursued Louis' retreating army into the Count of East-Friesland's territory and annihilated it at Jemmingen. After having made the town of Groningen feel his fist—he compelled it at last to receive its first bishop and had a fortress built there as at Antwerp—he was prepared to march South again and meet the Prince of Orange.

For Orange would not abandon the enterprise, even though his German relatives, thoroughly frightened, were now trying to hold him back. In the neighbourhood of Trier a numerous army was assembling under his command. It was indeed far too numerous. Even after pledging all that he and his brothers possessed and obtaining the meagre contributions of the consistories, he had been hard put to it to raise money enough for the first month's pay. A crowd of exiles marched along with the army hoping to return into their country under his leadership. There were Count Louis, escaped from Jemmingen, Hoogstraten, Culemborch, De Hames, and other noblemen members of the Compromise. Eloquent manifestoes announced to the people their liberation, and tried to rouse them to rebellion against their oppressors, against Alva in particular, who was alleged to be acting against the King's wishes. But the mercenaries were driven to join Orange by nothing but the hope of booty, and never did a more unruly and rapacious host set forth to liberate a country. Alva, who had his own smaller army in infinitely better control, decided not to risk a battle and merely kept the Prince under observation. It was certainly against his wish that Orange succeeded in crossing the Maas, but the striking feat (which was not accomplished until the 6th of October) led to no results. In the towns everywhere sympathizers were following the movements of Orange's army with tense expectations. The Spanish party felt that nothing but fear of the garrisons kept the people in check, and every precaution had been taken. In all the most exposed towns—Thienen,[1] Leuven, Brussels, Mechlin—Alva had placed reliable governors, Walloon noblemen every one of them— Hierges (Gilles de Berlaymont, the eldest son of the President of the Council of Finance), Beauvoir and Robles, Bournonville, Aerschot, Du Roeulx, and de Crecques (the last three belonging to the house of Croy)—all with Walloon troops. No doubt, moreover, the excesses committed by the liberators created a bad impression. In any case, not a town stirred. In North Holland a movement in the country-side, not dissimilar to that of the Wild Beggars in West Flanders, but which used the name of Orange, was suppressed by the citizen guards of Hoorn and Enkhuizen. Thus the Prince soon had to retreat without having achieved anything, his army degenerated into an undisciplined mob, starving in the inclement winter, burning, ravishing, and murdering. After having escaped on to French territory he wandered about for months, pressed for payment by the soldiery, until he fled from them by stealth. No more pitiable failure could

[1] Thienen: in French—*Tirlemont*.

be imagined. Profound was Orange's disappointment at the inaction of the Netherlands people. He himself had become the laughing-stock of his enemies. Yet, "my heart hath remained constant in adversity": so the Beggar poet made him speak in these very days. There exists no more noble expression of acquiescence in misfortune, coupled with unshakable faith in the future, than the *Wilhelmus* song, which is still a national anthem in Holland, while the Flemish Nationalists, too, love it as a true expression of their aspirations. A cause which was able to find such a voice at such a moment disposed of greater reserves of power than was guessed at by Alva and the men who humbly did his bidding.

For the time being, however, Alva's authority was firmly established. The reign of terror continued. The Blood Council was still hard at work. The forfeitures constituted a source of revenue that the Government could not do without. But it was one which from its very nature could not flow indefinitely, and so the Duke proceeded to tackle the chief purpose of his mission—the completion of the absolutist system—by making the Government financially independent of the States for good and all. At bottom Alva's extraordinary powers were intended only to make the true Burgundian-Habsburg principles triumph over opposition which in normal times had to be respected. He carried farther the organization of the new bishoprics from the point at which it had been left by his predecessor. He also attempted to create order out of the chaos of the law, which was still purely medieval and differed from province to province. In 1570 the Ordinance of the Penal Law was issued; drafted by the jurists of the central councils, it was to have legal force for the whole of the Netherlands. In many respects it was an excellent piece of work, but its introduction met with powerful obstacles. The financial independence of the Government, however, was conceived as the basis of everything.

Alva had in mind the introduction of a tax which was to be granted by the States once for all. In March 1569 he summoned a meeting of the States-General and demanded their consent to a tax called the Tenth Penny, which had been devised after a Spanish pattern, and by which 10 per cent. was claimed of the value of every article whenever sold. Recalcitrant towns were brought to reason by having the hated Spanish soldiers quartered on them. The States of Utrecht refused obstinately, on the ground that they formed no part of the Patrimonial Provinces, to which with this exception the tax was confined. Alva knew how to deal with such disobedience. The entire States of the province were summoned before the Council of Blood on the charge of having neglected their duty in the troubles of 1566, and after long legal argument were found guilty and declared to have forfeited all their rights. Small wonder if the other provinces, however reluctantly, gave their consent. As usual the real struggle was fought over the execution of what had been formally decided upon. What roused the Netherlanders to opposition against the Tenth Penny was not only the principle of a permanent tax but the nature of that tax, which, suitable as it might be to Spanish conditions, menaced ruin to an industrial and trading country. Even so economic life was seriously incommoded by the troubles, the forfeitures, and the emigration. Now the air was thick with complaints and protests, and the Government officials at Brussels added their own grave warnings. For the time being, therefore, the Governor contented himself with an extraordinary grant raised by the provinces after the old fashion in lieu of the tax; meanwhile the matter was to be further investigated. The period of grace came to an end in 1571; and now Alva, regardless of the difficulties raised by his councillors and of the objections moved by staunch loyalists like Noircarmes and Berlaymont, and even by the Bishops, announced the introduction of the Tenth Penny—in a considerably toned-down version, it is true. In the spring of 1572 a beginning was to be made with the collection.

But the situation was no longer what it had been two years ago. In 1570 a Pardon had at length been issued. It is true that the exceptions enumerated in it embraced practically all the real malefactors, so that it was still out of question for the exiles to return except under the leadership of Orange.

But even so Alva had divested himself of that extraordinary authority which we saw him using against Utrecht, for instance, and men plucked up courage more readily to resist him and his schemes. The spectacle of the divisions of the Central Government, which could scarcely remain concealed, revived the courage of urban and provincial authorities and of all who, whatever their reason, hated the foreigner's system of government. The temper of the Netherlands people was in a ferment.

Scathing remarks have frequently been made to the effect that the Netherlanders suffered the torments to which they were put on account of religion, and only rose in revolt when they felt their purse to be endangered. At the time a Beggar song represented Alva as scoffing:

> They did not care about the ruin of their country
> As long as I let them stay with their fleshpots,
> But now that I lay violent hands on their Mammon
> They want to drive me out of these lands.

And indeed one can understand the exiles feeling thus bitterly. They always talked as if Protestantism was, or ought to be, the cause dearest to the heart of all Netherlanders. But in reality the religious question, far from being a unifying factor, could not but make for disruption amongst the Netherlands people; at least from the moment when, however briefly, the menace of a Calvinist domination had shown its face. Nothing is more natural, on the other hand, than that the Tenth Penny should have proved an efficient means to heal the cleavage. And yet even now the situation remained such that it must inevitably be the Calvinists who would avail themselves of every fresh opportunity, and thereby the others were sure to be deterred once more. The Calvinists were the bitterest enemies of Spanish rule, and in the exiles, who had nothing more to lose and who were all the time looking longingly across the frontier, they possessed a peerless band of picked shock troops.

It is true that Orange was still the one and only leader, or rather, that had once more become his position since he had been able to free himself from the most embarrassing consequences of the disastrous campaign of 1568. He had now come to an arrangement with his creditors which at least permitted him to go and live at Dillenburg again. But Orange had himself drawn closer to the Calvinists. No other allies equally zealous and reliable offered themselves to him. Even before setting out on his campaign of 1568 he had concluded an intimate alliance with the leaders of the French Huguenots, Condé and Coligny. In view of their Kings' design to root up "the true religion" and "to establish an unlimited tyranny on the ruin of the nobility and of the propertied classes," the two sides had promised each other assistance, and whoever witnessed the triumph of liberty of conscience in his country first was to exert himself on behalf of the other as if he were still in danger himself. Thus, after the failure of his invasion into Brabant, the Prince had for a while fought in the ranks of the Huguenots. Since then peace had been restored in France, and now that Coligny's influence at Court was plainly rising—Condé had been killed—Orange kept his eyes fixed on him full of hope for the fulfilment of the agreement of 1568. In the meantime he also entertained close relations with the Netherlandish Calvinist communities in the German frontier towns. His most useful personal assistants, too, were Calvinists, namely, the exiled pensionary of Antwerp, Wesembeke, who entered his council early in 1570, and from the end of that year Marnix of St. Aldegonde, who had just issued that bitterly antipopish pamphlet *The Beehive*, which has a place of its own in the history of Dutch prose. As the representative of Orange, Marnix went in 1571 to a synod of exiled Calvinists held at Bedtbur in the County of Gulich, where he urged the need of unity, if possible even with the Lutherans.

Yet Orange continued to work for the nation as a whole, and, indeed, out of its midst non-Calvinist elements did enter into relations with him. In January 1570 he received an unexpected visit from Paulus Buys, the pensionary of Leyden, whose unfavourable verdict on the effects of the Reformation will be remembered. The pensionary faced the dangers of that journey in order to inform the deposed Stadtholder of Holland of the temper created among the urban magistrates of that province by Alva's reign of terror and the threat of the Tenth Penny. A scheme was worked out for the organization of a revolt in the northern provinces; in Utrecht, whose States had suffered more than any from the tyrant's rough handling, even the clergy was involved in the conspiracy. Attempts were planned on a number of towns, money was collected in order to enable the Prince to come to the assistance with an army. It all ended in disappointment. Grievous mistakes were committed, money proved hard to come by, and Orange wrote bitterly that even the German princes asked themselves what had become of the famed love of liberty of the Netherlanders, a people who were reputed to be ready for any sacrifices in the preservation of their privileges.

Why was it that the Prince and his Brabant councillor— for Wesembeke displayed tremendous activity on behalf of these schemes—directed their attention to the northern provinces so specifically? The visit of Paulus Buys, Orange's particular relations with provinces of which he had been Stadtholder, these were contributory causes. But the main considerations were of a different nature, and in order to grasp this fact it should be realized quite clearly that the problem as it presented itself to Orange and his advisers was above all a strategic problem. Protestantism and disaffection were distributed fairly evenly over the whole of the Dutch-speaking Netherlands. The liberator could count everywhere on the sympathy of the population, and no doubt its character was everywhere composed in similar proportions of courage and cowardice, public spirit and egoism. In those respects there was nothing to choose between Hollanders and Brabanders, Flemings and Groningers. The question was, Where could an attacker cause the greatest embarrassment to the occupying Power?

In 1568 Louis of Nassau's raid in the province of Groningen had proved how easily an initial success could be gained in that outlying and inadequately garrisoned region. On the other hand the Prince's own expedition had shown only too clearly that the South, held immediately in the grip of the conqueror and his troops, was unable to do so much as to stir. In 1571 another Brabander, Geldorp, then rector of the Latin school at Duisburg, drew up a statement for the Prince, in which he characterized the invasion of Brabant as a strategic mistake:

country and circumstances were nowhere so favourable for the enemy as there, while, on the contrary, once you have got a foothold in the maritime provinces, it will be easy to resist all attempts at expulsion. Next time, therefore, Holland should be the objective. There is to be found the converging-point of trade routes which he who obtains a firm footing there will be able to command. It will be unnecessary to occupy more than a few towns, by preference in the neighbour-hood of the Zuider Zee. That will at once give to our privateers a safe retreat and a market. The enemy, hampered by the rivers and lakes, will not easily surprise us there. Town after town will choose our side and a free trading commonwealth will arise, which will be an example to Brabant and Flanders, tempting them similarly to throw off the yoke, or which, if they prove incapable of doing that, will be able to keep them cut off from all trade and traffic.

Evidently these were the ideas which the year before had guided the enterprises of Wesembeke. They had been aimed mainly at Enkhuizen, which was to have been connected with Germany by means of Zutfen, Deventer, and Kampen; the Maas towns, Rotterdam, Dordt, had also been thought of. It is easy now to see that this was a purely strategic conception, in which the desire to supply the Sea Beggars with dependable harbours had played a considerable part.

Among the forces at the disposal of Orange the Sea Beggars were indeed of the utmost importance. Even when Louis of Nassau advanced into Groningen land in 1568 he had been joined by supporters who had come by sea in their own ships. After the defeat these had turned Emden into their centre of operations, and, sailing along the coasts of Groningen and Friesland, had been plundering monasteries and churches, somewhat after the manner of the Wild Beggars in Flanders. When Orange was forced to disband his army, a number of noblemen joined them. Soon Orange himself, in his capacity of sovereign Prince of Orange, regularized their position by providing them with letters of marque. At the same time he tried to cure them of their fierce pirates' habits and accustom them to order and discipline. A Flemish nobleman,

Dolhain, was commissioned by him to organize them, using England, which was at that time on bad terms with Alva, as his base. That attempt proved a failure. In 1570 Louis of Nassau established a new centre at La Rochelle, the strong port of which the Huguenots had then just made themselves masters.

At a time when the obligations of neutrality could be stretched so far, while moreover the Spanish Government in the Netherlands disposed of no naval power of any importance, it was possible for the privateering of the Sea Beggars to develop considerable activity. Their prize-money was to help the Prince in raising another army. They caused, moreover, great damage to Netherlands shipping, creating a general sense of insecurity and increasing the unrest in the country kept down by Alva. As long, however, as they depended on the favour of foreign rulers who were exposed to the pressure of Spain, their position remained precarious. The advantage which the Huguenot cause gained by the possession of La Rochelle was not lost on the Netherlands rebels.

And yet Geldorp's scheme was no longer consonant with the Prince's intentions in 1571. It is true that he did not disguise from himself the strategic importance of the coastal towns of Holland, but the failure of the attempts of the previous year had caused him to doubt the capacity of the Netherlands people to start a rebellion of their own accord. He therefore based all his calculations on the European situation. Assistance from France—it was this which seemed to hold the only promise of salvation, and it was with a view to this that the warning memory of 1568 was to be disregarded and another direct attack launched on the main position of Spanish power in Brabant.

In France Coligny, the leader of the Huguenots, had since the peace of 1570 gained considerable influence over the mind of the young King, Charles IX, an influence which he used to direct his ambition to the resumption of the old struggle with Habsburg. In 1571 Louis of Nassau came over to Fontainebleau from La Rochelle in order to discuss with the King schemes for the expulsion of the Spaniards from the Netherlands. The secret of these interviews could not be prevented from leaking out, and the indignation and uneasiness of Alva may be imagined. But France as champion of the cause of Netherlands independence? No doubt in the forthcoming contest the Netherlands rebels managed more than once to play off successfully against their oppressor the rivalry of Habsburg and Valois. But these tactics were never without peril, and if the projects of 1571 had come to be carried out, Netherlands nationality, still only striving towards consciousness, would at once have fallen into worse jeopardy than that with which Habsburg domination threatened it.

According to the English Ambassador at the French Court —who was informed because the participation of his Queen was hoped for—it was intended to divide the liberated Netherlands. Flanders and Artois were to fall to the share of France (it was at least hoped that Charles IX would content himself with those provinces which had still owed allegiance to his grandfather), Holland and Zealand were to go to England, while the government of the remainder was

to be committed to some prince of Germany, which in reason cannot be but to the Prince of Orange.

In judging this project it should be borne in mind that Louis of Nassau, in spite of his having devoted his life to the cause of Netherlands Protestantism, was a foreigner, while it is improbable that Orange had any knowledge of it. It is certainly a fact that the movement in the grip of which the Netherlands now found themselves was by no means exclusively governed by national sentiment, and few were able to distinguish behind the catchwords of "the privileges," "religious liberty," or "Protestantism" the positive aim of an independent Netherlands state. Yet it may well be considered significant of the latent strength of the nationalist factor that in the stormy times which were beginning no Netherlandish leader ever meddled with schemes like the one mentioned, and that in the end the idea of Netherlands unity was only given up under the stress of superior military power. Nevertheless at the opening of the War of Independence this incident rises up as a reminder of the dangers to which French, English, and German interference had exposed the development of a Netherlandish nationality in former centuries, and as a warning that in the travail through which it was now to pass these dangers might well be revived.

Be this as it may, in the year 1572 events chose their own course without minding the deliberations of statesmen.

First of all, against the intention of Orange and Louis of Nassau, the game was set going in Holland, and that far too early, by a force of Sea Beggars who on April 1 captured The Brill, which in those days commanded the entry into the lower Rhine. Queen Elizabeth, who in the end felt not enough confidence in the French to risk the rupture with Spain, had ordered the Beggar fleet away from her ports, and the sensational feat had been the action of hunted and despairing pirates. Their commander was Lumey de la Marck, head of a great Liège family, who through his Holland mother also possessed estates in Holland. It was not he but his second-in-command, Blois van Treslong, a Holland nobleman, who first realized the possibilities of the capture, and at whose instance it was decided to hold the little town in the name of the Prince of Orange.

The true significance of what had happened became apparent only when Flushing called in the Beggars a few days afterwards, and especially when still a little later Enkhuizen broke out into rebellion. Then exiles, provided with commissions of the Prince, came streaming back, and in June and July the Beggars, starting from Enkhuizen, The Brill, and Flushing, brought most of the towns of Holland and Zealand under the authority of Orange.

Meanwhile the Count of Bergh had invaded Gelderland from Cleve. In the course of the summer he subjected town after town in that province and in Overysel, while in August the Frisian towns, too, were beginning to fall into the hands of the Beggars. The entire country north of the rivers was weakly garrisoned, and Alva felt himself compelled, in spite of the growing defection, to denude it still more when on May 24 Louis of Nassau surprised Mons in Hainaut with a band of Huguenots, thereby opening a suitable gate of entry to the threatening French invasion.

Yet this French invasion, on which centred the hopes of Orange as well as the fears of Alva, continued to be postponed. Orange himself, who was raising a large army in Germany, was delayed by lack of money no less than in 1568. On July 23 he took Roermond on the Maas, but had to wait for contributions from the revolting Holland towns before his soldiers, who were clamouring for their pay, consented to be led farther west. During all that time Louis was invested at Mons. A little Huguenot army, which attempted to come to his assistance, had been cut to pieces. After weeks of inactivity at Roermond, Orange at last crossed the Maas on August 27. Unknown to him, the French King, for a sign from whom he had been waiting hardly less than for money, had then given awful proof of his emancipation from the Huguenots and their counsels. On August 24, in the night of St. Bartholomew's, Coligny and his supporters had been murdered. There could be no question any longer of a French war against Spain. Even before his campaign had really started the ground had been cut from under Orange's feet. When he attempted to relieve Mons, the Spaniards on September 9 and 11 dealt severe blows to his army. Nothing remained but to return.

More successful than in 1568, Orange had made himself master of a few towns in Brabant and Flanders. Diest, Zoutleeuw[1] and Thienen had at once opened their gates for his army. Oudenaarde and Dendermonde,[2] had been brought to his side by sympathizers within co-operating with friends without. But to whatever pitch of excitement the temper of the people rose in many other towns, at Brussels, Brugge, Ghent, Breda, prospects were now too cheerless for any further defections to occur. Soon the army of "Duc d'Alve, the tyrant," was released from Mons—Louis of Nassau capitulated on September 19—south of the rivers that army was in complete control of the situation, and popular feeling counted for nothing. Orange, with his scratch lot of mercenaries, was powerless

---

[1] Zoutleeuw: in French—*Léau*.
[2] Dendermonde: in French—*Termonde*.

against it. At the beginning of October he led his army outside
the Netherlands, dissolving it near Orsoy. He himself travelled
over Kampen and Enkhuizen to Holland. There and in Zealand
—so he wrote to his brother John at Dillenburg—he meant
to make a stand and to see what was God's will. There—so
he expressed himself a few days later in a more gloomy strain—
he meant to find his grave.

HOLLAND AND ZEALAND IN REVOLT

The Prince was right in thinking that Holland and Zealand would alone be able to offer resistance. As soon as Mons had surrendered, Alva turned northward against Mechlin, which although abandoned as indefensible by Orange's governor Merode, was nevertheless, as an example for others, given up to the brutality of the soldiers. Unspeakable horrors were committed upon the defenceless citizens. The submission of other disaffected towns in Flanders and Brabant was graciously accepted by Alva. He had meanwhile advanced as far as Nymwegen, and from there sent on his son Don Frederick with the main body of the army.

To a greater extent even than elsewhere, external force had in Gelderland and Overysel been the determining factor in the rising of the towns. As we saw, it was the Count van den Bergh, Orange's brother-in-law, who had invaded those provinces with a little army from Germany. For a start he had, in concert with some citizens within, got hold of Zutfen, but all the other towns were simply captured. Deventer and Arnhem he found garrisoned too strongly to undertake anything against them, and from Zwolle and Kampen, even after the conquest, he experienced more hindrance than support. When, pushing forward, he reached the small northernmost towns of Overysel, some Frisian towns, long prepared by agitators returned from exile and at the same time exposed to Beggar attacks from Enkhuizen, began to join the revolt. At the approach of the Spaniards, however, it did not take the Frisian Stadtholder long to restore order in his province, while farther south there was hardly a thought of resistance against Don Frederick. Only in Zutfen did the Prince's garrison, at whose hands the citizens had suffered a great deal, remain just long enough to provide the Spaniards with the pretext for another spectacular act of severity. The sack of the town was attended with rape, murder, and arson; tremblingly the inhabitants of

neighbouring places told each other of "cries of woe" heard
over unfortunate Zutfen. The Count van den Bergh fled back
to Germany in unseemly haste. Town after town threw itself
at the feet of the despot. The magistrates of Kampen even
wrote to those of Enkhuizen to counsel them to submit.

But Holland, whither Don Frederick now marched, mas-
sacring the inhabitants of Naarden on his way—Holland was
another matter entirely. Not because the Hollanders were more
anti-Spanish or anti-Catholic, nor because they were more
courageous or tenacious than the people of Gelderland or
Overysel or Brabant or Flanders. But here stood the great
leader of the revolt, with his Beggars and mercenaries, the
concentrated power of resistance not of this province only but
of the whole Netherlands people, and they were determined
to put up a desperate fight. Nor was Holland an indefensible
post, but on the contrary a country with unequalled natural
advantages for defence and in open communication with the
sea. Moreover the Prince and his men were in possession not
of a few scattered towns but of the whole province, with the exception—a very important exception no doubt—of Amsterdam,
which continued to keep on the Spanish side; and they had
had time to place their party in power, sufficiently at all events
to enable them to continue the ejection of pro-Spanish elements
as soon as it might prove necessary. The Prince and his armed
followers it was in any case who made resistance possible; and
their party, the party of resistance, was a small party which
would not have been able to do anything without them.

Too often when Dutch historians consider those heroic four
years during which Holland and Zealand defied the armies of
the King of Spain while the rest of the Netherlands looked
on, patriotic and romantic rhetoric prevents them from clearly
recognizing that this was so. Yet the fact that the actual course
of events was in accordance with what history and human
nature would teach us to expect does in no way detract from
the grandeur of the spectacle. Let us look a little more closely
at the happenings of the summer of 1572, when the Holland
and Zealand towns came over to the side of the Prince.

It all began with the capture of The Brill, and in this the

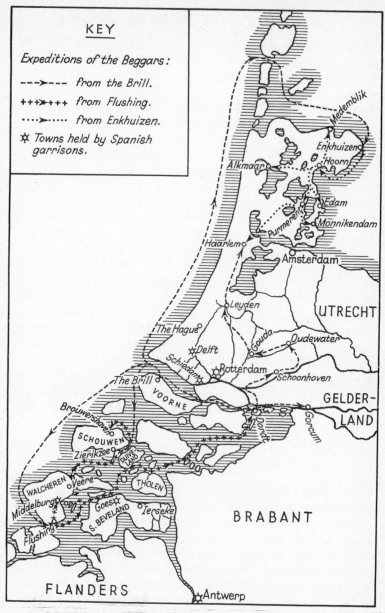

KEY

Expeditions of the Beggars:

--->--- *from the Brill.*

+++>+++ *from Flushing.*

······>······ *from Enkhuizen.*

☆ *Towns held by Spanish garrisons.*

Medemblik

Enkhuizen

Alkmaar   Hoorn

Edam

Purmerend   Monnikendam

Haarlem

Amsterdam

Leyden   UTRECHT

The Hague   Gouda   Oudewater

☆ Delft

Schiedam   Rotterdam   Schoonhoven

The Brill   VOORNE   GELDER-
                                        LAND

Brouwershaven   Dordt   Gorcum

SCHOUWEN

Zierikzee   DUIVE
            LAND

            THOLEN

WALCHEREN   ○Veere

Middelburg   Goes   ☆Terseke

Flushing   S. BEVELAND   BRABANT

FLANDERS   ☆Antwerp

MAP III HOLLAND AND ZEALAND IN 1572

citizens had no share whatever. The Sea Beggars, far from being received with open arms as liberators, caused a general panic by their sudden appearance, and the magistrates and all the wealthy citizens, together with the clergy, secular and regular, fled with what possessions they could carry. Less than a week afterwards the defection of Flushing from obedience to the King began, and here we have indeed a different case, although here, too, the scale was tipped by influences from outside. Here, when Alva, mindful of the strategic importance of the place, but just too late, wanted to introduce a Spanish garrison, a real popular commotion was the response to the incitements of Jan van Cuyck, Lord of Erpt, an emissary of Orange's. The construction of a citadel, which was still unfinished, had already caused great resentment in the town. But it was on the fishermen, who were restive on account of the interruption of their trade, that Van Cuyck made the most impression. In vain did the town magistrates strive to keep the movement within bounds; they themselves were pushed onward by the captains of the citizen guards. Van Cuyck went to The Brill for help, soon Treslong brought troops in three vessels, and foreign auxiliaries, too, came pouring in. Tseraerts, a Brabant nobleman, sent to act as Orange's governor, came over sea from France with Walloon and French troops. English troops sailed with the secret approval of their Government and helped to garrison the town:

So that the people of Flushing grew very courageous and had no more thought of opposing the war.

Small wonder if the citizens had at times experienced a sinking of the heart when they reflected on the consequences of their impulsive rebellion; but the influx of soldiers, which they owed to their free connection with the sea, not only raised their courage, it also dragged them irresistibly along into further adventures. From Flushing as a starting-point in the first place the whole of Walcheren must be brought under the Prince. The magistrates of Veere refused to let the Beggar troops in, but here too Van Cuyck succeeded in rousing the fishermen, so that the gate was opened for a company from

Flushing. Middelburg, the seat of the provincial government, was held by a Spanish garrison and had to be laid siege to. In spite of the Beggars' command of the waters it could get supplies from South Beveland via Arnemuiden. Tseraerts therefore attempted to get hold of Goes in order to cut Middelburg's communications with the Continent, the basis of Spanish power. It was then, in October 1572, when the recapture of Mons and the withdrawal of Orange's army had freed Alva's hands a little, that the Spanish commander Mondragon, with three thousand men, made that famous march from Tholen (which can easily be reached from the Brabant mainland) to Ierseke, right across the water of the East Scheldt at low tide. Goes was relieved and the pressure on Middelburg lightened for the time being. Truly a brilliant feat of arms! It had taken five hours to cross the chilly autumn water, which sometimes rose as high as the men's lips. How the affair makes one realize the inestimable advantage which their superiority on the water in that island province gave to the insurgents!

Without the Spaniards being able to do anything to prevent them, the Beggars' fleet had meanwhile raided now this now that part of Schouwen-Duiveland from their bases at The Brill and Flushing, finally laying siege to Zierikzee, where the magistrates and the garrison with one accord offered resistance. For the citizens of that considerable port the situation soon grew unbearable:

We are caught like mice in the trap [so the town government wrote to Brussels]. Many citizens have gone away with their ships, wives, and children, some towards the enemy, some elsewhere. The citizens of good will who have remained in the town are becoming unmanageable.

A summons from the Beggars of Veere that they might free themselves from "the eternal slavery in which you wallow" and might not wait until they, the Beggars, forced their way in, made an impression, although when the end came in August 1572 it was still force to a certain extent which decided the issue. Even though they had been able to relieve Goes, Walcheren remained as inaccessible to the Spaniards as

Schouwen-Duiveland; when the Beggars began to besiege Middelburg next year in real earnest, the town could not be held. Before acquiescing in its loss the Spaniards made a desperate effort to assert themselves on the water. But while warfare on land could be carried on with foreigners, for the fleet they fitted out on the Scheldt they needed Zealanders. It was difficult to procure any while Flushing, Veere, Zierikzee, and Brouwershaven were in the hands of the rebels, quite apart from the fact that the sailors preferred service under the Prince to service under the Spaniard. The fleet which had been assembled at Antwerp with so much difficulty for the purpose of breaking up the blockade of Walcheren suffered a crushing defeat in December 1573 against the Beggars' fleet under its new admiral, Boisot (a Brussels nobleman, with estates in Flanders). This sealed the fate of Middelburg. The citizens of that town had suffered little less for the Spanish cause than those of Leyden were soon to do for the cause of the country.

In Holland events had meanwhile followed a similar course. The capture of The Brill had been far from leading immediately to further defection. On the contrary, Bossu, Alva's Stadtholder for Holland, Zealand, and Utrecht, on the first report of what had happened had crossed over to Voorne with ten companies of Spaniards in order to expel the invaders, but he had been forced to evacuate the island again somewhat hurriedly when the Beggars began inundating it. Yet he had been able to summon the States of Holland to The Hague and to obtain a subsidy from them for the war against "the pirates." This in spite of the fact that what was called "the Rotterdam massacre" had already occurred on his retreat from Voorne: instead of marching through Rotterdam as had been agreed upon, he had, at the cost of the lives of several citizens, taken possession of the town, a deed which had everywhere intensified the hatred against the Spaniards as well as the fear of garrisons.

The first town where anything happened was Enkhuizen. Just as at Flushing, the fishers and skippers were in a disturbed mood through lack of employment. The burgomasters, scenting danger, wished to take in a garrison from the Count of Bossu, a precaution which seemed to be all the more necessary as Enkhuizen was the principal naval port on the Zuider Zee, and the Stadtholder was at that very moment having men-of-war fitted out there. But on the first suspicion of their magistrates' intention the citizens flew to arms. For weeks Enkhuizen vacillated between Bossu and Orange. At one time the citizens seized the Spanish warships, or even laid hands on the admiral, then again on the admonition of their burgomasters they let them go. A company of townsmen taken into pay by the burgomasters proved insufficient to keep order. The citizens' guard was indispensable, but it was so divided as to be in constant confusion. The first report of the disorders had caused a number of exiles to hurry to Enkhuizen. The Lord of Sonoy, whom Orange in anticipation of possible developments had appointed to be his lieutenant in North Holland, was levying troops in East Friesland. Beggars' ships made an appearance off Enkhuizen. At last, on the 27th of May, matters came to a crisis, in which former exiles played a leading part. The magistrates were placed under arrest in the Prince's name, appeals for help were sent to the Beggars in the Vlie and The Brill. On the 2nd of June Sonoy arrived in the town and took command.

It was his first task to provide the revolt with a broader foundation. By June 8 Medemblik had been taken; nearly the whole body of the citizens fled into the castle, but by pushing their wives and children in front the Beggars compelled them to surrender. Next came Hoorn, where the citizens were facing each other in arms, and after this one little town of the Northern Quarter after another was brought over to the side of the rebellion.

If Bossu, already hard pressed by The Brill and Walcheren, had any intention of venturing between the lakes and meres of North Holland against this second set of intruders, it certainly did not survive the emergence of yet another threat, for soon a thrust was aimed against the very heart of his provinces—against South Holland. On the 18th of June the Lord of Swieten, a nobleman who as a landed proprietor

E

had possessed considerable influence in the neighbourhood of Leyden, but who had been attainted by Alva, threw himself into Oudewater with a little band of Beggars, all come from The Brill. A few days afterwards he came and occupied Gouda by agreement with the citizens; the town had long been in a disturbed condition. Now disaffection suddenly began to stir on all sides. At Leyden returned exiles appeared in arms before the town hall in order to prevent the magistrates from taking in a Spanish garrison. For a few days longer the town government opposed the admission of a Beggar garrison either, then they twice let in a few hundreds. At the same time (June 23) Dordt, where "the commonalty" had long been agitated by letters from Flushing, concluded an agreement with Jonkheer Barthold Entes, a lieutenant of Lumey's. Bossu, all the time entrenched at Rotterdam, did not dispose of the naval power needed to cut those communications. Without loss of time a Beggar expedition set out from Dordt against Gorcum, which by reason of its situation on the confluence of Maas and Waal was of great strategic importance. Here the castle, where the clergy and Catholic citizens had sought shelter, had to be taken by dint of hard fighting. Simultaneously from Enkhuizen and from Leyden pressure had meanwhile been put on Haarlem. On July 3 burgomasters and corporation, impressed by what they had been told of the growing power and the plans of Orange and urged on by part of the citizens, concluded with the Prince's plenipotentiaries (former exiles of their town) an agreement similar to that of Dordt. A few weeks afterwards Dordt took it upon itself to call together the first assembly of the insurgent States of Holland. On July 19 Marnix appeared before it as the representative of the Prince of Orange, who was recognized in his former capacity of Stadtholder. About that very time Alva, in order to concentrate the whole of his forces against the menace on the French frontier, summoned all troops from Holland. Rotterdam, Delft, and Schiedam were evacuated; and with the troops, the Court of Justice and other official bodies from The Hague, together with many priests and faithful Catholics, four thousand people in all, retired to Utrecht in seven hundred carts. The three evacuated towns at once joined the revolt, which now embraced the whole of Holland, with the notable exception of Amsterdam.

One thing appears at once from this outline—namely, that in the extension of the revolt the Beggars fulfilled a function of the greatest importance. Everywhere the magistrates had to be compelled to recognize the Prince, and it was not often that the party of the revolution, which most easily found support amongst the lower classes, was able to apply sufficient pressure from within the walls. It was the Beggars, under their aristocratic chiefs, who spread the revolt from town to town; and if occasionally a town did come over to the Prince spontaneously, their assistance was immediately required to confirm it in its choice. Nor should it be thought that all these Beggar bands did was to reveal the towns to themselves. The two were by no means animated by the same spirit. The Beggars were the men of '66, the Iconoclasts; men who had suffered on account of their faith and who bore a grudge not merely against the Spaniards but against the Church; men whose Calvinist faith found vent most readily in hatred against priests and papists. But the bulk of those who called in the Beggars most certainly had no thought of breaking with the country's Catholic tradition. To the town populations on whom Orange called in the summer of 1572 his cause meant detestation of the Spanish garrisons and the Tenth Penny. We have seen how the fear of garrisons helped to set Flushing and Enkhuizen on the road to revolt. When the burgomasters of Gouda, in their anxiety at the approach of the Lord of Swieten, cautiously sounded part of the citizen guards as to whether they were ready to defend the town, all the reply was:

No; for the Tenth Penny we won't lift a finger.

The Beggars on their part soon made it clear that five years of a piratical life had not softened their manners. The Brill, under Lumey, became a veritable den of robbers, whence the Beggar vessels sailed to plunder churches and catch priests and monks. Treslong's troops entered Flushing dressed up in desecrated vestments. The whole of Europe was horrified by the massacre of twenty monks captured at the conquest

of the Castle of Gorcum and thence dragged to The Brill. Here
Lumey showed great personal interest in their fate. He himself interrogated the unfortunate captives, placing before them
the choice of apostasy or death—for no crime but that of their
faith and calling was brought up against them—harassed them,
put them to the torture, and in the end had them hanged:

to the great dissatisfaction and annoyance of the good citizens, who
had a great aversion from such cruelty.

The good citizens had only too much occasion for annoyance
in those early days. The clergy and faithful Catholics suffered
most in those towns where the Beggars had made a forceful
entry with the help of sympathizers from within. But in many
cases, as we saw above, at Dordt, Leyden, Haarlem, for
instance, the town government concluded an agreement with
the Beggar chief who came to liberate them from Alva before
opening the gates for him, and in these agreements there was
always an express guarantee for the safety of the lives and
goods of ecclesiastics and for the exercise of the Catholic
religion. But no sooner was the Beggar chief inside than the
agreement, which was nevertheless in such complete harmony
with the wishes of the Prince, was violated, churches and
monasteries were plundered, and priests murdered. Next there
came, sooner or later, the expulsion of magistrates who were
considered too favourable to Catholicism. Generally some men
who had just returned from exile were waiting to take their
places. In any case these were filled with reliable Calvinists.

Lumey, who looked upon himself as the begetter and leader
of the revolt, appeared before the States assembly at Dordt,
not a fortnight after having cooled his courage upon the
"Gorcum martyrs," armed with a commission by which
the Prince of Orange appointed him to be his lieutenant in
the Stadtholderate of Holland. It had not been forgotten in
that document to enjoin him to protect Catholics as well as
Reformed and compel the two to live in peace. That was indeed
putting the wolf in charge of the sheep! When Lumey soon
afterwards went north to besiege Amsterdam, it was not long
before the lamentations of the country people round Haarlem

reached the States, who dispatched their secretary to investigate. This was no less a person than Coornhert, who after his imprisonment in 1566 had secretly served the Prince. Now he soon fled from Holland to escape the rage of Lumey.

Orange, when he appointed Lumey, could not yet have had any knowledge of the Beggar chief's goings-on at The Brill. As soon as he arrived in Holland, towards the end of October, the Prince at once became the protector of all the oppressed, the support of all who wanted to found the new order on respect for private rights. Sonoy, whose conduct in North Holland had been little less reprehensible than Lumey's in South Holland, mended his ways, for a while at any rate. With Lumey, after more shocking misdeeds—the murder of Father Muis on his flight being the most wicked—matters came to a crisis. At the risk of goading the Sea Beggars to a rising on behalf of the chief with whom they felt their interests to be bound up, and of irritating the fanatics and the plunderers who saw in him a man after their own hearts, the Prince, in January 1573, after consultation with the States, had Lumey and a few of his lieutenants arrested. It was thought inexpedient to deal with Lumey, Prince of the Holy Roman Empire, after his deserts. In May 1574 he was allowed to retire to Germany, where he returned to the Roman Catholic Church.

It was easier for Orange to suppress excesses which threatened to bring the revolt, no less than the regime against which it was directed, into conflict with human and social order, than to realize the purpose of which he had formed so admirably clear a conception. No doubt this conception, so truly noble, which he expounded with such splendid eloquence in his manifestoes, speeches, and letters, had an elevating influence on the whole movement. It is due to this great leader more than to anyone else that the national significance of the revolution asserted itself in spite of everything. That the reality fell short of the ideal cannot, however, be denied. A free Netherlands community, safeguarded externally against the King and his Spaniards, by the ancient privileges under the watchful supervision of the States-General, and internally against divisions and civil war, by religious peace—such was the programme that William of Orange advocated. It was neither the introduction of Calvinism, still less the suppression of Catholicism, that he called upon the Hollanders to achieve, but

to restore the entire fatherland in its old liberty and prosperity out of the clutches of the Spanish vultures and wolves.

"The entire fatherland." In the assembly of the insurgent States at Dordt the Hollanders had not merely recognized the absent Prince as their provincial Stadtholder and leader against "the Albanian tyranny"; in pursuance of his instructions the Prince's commissary, Marnix, himself a Brabander, made them, as it were, abjure their provincial particularism and promise that they would also support Orange in his task,

as a principal member of the General-States of this Netherland, to protect the said Netherland against all invasions and oppressions on the part of foreigners, they being ready, as far as lies with them, to consult and agree thereupon with the other regions and provinces.

That same day (July 20, 1572) the States resolved, in accordance with what Marnix had "stated to them to be the intention of his Princely Grace":

that freedom of religions shall be observed, as well of the Reformed as of the Roman religion, and that everyone in his house or in public, in churches or chapels (such as shall be ordained to be most convenient by the local authority) shall enjoy free exercise of his faith, and that the ecclesiastics shall be left in their state and unmolested. Unless they proved to be hostile.

The *unless* sounds an ominous note. As a matter of fact the fair promise of this resolution was not long honoured. Even now that the Beggars' rule of terror had been ended, the mob showed an inclination to break out against all manifestations of Catholicism. Conscience remained free, this was a precious gain of the revolt which was never again to be lost, but in the spring of 1573 the exercise of the Catholic religion was prohibited on the pretext of the interests of public order.

Meanwhile the replacement of Catholic by Reformed magistrates proceeded apace, and the complexion of the States of Holland, which were nothing but a reflection of the town governments, grew ever more Reformed in consequence. In April 1573 Orange himself joined the Reformed Church; yet he was never completely identified with the stricter sort. Among the town "regents"—as the magisterial class was called —there were many who left the Catholic Church without ever joining the new community, while others conformed but outwardly.

At first sight the Protestantization of Holland is an amazing spectacle. There can be no doubt that the Reformed constituted a minority, and even a small minority, and this continued to be so for a long time to come, for generations in fact. As late as 1587 they were estimated at one-tenth of the population of the province. How did they manage to retain the ascendancy which in 1572 they had obtained by surprise, because they happened to be the only armed force in the country? How was it that in the long run they even succeeded in winning the majority over to their side? This phenomenon becomes intelligible only through the state of war, a condition under which detestation of the enemy can cause a society to submit to harsh but purposeful leadership against its real inclinations.

At the beginning of December 1572 the enemy had set foot on Holland soil. They came by way of Amsterdam. It was not by any garrison that Amsterdam was kept on the Spanish side; on the contrary, it had obstinately refused to take in a garrison. The magistrates maintained order with companies levied in the town itself. A number of the wealthiest merchants, who had some years before complained to the Governess about corruption in the municipal administration, had in 1567 been forced to flee and had since served the Prince of Orange ashore or afloat. If Amsterdam went over to the Beggars they would inevitably come back into power. It was only in accord with Spain, therefore, that the magistrates could maintain themselves, and none realized this more clearly than they. That their citizens continued to follow their lead in spite of the disastrous effects on the city's trade resulting from the

Beggars' control of the Zuider Zee, is a most remarkable fact. It proves, just as does the case of Middelburg, that there existed in Holland and Zealand, no less than in the other provinces, a strong anti-Beggar undercurrent, which could easily have come to the top had the war taken a different course. Lumey's attempt to gain possession of the town had failed, without giving rise to disturbances within. And now Amsterdam opened to the Spaniards a road straight into the heart of Holland.

Here Orange, in the six weeks since his arrival, had done what was possible to bring order out of the chaos caused by Lumey's misrule. His first task had been to inspire even his supporters with the will to resistance, for under the impression of the defeats in the South the most prominent and active among them were thinking of flight.

But with the coming of the Prince the faint-hearted were now so much encouraged that they no longer flinched from peril. To the States (whom he met at Delft) he afforded such hope and satisfaction in everything that they declared themselves content to venture with him all that they possessed in the world.

Yet the very first town against which Don Frederick led his troops from Amsterdam—Haarlem—nearly opened its gates for him. On the approach of the army stained with the blood of Mechlin, Zutfen, and Naarden, the frightened corporation had decided by a majority to send delegates to Amsterdam to arrange a surrender. Behind their backs, however, the Beggar commander of the town, the Groningen nobleman Wigbold van Ripperda, engineered a local revolution. It was possible to argue from the past massacres the uselessness of surrender as well as that of defence. Ripperda's advocacy of resistance made an impression on the citizen guards. The garrison, too, was quickly strengthened, and Orange informed of what was happening. The Prince sent Marnix, who changed the magistrates in his name. The delegates were arrested on their return, and, notwithstanding their plea of having acted on the instruction of the corporation, they were beheaded at Delft.

For seven months Don Frederick lay before Haarlem,

though he had not expected that seven days would be needed. Assaults were beaten off. To exhaust and starve the town proved difficult on account of its communication with the Lake, across which fresh troops and provisions could be freely carried to it from Sassenheim. With all its lakes still awaiting reclamation Holland was hardly less an island province than Zealand, and operations on water covering a wide area played a decisive part in the siege of Haarlem, as in those of Zierikzee and Middelburg. In the end the Spaniards, at great labour, transported the whole of their Zuider Zee fleet under Bossu to the Haarlem Lake. Sonoy at once tried to utilize the command of the Zuider Zee, which was thus left to him, by making a move from Enkhuizen and occupying the Diemen Dyke, in order to cut the communications between the Spanish army and its base in Utrecht. But Amsterdam citizen companies drove the Beggars from that post, and at the end of May the Beggar fleet on the Lake suffered a crushing defeat at the hands of Bossu. It was only then that the investment of Haarlem could be made watertight, and when an army which attempted relief overland was scattered in an engagement on the Manpad (end of June 1573), the town was doomed irretrievably.

Since earlier severity seemed to have inspired Haarlem with the courage of despair, Don Frederick decided to try moderation this time, and the citizens' lives were spared. Five executioners were nevertheless set to work on the soldiers, and finally, when arms had grown too tired to wield the sword, those that remained were thrown, bound back to back, into the River Spaarne. Ripperda was beheaded.

The long duration of the siege was almost as serious for the Spaniards as failure would have been. Consumed by impatience, Alva had been waiting in the South, knowing full well that only by a show of power were the obedient provinces kept quiet, and at his wits' end how to obtain the money required to satisfy his soldiers. Yet it seemed reasonable to hope that the fall of Haarlem, which with Amsterdam cut Holland in two, would dishearten the other towns. And indeed when a few days later a small contingent of Spaniards appeared before Alkmaar, which could be reached from Haarlem by a march along the border of the sea downs, that little town fell into the greatest confusion and panic. It had for some time refused to admit within its walls Jonkheer Jacob Cabeliau with his troops, whom Orange had designated to be its governor. (No more than Marnix, Lumey, Boisot, Sonoy, or Ripperda, by the way, was he a Hollander: he hailed from Ghent.) And now neither the magistrates nor the citizens knew what to do.

If the Prince has been unable to relieve the brave town of Haarlem, what will he do for us?

This plaintive question was asked of the Beggar chief himself, when with Ruychaver and a few more officers he appeared before the corporation, assembled in the town hall, in order to press them to take in his troops who were waiting before the Friesland gate, rather than the Spaniards who were knocking at the Kennemer gate. The chronicler, Bor, tells a vivid story of the irregular way in which the decision was at last forced through by one of the burgomasters supported by a group of citizens.

They were so frightened that they could not resolve anything. A great crowd of citizens had assembled in front of the town hall, waiting for the resolution of the magistrates. When this had gone on for a long time, Ruychaver said with anger in his heart: "This is not the time to deliberate any longer, tell us briefly what you will do or not do." Upon which Floris van Teylingen, one of the burgomasters, said: "With Prince and citizens I live and die," and immediately he went with Captain Ruychaver out of the town hall. Many citizens crowded in front and behind, Meerten Pietersen van de Mey, the town carpenter, among them, with axes and sledge-hammers, and they hacked the Friesland gate open and let in the men of the Prince of Orange, and the next moment the Kennemer gate was opened so that these soldiers could make a sally against the Spaniards.

The Spaniards slunk back, but after a few months (wasted in a mutiny) they returned for a regular siege. Now, however, Cabeliau had the situation well in hand, and there was no more question of hesitation. After three assaults had been beaten off, Sonoy, careless of the opposition of the peasants, had sluices opened and dykes cut for the purpose of flooding the land. The Spaniards, who had never felt at ease between the canals and meres of North Holland, retreated before the rising tide, just as a year and a half earlier Bossu's troops had fled from Voorne. Thus, as people said, "at Alkmaar began victory." Almost at the same time the Amsterdamers were disappointed in their hope that the Zuider Zee fleet, which had returned from the Haarlem Lake, would succeed in opening up a passage to their trade again. Although a huge effort had been made to reinforce that fleet, it was defeated and Bossu carried to Hoorn as a captive. Before the year came to an end, Boisot, as has been mentioned above, won the battle on the Slaak, and early in the next year Middelburg had to surrender to the Beggars.

Not two months had elapsed before tragic proof was forthcoming of the strength which Spanish military power could still display when circumstances were less unfavourable than those provided by the soil of Holland and Zealand. Orange, who never cherished the illusion that the two provinces would be able to continue the struggle indefinitely on their own resources, not only made tireless attempts to move France and England to come to their aid, but also managed once more to raise a mercenary army in Germany. Louis of Nassau was to lead it into the Netherlands. Hurriedly the Spaniards withdrew their mobile troops from Holland and elsewhere, and close to the frontiers of the Netherlands, near Mook, on April 15, 1574, a battle was fought, in which the German auxiliary army was annihilated, and in which Louis of Nassau and another brother of Orange's were killed. But at the same time it became apparent that Spain, through lack of money, was beginning to lose control of that admirable weapon which was the Spanish Army. After the victory, instead of taking immediate advantage of the dejection it caused in Holland, the Spanish soldiers demanded the pay still owing to them and began to mutiny. It was a repetition, only much worse, of what had already occurred after Haarlem. Under an *electo* the mutineers marched through the subjected provinces, robbing as they went, and finally entered Antwerp, which they proceeded to terrorize, until the Central Government succeeded by a great effort in finding some money to satisfy them. Then they were once more sent into Holland, and before long the main body was again immobilized for months by another siege —that of Leyden.

Alva had departed in November 1573. The fact could scarcely be glossed over that his rule had ended in dismal failure. He was replaced by Don Louis de Requesens, also a Spaniard, but at least not so detested that his name alone was enough to frustrate every attempt at reconciliation; for a change of policy was now announced with much blowing of trumpets. In reality this signified nothing. Requesens might have been found ready to grant real concessions. The new Governor was alarmed by what he discovered concerning the temper of the subjected provinces, which must provide him with his foothold for the struggle with the two rebellious ones. Moreover, he experienced the public penury directly, so much so that there were moments when he was unable to pay the tradesmen of his own household. But it was the King, shut off from all contact with reality in his convent-like palace, from no reality so distant as from that of his Netherlands, who nevertheless indicated the lines along which Netherlands affairs had to move; and on the point of religion, at any rate, he was immovable. Requesens himself, it is true, believed that the Tenth Penny was the real cause of the revolt. However much truth there might be in that view, the abolition of the Tenth Penny and a General Pardon were no longer sufficient to pacify public feeling even in the subjected provinces, and at any rate to the Calvinists who had got control of Holland and Zealand the religious question was of no less importance than it was to the King. There was nothing for it but to continue the trial of strength.

The siege of Leyden put the revolt to another hard test. The town could be approached by the Spaniards via Amsterdam and Haarlem, and in order to close it in towards the south a wide circle of the country-side was occupied. Part of the population of The Hague, which was unfortified, fled to Delft; the rest welcomed the Spaniards with manifestations of joy. Leyden had no garrison, but the citizen guard had been reformed in 1572, and consisted of zealous adherents of the new state of affairs. The town government, too, which in that year had given so hesitating a consent to the introduction of the Beggar regime, had undergone some change. Van der Werff, a new man, returned from exile, during which he had served the Prince on missions full of danger, had been included among the burgomasters. Yet, on the whole, the government was still lukewarm and lent a ready ear to refugee citizens— "glippers" as they were called—who transmitted from the Spanish camp promises of mercy in case of submission. In September, after more than three months of the siege, distress was already gripping the population while there were no signs yet of the relief announced by Prince and States. If in those circumstances surrender was not decided upon, it was due to a few men of determination, who could count on the civic guard. These were, besides Van der Werff, the secretary of the town, Jan van Hout, and his literary friend, the noble-man Jan van der Does (both of whom we shall meet again, Van der Does under his scholar's name of Douza, when considering the intellectual activities of the period); and the latter's cousin Jacob. The Prince's governor, Bronkhorst, who had caused a gallows to be erected in the Breestraat as soon as any murmuring began, died in these same critical days. Jan van der Does, writing to the Prince, spoke bitterly of

the great unfaithfulness of some from among the magistrates, who presume daily more and more to incite the needy and hungry commonalty to disobedience by means of idle and false promises taken from the enemy's letters, contrary to the oath they have sworn to your Excellency and to the States.

But he and his friends stubbornly resisted all such attempts, and the town held out until Prince and States saw the fruits of their efforts. Towards the end of September the autumn winds swept the waters of the Maas, through the gaps cut in the dykes, over the land of Schieland and Delfland, and at last of Rijnland also, so that the Zealand Beggars, under Boisot, in their flat-bottomed vessels, were able to approach the town.

The soil of Holland's polder-country becomes living history in the story of that expedition. The advanced posts of the Spaniards at Zoetermeer and Zoeterwoude suddenly saw the water rising all around them, the Beggars in boats and armed galleys threatening to cut off their retreat across what yesterday was land. As at Voorne, as at Alkmaar, the Spanish Army fled terror-stricken. For a while they continued to hold The Hague; but they soon broke out into mutiny again, and marched through Haarlem and round Amsterdam to Utrecht, subsisting on the peasants there and in Gelderland, at times engaging in bloody fights with the troops of the royal Stadtholders, until Requesens had once more scraped enough money together to come to some arrangement with them.

The relief of Leyden was a great event. The courage and self-confidence of the rebels were immensely stimulated. Very gradually their position acquired a certain stability. The country-side had naturally suffered terribly from the inundations and from the expeditions of the Spaniards right across the province. The trade of the towns, too, was impeded. And yet they were better off than the trading towns still on the Spanish side, Amsterdam and Antwerp, for the Beggars held the sea, preventing any ships from passing in or out, so that if the inland provinces wanted overseas goods, they had to connive at importation from the rebel towns. It is a curious spectacle to see a new social order in course of formation in the midst of the convulsion of war. Nothing is more striking in this connection than the foundation of a university—at Leyden, as a reward for the perseverance shown during the siege—which was to be for the new Reformed Church what Leuven was for the Catholic Church. But this was no more than a detail in the great work of building up a Reformed Church organization. Calvinism had been weak in Holland before 1567. At a general Netherlands synod held at Emden in the period of exile shortly after that of Bedtbur, the Holland ministers had joined in signing the confession of De Bray as an instrument of unity. Now that Holland and Zealand were an open field for their activities, nothing could stand against the rigid organization and determination of the Calvinists.

They had laid hands on the positions of power in the two provinces; for their part the authorities recognized the Reformed organization as the State Church which could unite the people in the struggle against Spain, and on whose behalf the goods of the old Church were seized. In 1574 a general synod took place at Dordt. In close co-operation with the local authorities Reformed congregations were organized in all the towns. At first the Reformed Church was almost exclusively an urban affair, and, indeed, in this new order of society the towns were of even greater importance than they had been in the old.

This was emphasized by the political developments as well. In the peculiar position of a Stadtholder representing the sovereign against whom the country was waging war without having repudiated him (for the fiction was that arms had been taken up against "the Duke of Alva and his adherents"), the Prince of Orange was, practically speaking, the depository of sovereignty, and in 1575 the States actually invested him formally with it, using the expression "High Authority"; this was after the breakdown of the negotiations, about which more hereafter. But he never strained their confidence unduly, and did nothing without consulting them. The result was that the States came to exert not only a political influence but immediate administrative powers such as they had never possessed before. Now in these States the urban oligarchies ruled supreme. The popular uprising had not found expression in any greater and more regular popular influence on the Government. The oligarchies in power had bowed so low before the storm that they had not been broken. In so far as changes had taken place, they had been changes of individuals. Many "regents" of too pronounced Catholic sentiments had been removed, and their places had been taken by exiles and other new men whom the Reformed party trusted, and to whom, once placed into power, they left the management of affairs. The nobility had been greatly reduced in numbers by proscription and emigration, and their influence in the provincial administration was to a certain extent supplanted by that of the burgher oligarchy. Side by side with the six large towns which of old "had session" in the States of Holland, twelve small ones took part henceforward, so that the "College of Noblemen," purged of Catholic emigrants, was now only one—though it retained the dignity of being the first—of nineteen members of the States. The political power which had been set free mainly by the efforts of the nobly born Beggar chiefs and the lower class of the people thus fell to the share of the town "regents." The Reformed community found itself face to face with the States as a self-contained power, which later on would prove to be animated by quite other than Reformed ideals. Indeed, amongst the most daring and sturdy leaders of the revolt in its early days there were those—I need only recall Jan van Hout and Jan van der Does—who traced their spiritual descent from Erasmus rather than from Calvin, and for whom the aim of the struggle was not Reformed theocracy but liberty. After the wild confusion of the beginning, conditions in Holland thus developed under the banner of Calvinism in a remarkably quiet way.

The state of public feeling in the subjected provinces, on the other hand, was growing more and more alarming to the Spaniards. Negotiations, carried on for a year through various intermediaries, had really made it clear above all else that the programme of the revolt as formulated by Orange and the States of Holland and Zealand was the national Netherlands programme. While ready to acknowledge the King's authority, the Hollanders demanded the restoration of the privileges, the departure of the Spanish soldiers and officials, and liberty of conscience. As to the first and second points, these were the very concessions for which the States-General, summoned to Brussels by Requesens to assist him in his financial need, were clamouring without showing much gratitude for the dropping of the Tenth Penny. And while they certainly continued to speak fair words about the maintenance of the Catholic religion, the Governor noticed sorrowfully that there was no sincere dislike of liberty of conscience. All he could think of in that disastrous winter of 1574–75 was to make another attempt at negotiating, in a more formal manner this time. So desperate did the situation appear to him that he undertook to do this without the express consent of Philip, who, as so often at critical moments, took refuge in a profound silence. At Breda, in the spring of 1575, delegates of the two sides met in the presence of an Imperial Ambassador, a circumstance which added even more prestige to the rebels. The instructions of the States of Holland and Zealand to their delegates laid down that they must treat only in writing and use the Dutch language; three of these delegates were Brabanders: Marnix, Charles de Boisot, brother of the admiral, and Dr. Johan Junius de Jonghe. The object of their diplomacy—here we can detect the master-hand of Orange—was to bring out still more clearly the essential unity of interests and feeling between the rebellious and the other provinces. The religious question was not pressed to the front; nay, the Holland and Zealand delegates were empowered to declare their readiness to submit it to a free States-General, on condition that the Netherlands were first evacuated by the Spanish troops. When the other side had to admit that the King could not withdraw these until order and the supremacy of the Roman Catholic Church had been restored, the negotiations could safely be broken off. Orange had achieved his object.

However, despite the disapproval with which even official circles in the obedient provinces and towns regarded the policy of the Government, all exhortations to cast off the yoke addressed to them by the States of Holland—especially to Flanders and Brabant, and to Amsterdam—remained without effect. In that same year, 1575, indeed, the Netherlanders saw a striking demonstration of the formidable strength that the Spanish military forces could still display. Although many foreign bankers had been driven away from Antwerp by the disturbances and uncertainty of the last few years, so that the money market was woefully weakened, Requesens had once more managed to raise enough funds at a high rate of interest for a desperate attempt to break down the revolt by main force. Attacks were launched at three points. An invasion of North Holland led to nothing—except to the infliction, on Sonoy's responsibility—of horrible tortures on a few Catholic peasants who were wrongly suspected of an understanding with the enemy.

Hierges, who had been appointed to replace Bossu, after the latter's capture, as royal Stadtholder of the provinces of Holland, Zealand, and Utrecht, next proceeded from the town of Utrecht and captured Buren, Oudewater, Schoonhoven, and the fortifications near Krimpen on the Lek, only to be held up by Woerden. In the autumn the Governor-General himself undertook the conquest of the island of Schouwen-Duiveland, marching through the water from Tholen, as Mondragon had done a little more towards the south three years before. Bommenede and Zierikzee, both strongly garrisoned, offered heroic resistance, and after a winter spent in hard fighting—both the Boisots were killed in attempts at relief—the troops were still lying before Zierikzee when Requesens died, on the 5th of March, 1576. Thus the government of the Netherlands devolved upon the Council of State, which soon gave proof of being unequal to it.

Yet as late as the end of June the Spanish troops, now under Mondragon, managed to get inside Zierikzee, but immediately afterwards they broke out into mutiny and abandoned the conquest which it had taken them nine months to achieve. That mutiny caused the practical collapse of the Spanish dominion over the Netherlands. The Beggars of Holland and Zealand had not brought about this great event directly by force of arms, but it resulted from the financial exhaustion into which their obstinate perseverance had plunged the entire Spanish Empire. For it was not the Netherlands provinces alone which were suffering from the penury owing to which the soldiers' pay was twenty-two months in arrear. On the contrary, Requesens bitterly reproached the States-General for the close-fistedness which compelled the King to send millions, far above his means, from Spain. As a matter of fact, by declaring in the autumn of 1575 a bankruptcy of his exchequer, Philip had dealt the final blow to the credit of his Governor as well; his precaution of soliciting beforehand the approval of the Pope, who gave it in consideration of the extortionate rates of interest paid so far, did not sufficiently impress even the most faithful Catholics among the bankers.

The changed state of affairs in the rest of the Netherlands suddenly freed Holland and Zealand from all immediate danger. Seventy years were to pass before Spain gave up all claims to sovereignty over those provinces, but never again was a Spanish force to tread their soil. There was to be plenty of time for the stabilization of the condition which we have seen growing up with and as a result of the armed resistance against foreign domination; the Reformed ruling class was given the opportunity of consolidating its position.

The phrase "ruling class" does not do justice to the actual state of affairs. There was a community of active citizens, the only ones who, according to their own opinion, had a right to activity, and who as emphatically identified themselves with the nation as do the Fascists in present-day Italy. For while the Reformed accepted William of Orange's nationalist ideology, they permeated it with their particular notions, and then went on to lay exclusive claim to it. In that way the Catholics were pressed down relentlessly to the position of second-class citizens. A most unnatural state of affairs—yet it is difficult to see how the revolt could have stood this four years' test of fire had it not been for the iron courage and energy which the Reformed owed to their faith in the country's being elected to become a temple for God's word. Later the divergence within the ascendancy party, which has been hinted at above, was to become apparent and to cause great strife and trouble in Holland. For the time being nothing was shown outwardly but Calvinism and an inclination to spy in every Catholic a suspect, a potential friend of Spain.

The problem presented in 1576 with pressing insistence by the sudden but temporary breakdown of Spanish power was the problem of "the entire fatherland." The independent position, however, which Holland and Zealand now occupied in the Netherlands, and the peculiar politico-religious character they had been developing, complicated this problem not a little. William of Orange was already familiar with the difficulty of uniting the two religious parties against the Spaniard. Would it prove an easier task now that one of them had acquired a firm foothold in a particular region? The Prince was the man

called by fate to undertake the attempt in the new circumstances created by the death of Requesens, but at no time
would he be able to forget that Holland and Zealand, such
as the last four years had fashioned them, provided him and
the revolt with the most reliable support.

III

"THE ENTIRE FATHERLAND" IN REVOLT

a. UNDER THE PACIFICATION OF GHENT

After having taken Zierikzee the Spanish troops, as mentioned in the previous chapter, began to mutiny, and in spite of Mondragon's objurgations marched off to the Continent. At Roosendaal their comrades from Goes joined them, and together they went farther into Brabant, threatening Mechlin, then Brussels, and when both towns made brave preparations for resistance they turned westward and suddenly entered Aalst, where they entrenched themselves strongly. This was not the first time that the bloodhounds of Philip II had broken loose and wildly attacked his obedient subjects. Indeed, these Spanish mercenaries were men of convictions, and, without making much distinction between the rebels and the other Netherlanders, they looked upon that whole nation as sullied with heresy and turbulence, heinous vices which inspired them with a sincere aversion. Not all the horrors they perpetrated had weakened their faith in the cause for which they fought. The less fiery Catholics of the Netherlands looked on astonished at their scourging processions. Even during their mutinies their piety asserted itself. Their *electo* and his advisers were solemnly sworn in at the altar. They prepared for their worst massacres with prayer and carried them out under a banner from one side of which Christ, from the other the Holy Virgin, looked down on them. This time, the more readily because the Central Government, under the care of the many-headed Council of State, was clearly seen to be tottering, their excesses called forth a violent reaction.

Brussels took the lead. The furious and excited citizens brought so much pressure to bear on the Council of State that this body, notwithstanding the protests of the Spanish member De Roda, towards the end of July, declared the mutineers to be public enemies. At the same time the States of Brabant had already begun levying troops on their own account. Orange came to Middelburg, so as to be nearer the fire, which he fanned with all his might. The Lord of Heze, who commanded the Brabant troops, carried on a frequent correspondence with him. The Abbot of St. Gertrude among the clergy, Heze and Glymes among the nobility, the pensionary of Leuven, Roels, among the town delegates—these were the leaders of a powerful party in the States of Brabant who looked to the Prince for salvation. Meanwhile a popular agitator, De Bloyere, was working for him among the Brussels citizens. The Council of State was powerless. Out of Spain there came no better comfort than the announcement, five months after the death of Requesens, of a new Governor: no less a personage than Don John, the King's bastard brother, was to come—only patience!—and he would, so Philip assured, bring with him "the true remedies" for a disease which nevertheless under the King's doctoring had for twenty years been going from bad to worse. Meanwhile the Spaniards at Brussels went in danger of their lives. A secretary of De Roda's was murdered in the streets. De Roda himself sought safety elsewhere, and now Heze, without a doubt at the instigation of Orange, placed the remaining members of the Council of State under arrest.

At this moment the States of Brabant made a move which recalls that of Dordt in July 1572: they addressed a summons to the other provinces—excepting the two with which a state of war still existed—to send deputies to an assembly of the States-General. Soon, however, a few of the imprisoned councillors were released—not Viglius or Berlaymont, who were still kept in confinement—and the Council of State, thus doubtfully restored, in which the Duke of Aerschot was the leading personage, lent its authority to give that summons a semblance of legality. This had already proved to be indispensable. Only Flanders and Hainaut had appeared on the invitation of Brabant. The States of Gelderland, for example, who with the other north-eastern provinces did not join until a few months afterwards, took good care to underline the fact that the summons which they accepted had been sent to them by the Council of State, "charged with the general government of the Netherlands by His Royal Majesty our most gracious Lord."

Meanwhile the States-General, still representing only Brabant, Flanders, and Hainaut, had resolved at their first sitting (September 25, 1576), and as their very first act, that in the country's distressful condition a chief was required, and had appointed Aerschot to act in that capacity. Aerschot was a man of little perspicacity or character, whose importance lay wholly in his rank and fortune. It will be remembered that he had taken little part in the national movement of the magnates before the coming of Alva. The rivalry of his own house of Croy with Nassau-Orange obscured his understanding of the greatest national problems. In accepting the commission of the States-General he caused the Greffier of Brabant to take good note of his declaration

that he does by no means understand to take upon himself this charge for any object but the maintenance of God's service and of the old Catholic Roman religion and of the service and obedience of our Lord the King and to the greater profit and prosperity of the country.

Yet at that moment the movement had already gone beyond taking measures against the Spanish mutineers. De Roda, who was now lodged in the citadel at Antwerp under the protection of its Spanish garrison, declared the full power of the Council of State to be residing in himself as its only member not exposed to violence or undue pressure, and he protested his utmost against the action of Aerschot and his colleagues. The Spanish commanders, not only in the citadel of Antwerp but also at Haarlem, and in the citadels of Ghent, Valenciennes, Maastricht, and Utrecht, obeyed De Roda, and so did, though more hesitatingly, a number of German and Walloon garrisons scattered over the whole country from south to north-east. The consequence was that the mutineers were no longer isolated, and the States-General therefore began its career with the prospect of a serious war. Troops had to be hired. For that matter, among the noblemen siding with the States-

General there were, since Aerschot covered the movement with his name, several in official positions, and these sometimes carried their soldiers, especially the Walloons, with them. Hierges, the Stadtholder of Utrecht and Gelderland, for instance, joined in the hope of obtaining the release of his father Berlaymont.

Nothing more natural than that others, whose dislike of Spanish rule was more sincere, at this critical juncture looked towards Orange, the master of tried troops, with which during four long years he had kept the Spanish armies in check. Soon there came to Middelburg the Lord of Haussy, a brother of Bossu (himself still a prisoner at Hoorn), to ask, in the name of Du Roeulx, the Stadtholder of Flanders, for help against the Spaniards in the Castle of Ghent. Orange was eager to comply with the request. And, indeed, the States-General themselves had placed the restoration of peace with Holland and Zealand in the forefront of their programme; and in October, in that very town of Ghent where Orange's troops had already entered to help besiege the Spanish garrison, negotiations for that purpose were begun. Don John, the new Governor, was now on his way. It was essential that the negotiators should reach a conclusion before his arrival.

The veneer of legality which the authority of Aerschot and his Council of State was intended to spread over these activities cannot really hide the fact that with the unauthorized meeting of the States-General the Netherlands had taken the first step on the road towards rebellion against the King's rule. It is nevertheless well worth our while to observe how profound was the difference between the beginnings of this revolution and of that which four years ago had overtaken Holland and Zealand. That difference did not proceed from any inherent difference between the two maritime provinces and the rest of the Netherlands, but from the circumstances in which the two events took place.

In Holland and Zealand we have seen that the revolution was brought about by the Beggars, who came in from outside and directed developments. The revolution of 1576, on the other hand, was made by the established authorities under the pressure of their own people. An attempt could therefore more readily be made to consolidate it on the basis which before the coming of the Beggars had existed in Holland and Zealand too—namely, on a Catholic and conservative basis. The slogan announced by Aerschot gave complete satisfaction to most members of the States-General. All they wanted was the restoration of prosperity, and no one objected to the service of the King and the maintenance of the Catholic religion. In Holland the Beggars had constituted the only armed force. In the other provinces, on the contrary, it all began with the raising of an army by the States themselves, and the noblemen who were placed in command over it bore little resemblance to those country gentlemen returned from their exile for religion's sake who had played a leading part in the revolt of Holland and Zealand; they belonged to that nobility of courtiers and officials which possessed such power in Flanders and Brabant, although, as we know, generally not of native but of Walloon origin; even more exclusive, indeed, was its ascendancy in the Walloon provinces. This does not mean that the Netherlands outside Holland and Zealand knew no Beggar movement. On the contrary, feeble though it was, for example, in Gelderland, Overysel, and Groningen, and hardly noticeable any longer in that Walloon region which ten or fifteen years ago had been active in introducing Calvinism into the Netherlands, it was vigorous in Flanders and Brabant. But in order to come into power it had to wage a severe struggle with a social order whose powers of resistance had not been taken by surprise.

In these circumstances there could be no question of any recognition of Protestantism in the provinces now seeking a *rapprochement* with Holland and Zealand, nor could Orange even ask for such recognition. The negotiations at Ghent were regarded as a resumption of those of Breda, which only the King's obstinacy had caused to fail. The principals at Brussels were still hesitating whether to ratify what had been arranged by their delegates, when all scruples were removed by a terrible event at Antwerp. A few weeks earlier Maastricht had had to suffer a massacre for risking an attempt to rid itself of the Spanish garrison in the castle. Now it was Antwerp's turn. Simultaneously the troops of De Roda from the castle and the mutineers from Aalst fell upon the town, expelled the troops of the States, and plundered and murdered for days on end. The so-called Spanish Fury struck a heavy blow at Antwerp's long-threatened prosperity. Less than a week later the Pacification was signed.

It was a treaty of peace between the provinces of the States-General on the one side and Holland and Zealand on the other, and at the same time an alliance for the repulsion of the Spanish soldiery and other foreign oppressors. The Prince of Orange was recognized in his Stadtholderships dating from before Alva's time; the towns belonging to them which had not yet accepted his authority (Amsterdam being the principal) were to do so after having received "satisfaction" from him on points in dispute. An extraordinary assembly of the States-General was to be called together in order to settle everything, the religious question included, and this in Holland and Zealand no less than elsewhere. Until then the Edicts against heresy were everywhere to be suspended. The States of Holland and Zealand promised not to undertake anything against the Catholic religion outside their provinces. The exclusive rule of Calvinism in the two provinces was, for the time being at any rate, recognized implicitly; in a clause about secularized Church lands almost explicitly.

Here was a victory indeed for the rebels of 1572! But at this very moment the new Governor had arrived in Luxemburg, and the question arose what was to be done. The States-General did not dream of admitting him without imposing their terms. The fame of Don John's martial glory and of his attractive and romantic personality were far from making that impression on which he himself had counted. There were other facts which had more weight, as, for instance, that he came without troops and without money, and that he could not hope to achieve much, even if they were of a mind to obey his orders, with the scattered Spanish garrisons—that of Ghent capitulated in these very days. The noblemen who had the lead in the States-General, the Croys, the Lalaings, the Hennins, Catholic and Royalist as they were, intended to make the most of this splendid opportunity to carry out the traditional programme of the nobility and to shackle the representative of absolutism. Don John would have to treat. For that matter, he had been authorized to treat by his brother the King. To the ambitious dreamer, who had coveted the Netherlands government especially because he wanted to cross over from the Scheldt to England, and to set free and perhaps marry Mary Queen of Scots, the humiliating delay in Luxemburg was a grievous disappointment. The most galling demand made to him was that he should ratify the Pacification and send away the Spanish troops, which alone could help him to secure real power. Meanwhile, province after province joined the States-General, and in January 1577 a Union was concluded at Brussels by which nobles, abbots, and town deputies signed their names to a pledge to stand by the Pacification. Don John realized that there was no other way for him. In February he accepted the Pacification, by the so-called Eternal Edict, and the Spanish troops were ordered to leave the country. Only when they had actually departed was Don John permitted to make his festive entry into Brussels. It was then May, and the Governor's patience had worn very thin. The capital in which the States received him was still guarded by their own troops.

But if the situation was far from agreeable for the Governor, Orange, too, had plenty of reasons to feel uneasy. He had been against all negotiations. In his frequent correspondence with adherents and prominent men outside Holland and Zealand he had been tireless in sowing the seeds of distrust against Don John. He had caused intercepted letters to be published so that all might see that treason was brewing. Nor had his attempts been fruitless. A burgomaster of Zutfen, Van Thil, travelling to Brussels to attend the States-General, went by way of Middelburg to meet the Prince. Afterwards, writing to his principals from Brussels, this man expressed the greatest concern at the decision, which had then just been taken, that the assembly should move to Namur in order to speed up the negotiations. The citizens of Brussels insisted that only part of the deputies should go,

for they fear that if we came there all.in a body, it might end in a Paris affair [St. Bartholomew's Massacre].

Van Thil himself was no less fearful of it, but he comforted himself with the reflection:

Dulce est pro patria mori. If I do not return, your worships may have a mass read for my soul.

If this was how a staunch Catholic felt, with how much more anxiety must the Reformers watch Don John make his entry, even though the Spaniards marched away; especially because it could not be denied that the States-General, in their eagerness to come to an arrangement, had made light of the clause in the Pacification concerning religion. The Eternal Edict spoke of the restoration of the Catholic religion in the whole of the Netherlands without mentioning any previous extraordinary assembly of the States-General. That was the basis on which already in January the Union of Brussels had been founded. Now the agreement with Don John was concluded without the Brussels leaders awaiting the consent of Holland and Zealand.

There was not, in fact, much chance that this would ever have been given. About this very time a person sufficiently simple to expect that this clause in the Pacification might result in the expulsion of heresy was met by a Brabant Calvinist with the scornful reply:

Will the Hollanders suffer themselves to be robbed by means of a vote of what they have not suffered to be taken from them by force of arms?

Indeed, it was not likely. The Hollanders and Zealanders were still sitting behind their water defences, their army and navy ready to act, governing themselves under their States and Stadtholder, and not at all inclined to let themselves be dissolved in the community of the States-General except on their own terms. Haarlem (taken by the Spaniards in 1573), Schoon-

hoven (in 1575), and Goes (which had never as yet sided with
the Beggars) had received treaties of "Satisfaction," in accordance with the Pacification, and had submitted to the States
of Holland and of Zealand; in all these "Satisfactions" protection of Catholicism was asked for and promised; in Haarlem
the Bishop still resided. Amsterdam alone, blocked in now on
all sides, stubbornly refused to join the rest of Holland; it
still hoped for relief from Don John. Meanwhile the Prince
was trying to strengthen the outer defences of the position.
His troops still lay at Ghent, where he had supporters who
were ready for anything. Negotiations were being carried on
with Utrecht, which had been freed from the Spanish garrison
in the Vredenburg Castle only in January 1577, and which,
so the Prince maintained, by virtue of the Pacification ought
to revert under his Stadtholderate. The States of that province,
however, in which nobility and clergy possessed much power,
and which were traditionally afraid of being overshadowed by
Holland, preferred to keep Hierges. Holland envoys travelled
to Gelderland in order to put the States on their guard against
Don John's intentions and to propose a closer alliance with
Holland. At Brussels, at Antwerp, everywhere the Prince's
agents were agitating and intriguing.

Don John, who had started negotiations with "the arch-
rebel," soon discovered that he would never of his own free
will make any concessions on the point of religion. What was
worse, like Requesens, the new Spanish Governor found that
the Netherlands nobles who surrounded him were not averse
from liberty of conscience, and were little enamoured of the
prospect of a renewed struggle with the two maritime provinces. They irritated him terribly, these nobles, who were
holding him in strings. How different was this Governorship
from what he had pictured to himself:

fit for a woman, like Margaret of Parma. Only a renewal of the war
could make the situation bearable, only by possessing Holland and
Zealand and thereby commanding the trade of the Netherlands, can
one be Governor of the Netherlands in reality.

In fact, he was so far from enjoying any real power that already after a few weeks, aggrieved by the hostile and suspicious attitude of the citizens, he had left Brussels. For a time he resided at Mechlin, but his position became unbearable, and on 24th July, 1577, he unexpectedly captured with his body-guard the citadel of Namur. An attempt on that of Antwerp failed. From Namur he now demanded fuller power, the removal of suspect personages like Marnix from the States-General, and assistance against Orange. An outburst of popular rage was the response, and while Don John could only wait in impotence for the troops which he begged Philip to send back, but which were slow in coming, the citizens at Antwerp, Utrecht, and elsewhere pulled down the hated citadels, and the country threw itself into the Prince of Orange's arms.

The policy of co-operating with Don John, or rather of using him, had been the policy of the high nobility. The peace of the Duke of Aerschot, that was the name given to the Eternal Edict. As in the days of Margaret of Parma after Granvelle's departure, the nobles had under Don John carried everything with a high hand. Now that he himself tore up the Pacification and called back war and Spaniards, the party of the Catholic nobility was plunged into the greatest confusion. Some who had kept aloof from the States-General movement, or had no heart in the business, Mansfeldt, Berlaymont and his son Hierges, Meghen, and the others, rallied round Don John. The majority, Aerschot himself among them, could not so readily renounce the programme of the Pacification of Ghent and the Union of Brussels, but they now found themselves, half un-willing and somewhat disconcerted, more patently in opposi-tion to the King's authority than ever before. At the same time their prestige with the public had seriously suffered. The Prince of Orange was now the wise man who had foreseen it all. His adherents triumphed. Not only had his warnings been justified by the events, but, moreover, now that it was to be war once more, the two provinces of Holland and Zealand, strongly situated, vigorously led and formidably armed, offered an unshakable support in the rear that could not but appear of the utmost value.

For the time being there still prevailed in the States-General at Brussels a good deal of confusion and vacillation. In fact, it was from outside the circles of the politically privileged that the great moves towards drastic change were now to proceed. All over the Netherlands, in the towns at any rate, the people began to stir. First of all at Utrecht, where the burgher captains (captains of the civic guard) presented a threatening address to the endlessly deliberating provincial States, urging them to hasten the negotiation about a "Satisfaction," and even to invite the Prince to visit the town. The popular party at Utrecht had ever been turbulent. Yet there was not lacking, even in this address, the assurance that everything must be done

without injury to the Catholic Apostolic Roman Religion or to the due subjection to His Majesty.

Orange came to Utrecht even before an agreement had been reached over the Satisfaction, and was received rapturously. He also tried once more to establish relations with Gelderland. The States of that province, hard pressed by the garrisons of Kampen, Deventer, and Roermond, which remained loyal to Don John, were fain to concert common measures of defence with their Catholic neighbours of Utrecht, Overysel, and Groningen; but even so they were still a little shy of Orange.

Now, however, the citizens of Brussels suddenly broke the deadlock. The government of that town consisted of three "members," the third of which was that of the nine "nations" or guilds. These nations had appointed a committee of "Eighteen Men," and these, under the leadership of the lawyer Van der Straeten, who was in close touch with Marnix and through him with Orange, lorded it over the town and bombarded the States-General with petitions and opinions. It was under their immediate pressure that this assembly invited the Prince to come to Brussels in order to assist it with his counsel. The States of Holland were loath to see him go. Their independent position had become dear to them since 1572, and was it not to be feared that Brabant and Flanders, now that they rallied to the Prince, would resume their ancient leadership in the Netherlands community? All Orange's activities in the South in the ensuing years were to be watched with jealous eye by Holland and Zealand.

This was nevertheless a proud moment in the life of William of Orange, when he, the exile of ten years ago, after first having been received with tempestuous joy at Antwerp, made his stately entry into Brussels. At Vilvoorde already the Brussels rhetoricians welcomed him with their symbolic representations on barges—the journey from Antwerp to Brussels was made by water—the famous "Rhetorician" Jan Baptista Houwaert greeted the Prince in flowery Dutch rhyme, just the kind of poetry to which he had been treated at Utrecht; for the rest of the journey to Brussels a citizen guard of honour marched on either side of the canal; at the gate of the town were waiting representatives of the States-General, the States of Brabant and the municipal government; Aerschot himself rode beside Orange through the densely crowded and gaily bedecked streets, amid cheers and blessings, to the palace of Nassau, which, plundered and gutted by Alva, was yet home to its returning master. It was Aerschot again who welcomed him on the morrow in the States-General, although in effect the Prince had come to transplant the "chief" elected by that assembly a year ago.

He came just in time to frustrate negotiations with Don John into which the States had entered out of fear for the master they were giving themselves. Orange's strength lay in the people. He knew how to make himself liked. The Eighteen Men he invited to his table; in the street, on the walls, he talked to the civic guards familiarly and in a human way, using at times the great words of Liberty and Fatherland which went straight to their hearts. And when shortly afterwards another scheme came to light with which Aerschot hoped to deprive him of the power to harm; when it appeared that the young archduke Matthew, a brother of the Emperor's, nephew of Philip's, was on his way to the Netherlands, having been invited by a number of the high nobility to come and assume the governorship in order to save the country at least for the Habsburg dynasty and for the Catholic Church, then the people of Brussels were immediately ready to maintain the Prince against those intrigues as the trusted man of the nation. Reinforced with delegations from Antwerp, Leuven, and Den Bosch, the three other chief towns of the province, the men of Brussels pushed their way into the meeting-chamber of the States of Brabant and forced through the appointment of Orange to be "Ruwart" of Brabant—an office corresponding to that of the Stadtholder in the other provinces; as the residence of the Governor-General was in Brabant, that province had no Stadtholder in ordinary circumstances. The appointment was confirmed by the States-General acting under similar pressure. Aerschot and the entire conservative party were profoundly irritated.

Aerschot had just been made Stadtholder of Flanders by the States-General. He thought that post gave him a *point d'appui* for a counter-attack. In fact, he caused the provincial States assembly at Ghent to protest against Orange's appointment. But here his rival had the same kind of allies at his disposal. The popular party, fired by the recollection of the heroic traditions of their town's past, burned to imitate the example set by Brussels. Two members of the Ghent municipal aristocracy, Hembyze and Ryhove, aspired to the rôle of tribunes of the people, like in days gone by Artevelde, with whom Hembyze claimed family connection. He had long been in touch with Orange. It was with the Prince's help that he had just succeeded in obtaining from the States-General the restoration of the privileges which Charles V had torn up in 1540. This had caused great rejoicings at Ghent. The people expected next to see guild rule re-established in a legal manner. Aerschot, the new Stadtholder, looked askance on that claim, but Hembyze and Ryhove, having made sure of Orange's secret approval, now ventured upon their great attempt. On the 28th of October they arrested Aerschot and the principal members of the States of Flanders, among them the Bishops of Brugge and Yper. The old democratic town government was resurrected, but at the same time a revolutionary committee of Eighteen Men was instituted.

These developments caused not a little consternation in the States-General at Brussels, and everywhere they hastened that

F

estrangement from the cause of the revolt which had already begun among nobles, clergy, magistrates. While Orange had Aerschot (and Aerschot alone) released from prison, during a visit to Ghent he showed himself openly the friend and ally of Hembyze, Ryhove, and the guilds. Indeed, he had for a second time marched troops into the town from Zealand, and it was on these that the revolutionary regime now rested. Meanwhile the States-General were still entirely under the thumb of the Eighteen Men of Brussels, who declared masterfully that the national cause was the cause of the people, and therefore their concern. The Commune of Paris, two centuries and more afterwards, during the French Revolution, would not be able to put it any better.

It was in this confusion that the organization of the new government under Matthew, which was to be independent of Spain, had to be elaborated. The two most vital decisions were forced through by new tumults. It was in spite of themselves that the States-General included in the new Council of State avowed adherents of Orange like the lawyer Liesvelt and Marnix. And it was in spite of themselves that they appointed Orange to be Matthew's lieutenant, an arrangement by which in effect the Governor, intended by Aerschot to control him, was delivered into his hands.

A Netherlandish government was now in being. After Don John, after Orange himself, Matthew could make his festive entry into Brussels, and under him Orange was the real ruler. It was a government in which old national tendencies were realized. As we saw, the States-General had taken it upon themselves to appoint a Council of State. In spite of all loyal declarations with which even now they were not chary, they laid hands on a considerable part of the royal prerogative. The Governor took an oath to Philip, but also to the States-General. He promised that even when fortified by the advice of the Council of State he would consult them before committing any important act of government, and he acknowledged their right, as also that of the provincial States, to assemble of their own accord. In case these conditions were violated, the States would be at liberty to take up arms—who does not recognize here the inspiration of the Brabant Joyous Entry? It was a veritable constitution. But was this constitution of a nature to secure sufficient strength to the Central Government?

The Burgundian Dukes, as we have seen, had imposed the Central Government upon the Netherlands people as a foreign organism which—certainly not without great gain to national development—went right against historic subdivisions which may appear arbitrary now, but to which political life had accustomed itself. Now this superimposed Central Government was to a large extent pulled down and a new one formed, but as the vitality of these historic subdivisions was far from being exhausted, the new Central Government was conceived as the resultant of the old groups coming together in freedom. No doubt a true feeling of community manifested itself in opposition to the provincial particularism which had always caused so much trouble to the rulers, but the difficulty was that the States-General, without whom the Governor was nothing, were so much the immediate creature of the provinces that in cases of conflict they could do little but admonish and implore. As for the Prince of Orange, it was impossible that he, in spite of his eloquent declarations, should be generally accepted as a national leader; in the eyes of many he was bound to remain the chief of a party. The worst weakness of "the Generality," however, was its lack of money. The States-General reproached the provinces situated a little away from the Brabant centre with not contributing anything to the federal exchequer. These provinces retorted that the States left them to battle alone against their particular perils. Gelderland, for instance, still had serious trouble with the garrisons, mentioned above, of Kampen, Deventer, and Roermond, and the Gelderland deputy, Van Lier, wrote home from Brussels in his German-flavoured East Netherlandish:

According to my humble opinion there is but little help and comfort to be expected for us from their lordships the States here. I give your worships to consider, therefore, whether it might not be better that we provide ourselves with the help and assistance of the neighbouring provinces.

And the new regime, thus beset by the problems of these

strong centrifugal tendencies, had hardly begun to function
when the military power of Spain administered a blow to it
which set it tottering. The Netherlands were not to be left
to work out their own destiny.

Don John had had to use a great deal of patience, but at
length in January 1578 three thousand of the Spanish troops
which he had sent away after the Eternal Edict came back,
and without losing a moment he marched from Luxemburg
in a north-westerly direction. At Gembloux, just across the
Brabant boundary, he fell in with the much more numerous
army of the States. Many of its noble officers were at Brussels
attending a wedding. The Walloons threw away their arms
almost at once. The defeat became a rout. Nivelles, Diest,
Thienen, Leuven capitulated; Maastricht was held, like
Brussels, where the people insulted the nobles, calling them
traitors; Don John did not yet dispose of a sufficient number
of troops to attack the capital. Yet the States-General, with
Matthew and the Prince of Orange, withdrew to Antwerp.
What might not have happened had Don John been able to
follow up his success! But while the course of events in his
Netherlands was once again crying out for speedy decisions,
Philip was sitting lost in the disentanglement of his half-
brother's vague projects against England; he suspected him
of treason, had his agent Escovedo murdered in Madrid, and
instead of reinforcements sent him congratulations. The States-
General and the Prince of Orange obtained a respite to put
the country in a state of defence.

An almost desperate undertaking; not only on account of
the feebleness of central authority, which has been indicated,
but at this very moment, partly as a result of the shock of the
defeat, the country slid into an indescribable confusion. The
savage forces set free by the political and religious passions
of the time no longer let themselves be controlled by the
ingenious devices of the States-General and of Orange. Their
sudden irruption, which threatened society itself with collapse,
dealt shocks to the young community of the Netherlands which
weakened its powers of resistance not a little, just when it
needed them against the renewed attack from outside.

b. RELIGIOUS STRIFE AND SEPARATE UNIONS

The Pacification of Ghent, as we know, had attempted to settle the religious question on regional lines. A really satisfactory solution could hardly be obtained in that way, for even though the events of 1572 had brought the Reformed party into power in Holland and Zealand, there were Catholics there just as much as there were Protestants in the fifteen provinces that were officially considered as Catholic. Both sides now had the consolation that conscience was free, but for the rest all they were allowed to do in those provinces where they were not in control was "to keep quiet." Their respective attitudes showed how much the tendency of the time was with the Protestants. In spite of the fact that the suppressed Catholics in Holland and Zealand constituted a majority of the population, the Protestants stirred much more vigorously and created a far more urgent problem in the provinces where they were kept under, small minority though they were there too. The example of Holland and Zealand acted as an inspiration to them. Numerous Flemish and Brabant exiles, who had done their share in the building up there of the new Reformed State, now brought to their own towns the tales of the victory they had witnessed. It was inevitable that the democracy, which Orange had helped to put on its feet in Brussels and Ghent, and which he had let loose against the conservative and Catholic States assemblies, should move towards Calvinism. Both the Catholicism of its adversaries and the Calvinism of its Holland allies and of the returning exiles drove it in that direction. In the eyes of the democrats, too, the national cause, which they already identified with the cause of democracy, became one with the cause of the Reformation. At Ghent the report of the defeat near Gembloux had the immediate effect of causing the Eighteen to have the monasteries occupied by their soldiers, and this was only the first of a long series of acts of violence against the Catholics.

At Ghent, under the leadership of Hembyze and Ryhove, and after the fashion in which the same work had been done in 1572 and 1573 in Holland and Zealand, Calvinism was in the course of the spring and summer of 1578 raised to exclusive dominion. Monasteries were closed and their properties confiscated, monks sent into exile, all offices filled with Calvinists, churches emptied of decoration and whitewashed for the Reformed service, finally the exercise of the Catholic religion prohibited. Ghent's traditional claims, which had been vigorously revived by the revolution of the year before, combined with religious enthusiasm to drive the movement outside the town. Oudenaarde, Kortryk, Brugge, finally Yper as well, were surprised, generally with the help of sympathizers within the walls, and gradually the whole of Flanders was forcibly subjected to Calvinism, the democratic form of government, and at the same time to the hegemony of Ghent. Needless to say the process was attended with a good deal of violence. The Ghent preacher Regius—De Koninck, a native of Kortryk—on contemplating the finished work, found comfort in the thought that the worst things

were done by those who know of no religion. In fine (so he must nevertheless admit) Babylon (meaning Rome, Catholicism) could not be annihilated without a Babylonish confusion.

In July, when public preaching had only just begun, this man had felt very unhappy over an interview at Antwerp with Villers and Taffin, court preacher and councillor to the Prince, who had warned him that what was happening at Ghent "greatly displeased" Orange.

With many arguments and high words they begged of us that we should at once abstain, if we would not cause His Excellency the greatest trouble and to the Fatherland the most notable peril.

Nothing more natural than that the Prince should be alarmed to observe the breaking forth of Calvinism in Flanders. The entire Catholic and aristocratic party in the Netherlands were aghast and at the same time indignant, and protested with all their might against the tearing up of the Pacification. Orange had not scrupled, when there seemed to be a fair opportunity, to administer shrewd blows to these men, but now he judged, and rightly, that caution was necessary, especially because they were in almost exclusive control of the Walloon provinces, which consequently—and this was an exceedingly dangerous development—began to form a block in the States-General. But however readily one may understand the Prince's urging patience and moderation, no less obvious is it that the Calvinists could not at his bidding check themselves in midway. God's work must not be hindered by human considerations. Everywhere the Protestants began to stir, and after a synod at Dordt, presided over by Dathenus, a formal request for freedom of religious exercise was presented to Matthew and the Council of State.

The Prince now flattered himself with the hope that concessions would get the better of the extreme claims of the Reformed party. In July the States-General resolved to lay before all the provinces a project of Religious Peace. Even though this was merely a project, over which each province was to retain the final decision, the resolution met with the opposition of Hainaut and Tournai, and needed Orange's urgent insistence to go through. According to it, public exercise of the second religion would have to be conceded, of Catholicism where the Reformed were in control, of Calvinism where the Catholics ruled, in all places where a hundred families so desired.

At Antwerp, under the eye of the Prince, the project was introduced, and for the time being only there. One cannot wonder that the Catholics in those provinces where they still had the upper hand, especially the Walloon area and Groningen, Gelderland, and Utrecht, saw in it merely a sly contrivance for the introduction of heresy and in the long run for the dethronement of Catholicism. That was the way they saw things going all over the country! The example of Flanders and Holland and Zealand was instructive: there was no thought there of granting to the Catholics that liberty which in the Catholic provinces the Religious Peace was to bring to the Protestants. Thus the Walloon provinces grew more and more embittered, and events rolled on irresistibly in their fatal course. The Walloon troops which had acquitted themselves so badly at Gembloux had been removed to the boundaries of Flanders and Hainaut, and there, long unpaid, and declaring that they were intentionally neglected by the States-General, in August they began to mutiny. They had since been living at the expense of the peasants in southern Flanders. On September 28, under the command of the Baron of Montigny, a brother of the Count of Lalaing, who was Stadtholder of Hainaut, they captured the little Flemish town of Meenen.[1] Montigny gave them a watchword: they called themselves "Malcontents," and fought for the Catholic religion and for the Pacification. Soon the situation developed into a real civil war with the troops of Ghent under Ryhove, while the Walloon provinces acclaimed Montigny as their champion.

What complicated matters still more was the activity of John Casimir, the Elector Palatine, with his auxiliary troops. After the defeat of Gembloux the States-General had redoubled their efforts to obtain assistance from foreign princes. Lalaing had invited the brother of the French King, the Duke of Anjou, to Hainaut, but although the States-General had decorated him with the title of "Defender of Netherlands Liberty," he achieved nothing for the good cause. It was his interference nevertheless which, by rousing England's ever wakeful jealousy of France, made Queen Elizabeth forget both caution and economy so far as to subsidize the warlike and zealously Calvinistic Casimir towards leading his army to the Netherlands. The English money did not, however, go very far, and Casimir, having reached Brabant by way of Zutfen with his undisciplined troops, had nothing more urgent to do than to demand payment of the States, and when this was not forthcoming, achieved no more against the enemy than Anjou. With all the more fervour, however, did he throw himself into domestic party strife. In October, at the instance of Dathenus, who had been employed in the Palatinate during his exile after 1567, and who was now the minister of the St. Bavo church at Ghent, Casimir came to that town and backed Hembyze notwithstanding the admonitions of the States-General and of Orange. In the eyes of the Flemish Cavinist

---

[1] Meenen: in French—*Menin.*

he was the man of God. Orange, on the other hand, who wanted to tolerate Catholicism, who in spite of the St. Bartholomew's massacre was still hankering after an alliance with France, was for these zealots a worldling, an atheist. Dathenus rated him from the pulpit for making the State into his God, for changing his religion as other men would change a suit of clothes.

In these circumstances, and "having understood that the heretical provinces of Flanders, Holland, Zealand, Gelderland, and others are planning a separate union," the States of Hainaut in October took the initiative for negotiations with the other Walloon provinces in order to work out a similar alliance on a Catholic basis.

At that moment events escaped the control of Orange completely. The Spanish army had during the summer been driven back some way out of Brabant by Bossu, whom the States-General had entrusted with the command-in-chief over their troops. But while Don John, again in the neighbourhood of Namur, was eating his heart out over the way in which his brother the King was crossing his plans, the States Government lacked the cohesion it would have needed to collect its scattered forces for a decisive blow. Orange had to give all his attention to the war the Walloons were carrying on with the Flemings and to their threatening defection. It is true that he succeeded for a moment, by playing off Ryhove against Hembyze, in making Ghent submit to his policy. In December he came to the town in person and had the Religious Peace proclaimed. But in the meanwhile he had to leave the affairs of the North to his brother John of Nassau, who, no less zealous a Calvinist than Casimir of the Palatinate, was as little inclined to think of national unity, and in accordance with the Prince's policy to respect Catholic feeling.

John of Nassau, the eldest, and now the only surviving, brother of Orange's, had always assisted him in his perilous undertakings up to the extreme capacity of his lands of Nassau and beyond. When the Prince in 1577 went to Brabant, he had wanted to leave John as his lieutenant in the Stadtholderships of Holland, Zealand, and Utrecht, but the States of those provinces had not been agreeable. In June 1578, however, John

had become Stadtholder of Gelderland, which had been without a Stadtholder since Hierges had gone over to Don John.

How is it possible that the States of that eminently Catholic
province had let themselves be saddled with so vigorous a
Protestant? When they had begged Matthew to indicate a
suitable person for the post, they had been careful to stress
their desire to see the Pacification respected; that is to say,
they professed themselves to be averse from religious innovations. The fact is that Gelderland was in desperate straits.
Lords, knights, and towns, divided into four "Quarters," for
the most part disliked the idea of submission to Don John;
but even apart from a secretly pro-Spanish party, they were
torn by faction and could not unite on any decision, particularly not on a selection for the Stadtholderate. Yet at the same
time they were painfully aware of being unequal to the military situation created by the garrisons of Kampen, Deventer,
and Roermond. Only Orange, only Holland seemed to be in
a position to render assistance against those dangers. Orange's
brother appeared as the messenger of that assistance, and for
the moment his religion was overlooked. In Overysel, of which
province Hierges had also been Stadtholder, the States were
really making the same calculation when they asked to be
allowed to take as his successor the Lord of Rennenberg, who
was already, since the end of 1576, on behalf of the States-
General, Stadtholder of Friesland and Groningen. This was
indeed a more natural choice than that of John of Nassau, for
Rennenberg, a scion of the great Hainaut family of the Lalaings,
for all that he was closely connected with Orange, who loved
him as the younger brother of his late friend and fellow-exile
Hoogstraten, was at the same time a staunch Catholic. Between
them the two Stadtholders now obtained troops from Holland
—which were commanded by no less a person than Sonoy—
and in the second half of 1578 first Kampen and then Deventer
were besieged and captured under Rennenberg's direction.

This eliminated a serious danger, but there still existed the
chief menace, that from the South, where Roermond in Upper
Gelderland was still in Spanish hands. John of Nassau therefore applied himself vigorously to the task, entrusted to him

by his brother, of securing Gelderland by binding it more closely to Holland.

Mention has been made more than once in the preceding pages of this idea of a separate union between Holland and Gelderland and other northern provinces. It was promoted by Orange and Holland—there is no doubt that Van Lier's suggestion quoted above was inspired by the Prince—not because they felt more closely related in spirit to Gelderland than to the provinces south of the rivers, nor indeed because they had any intention of seceding together from those southern provinces. On the contrary, their insistence, repeated more than once, and each time suspiciously repulsed by the Catholic States of Gelderland, sprang from their realization of the strategic importance to Holland of the maintenance of Gelderland, coupled with their fear lest the province should prove too weak and too much divided to work out its own salvation. Against an attack from the south, Holland and Zealand were safeguarded by nature, but as soon as the enemy was able to take the offensive he was sure, just as in 1572, after a circling movement through Gelderland, to attempt an attack from the east. Gelderland was therefore described as "a propugnaculum," a bulwark for Holland, Zealand, and Utrecht, and attention was drawn to the fact that

the enemy directs most of his effort against Gelderland, thinking thereby to acquire the four rivers, to wit, the Rhine, the Maas, the Ysel, and the Waal, and in course of time to get at Holland.

It was John of Nassau himself who instructed an envoy of his to represent these facts to the States of Holland, it was he who, a little while after his elevation to the Stadtholderate, renewed the negotiations. In doing so he was by no means acting as the executor of the wishes of the Gelderland States. On the contrary, how to overcome their persistent opposition to the idea was his great problem. John of Nassau stood in Gelderland as an independent power, by many hated and feared in equal measure, but, strong through his relations with Holland, whose auxiliary troops now formed a potent factor in the struggle of forces in Gelderland, he carried through his policy with high-handed determination. This was the moment when the relations between Catholics and Protestants were becoming infinitely more strained than they had been since the Pacification; the events at Ghent by no means had that effect in the South only. If as a consequence many Catholics, affected by the temper of the Malcontents, began to look to the King's Governor, this again produced increasing suspicion on the part of the patriots against all Catholics indiscriminately. Nobody did more to strengthen this vicious circle than Count John. He exerted himself greatly to persuade the States of Gelderland to accept the Religious Peace, and when they obstinately refused, he yet helped the Reformed wherever possible to possess themselves of churches, overlooking antipapist violence on the part of the troops. A number of towns from the Quarters of Roermond and Zutfen addressed to the States-General a complaint about "the exorbitant innovations" with which, since the new Stadtholder had taken the oath, they were "overrun" by the action of the soldiers. The Stadtholder had on his own authority dissolved the Court of Justice of the province. No doubt this court was a hotbed of Spanish intrigues, yet in the eyes of many who had no use for Spain the deed was an unheard-of violation of the ancient constitution. In a similar fashion Count John, regardless of their kicks and struggles, forced upon the States that bitter medicine, the Union.

In September a meeting of the States was held at Arnhem, where, at the invitation of the Count, envoys of Holland and Zealand were present. Here the obstinacy of the men of his own province, who persisted in appealing to the Pacification of Ghent to justify their refusal, so angered him that he burst out:

Smear yourselves all over with the Pacification of Ghent, I see too well what is going on.

The Count of Culemborch, the Beggar of '66, who assisted him, gave even more explicit utterance to the suspicions of the Protestant party, fulminating:

"It is all due to the fact that a handful of idols have been thrown down [the military had been guilty of iconoclasm at Arnhem], that is why we see this distant manner. You had better take the Duke of Anjou, he will protect you, he is a Catholic, he drives the shaven band"—and more such words.

All these passionate sallies did not move the States of Gelderland to give in; but neither did their blank refusals make an end of the negotiations, which were continued by their Stadtholder. The project which served as a basis had been drafted by the Advocate of the States of Utrecht, Floris Thin, and had the approval of Orange. The Hollanders and Count John, however, altered it flatly against the Prince's intentions. Instead of, in accordance with his wishes, protecting and reassuring the Catholics as much as possible, the exclusive dominion of Calvinism in Holland and Zealand was first of all expressly recognized, while in the second place the Religious Peace was made the normal condition for the other provinces. The Religious Peace might not be in accordance with the Pacification, it had at least been sanctioned by the States-General. In the new project for the Union, however, a further step was taken: the provinces were allowed to do what seemed to them to be required by the interests of public order; at the same time, by clauses concerning the secularization of ecclesiastical goods, clerical apostasy was positively encouraged. So all that the opposition of the Catholic States of Gelderland effected was that the Union was prepared in Protestant conclaves, for in the end they were unable to prevent the alliance from being concluded.

· Don John had died in October 1578. Alexander of Parma, the son of Margaret, had taken over the government, an arrangement which the King confirmed. In the last days of the year he marched against the Upper Quarter of Gelderland. The Knighthood of the Upper Quarter (constituting one of the "members" of its States) declared at once

that this principality is entirely powerless to resist the enemy, and has fallen into such utter confusion that they cannot do without neighbourly assistance.

At the Gelderland Diet only Zutfen and the knights still opposed the despatch of delegates to Utrecht, where the final negotiations about "the Holland Union" were to take place. Fear of the Protestants, fear of Holland supremacy, everything had to give way before the need of Holland troops and Holland ships. On 23 January, 1579, the Union was signed at Utrecht. But even though the States of Gelderland had sent a delegation, they had not empowered it to sign, and it was Count John who with his solitary name on the document boldly represented the whole province. At Utrecht, shortly before, the municipal authorities had prepared for the conclusion of the Union by placing under arrest several of the clerical members of their States. Rennenberg and his provinces, who had taken part in the first discussions at Arnhem, abstained now that matters had taken this turn. Only the Ommelands, always at variance with the ultra-Catholic town of Groningen, at once participated. So also did Ghent, which had eagerly sent delegates to attend the final discussions and which formally adhered a few days afterwards. Holland and Zealand were the fixed point round which this so-called Closer Union crystallized.

As a matter of fact the alliance formed at Utrecht did constitute within the Pacification a far tighter organization. The participators bound themselves to be "for ever as one province." They organized a committee of their own to deal with military matters, and took into their service troops paid out of their own contributions and commanded by their own general, the German Count of Hohenlohe. The provinces allied at Utrecht continued to sit on the States-General, yet the latter were practically relieved from all responsibility in the territory of the Union, and it is only when one remembers how feeble was their rule and how incapable of acting with any speed that the founders of the Union can be understood to have been moved by other motives than a desire to secede.

The territory united on 23 January, 1579, while it was seeking to expand its boundaries, at the same time needed itself a good deal of confirmation and purification. In accordance with the opinion that had now come into sway, this meant the suppression of all influence of the Catholics, potential friends of Spain. It was practically by force that Count John got the Quarters of Gelderland to consent to the Union he had already concluded in their name. Into several town administrations he introduced Calvinists. At Zutfen, which remained recalcitrant longer than any other town, Sonoy's soldiers seized the churches for the Reformed. Sonoy admitted that

no doubt some idols were taken down somewhat roughly,

but nevertheless gloried in that work. Within the Union territory the public exercise of the Catholic religion was thus restricted more and more. So far in Holland and Zealand the towns which had come under the Prince's authority by Satis-factions had for some little while occupied an exceptional position. Amsterdam, whose citizens in 1577 had beaten off with considerable loss of life an attempted surprise by the troops of the States of Holland, had not come over to their side until February 1578, and then only on terms which included the continued suppression of all religious services except the Catholic. But these Satisfactions were torn up one after the other. At Amsterdam, as early as May 1578, the old government, together with the priests and monks, had been driven out of the town, where the exiles of 1567 now formed a new government and introduced Calvinism. They since supplied to the new regime in Holland, and even to the Union, some of the most prominent among many vigorous personali-ties; for example, Reinier Cant, who became a member of the Committee of the Closer Union. At Haarlem, on Corpus Christi 1579, the garrison assaulted the procession, invaded the cathe-dral, killed a priest, smashed the statues; the Bishop fled for his life. One of the offending soldiers was subsequently hanged, but in spite of the murmurings of the Haarlem Catholics, who appealed to the Satisfaction, public exercise of their religion was now prohibited and the churches were given to the Reformed. In the province of Utrecht, Amersfoort would not submit to the Union nor introduce the Religious Peace. Commissioned by the new regime, John of Nassau came to lay siege to the little town. On 10 March, 1579, it surrendered. New magistrates were appointed and the Religious Peace proclaimed. On the 11th of June following the statues were removed out of all the churches, and once again the Religious Peace had led to the exclusive domination of Calvinism. At Ghent, too, in March 1579, the Religious Peace which Orange had caused to be accepted there was brought to an end, and Hembyze and Dathenus were once more in control.

> They who at first asked for no more than to live in freedom,
> Now have their liberty, but will not give it to others.

Thus bitterly wrote Spieghel, the Amsterdam poet, who himself constantly refused to serve in any capacity under a regime based on the violation of the Satisfactions.

Orange—nothing else could be expected—looked on these developments with profound concern, and refused to join a Union which had been so utterly alienated from his intentions. Seen from where he resided, from Antwerp, the situation appeared gloomy indeed. In southern Flanders the Walloon Malcontents were advancing, while Parma's troops from the Upper Quarter of Gelderland marauded over the entire countryside of Brabant. Although the Prince, therefore, still considered "a good Union" to be imperatively necessary, at the same time he roundly declared to the envoy who came (at the end of February 1579) to ask for his signature to the Utrecht agreement and for his help in obtaining those of the magistrates of Antwerp:

this one is no good.

In spite of which, a little over two months later, he joined all the same, and not only Antwerp but Lier and Breda and the whole of Flanders followed suit. Circumstances were too strong for him. Once more his efforts to make Protestants and Catholics co-operate had failed; once more, now that there appeared to be no remedy for that, he had no choice but to go on with the Protestants alone. It was in any case too late to hold back the Walloons. No less by what had been done at Utrecht than by the proceedings at Ghent, they were irretrievably alienated.

We saw how the first rumours of a "heretical" Union had served as an excuse to the States of Hainaut in proposing a

Catholic one. This argument continued to be used, while in its turn the Union of the Walloons served the same purpose in the North. Here, too, was that vicious circle which Orange could not break through. In the end the Walloon provinces had come to an agreement at Arras before the others at Utrecht. At the basis of their Union was the wish to have the Pacification respected in a strictly Catholic sense. Since this was the very purpose of the Eternal Edict, which had been expressly confirmed by the King, the conclusion was obvious that between the Union of Arras and the legitimate Sovereign it ought to be possible to restore peace. The fact that Don John, who by his attempt on Namur had broken the Eternal Edict, was no longer among the living made an agreement even easier of achievement, and Parma showed himself to be an accomplished diplomatist. First, Montigny with his troops was reconciled—with him went that de Hèze who in the first stage of the revolt, not three years ago, had been Orange's man at Brussels—then the Walloon provinces of Artois, Hainaut, and Walloon Flanders concluded at Arras in due form a peace with the King. The great lords of those provinces made excellent terms for themselves. This was not a small temptation for their equals who still, at the cost of daily irritations and humiliations, held the side of the States-General. What a scene, for instance, when on Corpus Christi 1579 at Antwerp (where the Religious Peace was supposed to be in force), Aerschot and the Archduke Matthew himself, with all who took part in the procession, were, to the anguish of Orange, molested by the Beggar mob! For the rest, the peace of Arras, like the Eternal Edict, solemnly confirmed all the old privileges and promised the removal of the foreign troops. Was it not the true national policy which triumphed there? No, for the most precious thing was lacking, namely independence. But independence was not what the Netherlanders had set out to win with any clear consciousness of purpose, and in any case the triumph, under the Catholic banner, of the interests of the nobility and the States, of the old privileges, was bound to make a profound impression all over the country.

The secession of the Walloon provinces is an event in the

history of his people which rouses mixed feelings in the heart of the Netherlands historian. He is tempted to discern the possible beginnings of a sounder political organization. In the convulsions of the war of independence the French-speaking and the Dutch-speaking regions seemed each to be waking up to their own individuality. Not all was religion in these developments. That becomes evident at once from the exactitude with which the separation coincided with the racial boundary. After the Union of Arras the only Walloon deputies remaining in the States-General for a little while longer were those of Tournai. But, in fact, the Walloons were beginning to remember their ancient feuds with the Dutch-speaking Flemings, and became more conscious of their racial community as against that of the central and northern Netherlands. These for their part were heartily sick of the gallicization of the Central Government which had been the consequence of the conjunction with Walloon countries; this is true especially for the northeastern provinces, whose nobility and magistrates were less familiar with French than those in the others. The States-General—was it on account of the deputies from Tournai?—continued to use French for some time longer, but as soon as the Dutch-speaking provinces—from Flanders to Friesland —were left among themselves, Dutch was introduced as the official language. (In the provincial States, even of Brabant and Flanders, it had of course never lost that position, in spite of the influence of the nobility transplanted from Wallonia.) I am not suggesting that this linguistic and racial factor played any considerable part in the shaping of events, only that developments revealed its existence and sometimes fell in with it. The primary importance of the religious motive will clearly appear as soon as we come to consider affairs in the North-East. But even so we may, from the point of view of our later experience, point out what a blessing it would have been for the future of Netherlandish civilization in Flanders and Brabant—of the native civilization of those regions, in other words —if their leading classes had had to collaborate in politics with those of the North, and had been detached from the corrupting association with the Walloons. But while we cannot overlook these possibilities contained in the peace of Arras, even though they have not materialized, another reflection offers itself even more insistently. It is that if the Walloons had to cut loose from the Dutch-speaking Netherlands, they could not have chosen a more unfortunate moment. Their action hastened the development of a conflict between the cause of independence and the cause of Catholicism, a process as harmful to the one as it was to the other. And it provided the foreign ruler, whose commander so far had had to stay in the poor and distant region on the Maas, with far more important resources and a base of operations from which not only the towns of Brabant but those of Flanders as well came within his immediate reach. One circumstance, finally, deserves some notice, namely, that these Walloon provinces which by their defection were going to exercise so fatal an influence on the course of the war in the South and on the future of Flanders and Brabant, to-day for the most part do not even belong to Belgium. Of the four that made peace at Arras, two (Artois and Walloon Flanders) were wholly, while a third (Hainaut) was for about one-half, annexed to France, and for good, by Louis XIV.

The revolt thus found itself in a sad plight in 1579. Serious inroads were already being made on the Dutch-speaking Netherlands. Parma did not at once continue his attack on Gelderland, but turning round he first besieged Maastricht. After an obstinate resistance the town was taken, and suffered for the second time in a period of three years a horrible sack and slaughter. Meanwhile the Catholic party gained the upper hand at Den Bosch and Mechlin, so that these towns left the side of the States-General. A negotiation which was conducted at Köln that summer, once more under the Emperor's mediation, again stuck on the unsurmountable difficulty of the religious question. But this time a number of highly placed personalities, particularly the Duke of Aerschot and the Abbot of St. Gertrude, took the occasion of its failure to disengage themselves from an unbearably false position, and instead of returning to the States-General made their personal peace with Parma.

One most dangerous loss the revolt still had to suffer, as

a direct consequence of the unhappy contrast between Catholic and Reformed.

Friesland, Drente, and Overysel had joined the Union of Utrecht, district by district, and amid loud quarrelling. Rennenberg, who had at first resolutely refused to do so, invoking the example of Orange, had given in when the Prince himself changed his mind. He had then even forced the town of Groningen to submit and introduce the Religious Peace. Yet he did not feel comfortable when matters took this turn. It was not to be expected that he should! The Walloon nobleman could hardly remain insensible to the example set by his cousins the Baron of Montigny and the Stadtholder of Hainaut (Lalaings like himself), and by how many others! The faithful Catholic was greatly offended by the proceedings of Sonoy and of John of Nassau. Nor for that matter was he the only one. At Groningen, at Leeuwarden, Kampen, Zwolle, everywhere, the Catholics were afraid that the Calvinist minority, leaning on the Holland auxiliary troops, would proceed from Religious Peace to suppression of the Catholic services, and everywhere they felt their courage rise with the Malcontents movement, which had now found a protector in Parma. Members of the dissolved Law Courts of Friesland and Groningen, noble *émigrés* from the whole region east of the Zuider Zee and the Ysel, surrounded Parma and entertained relations with their friends who had remained behind, to whom they promised the King's and his Governor's pardon. The whole of that area, where many looked upon the Union of Utrecht as a yoke imposed by the Hollanders, was in a dangerous ferment. Rennenberg certainly must not be represented as the disinterested champion of an idea. Before taking the leap he made careful arrangements with Parma, as had done all his friends, about his rank and his possessions and his honorary titles. Nevertheless his "treason," as it is called in the North Netherlandish history books, was no mere personal act. It was an act of policy for which he could count on widespread acclamation in the provinces of which he was Stadtholder.

In March 1580, at Groningen, ever a stronghold of royalism in the North, he announced his defection from the States-

General. All his helpers and councillors were natives of Groningen, Friesland, and Overysel. His action caused a tremendous sensation. Everywhere the dislike of the patriots for Catholicism was doubled. At Leeuwarden, at Zwolle and Kampen, at Utrecht, priests were insulted and statues in the churches broken to pieces. The States of Friesland and those of Utrecht now prohibited the exercise of the Catholic religion in the whole of their provinces. The Catholics, on the other hand, longed only the more fervently for the coming of the liberator. But Rennenberg's intention had been guessed a good while before, and measures had been taken accordingly. The Prince of Orange, deeply shocked by the faithlessness of a beloved younger friend, had already come north as far as Kampen, accompanied by the Committee of the Closer Union. Holland was ready with an advance of money for the soldiers' pay, and the troops were withheld by Barthold Entes, the former Sea Beggar, from following Rennenberg. Erelong he was being besieged within Groningen by Sonoy and William Louis, John of Nassau's son; and even though without troops to overawe them, not a single town in Friesland, and especially in Overysel, could be relied upon, for the moment the defection had been checked. Only the Overysel country-folk, harassed by the States' troops little less than by the Spanish, rose to arms in their thousands, and had to be struck down in bloody fights by the Count of Hohenlohe's cavalry: seven hundred peasants were killed in the first engagement.

Immediately afterwards, however, Hohenlohe was faced by a harder task, when Parma sent a small army from the Upper Quarter of Gelderland round the east to relieve Groningen; it was led by Schenck van Nydechem, with a staff of Frisian and Groningen *émigrés*. Hohenlohe, trying to stop this force, was defeated, the siege of Groningen had to be raised, and now more than ever the entire North-East was in jeopardy. The majority of the citizens of Zwolle nearly succeeded in bringing the town over to the Malcontent side—for that name was now used here too. Oldenzaal threw its garrison out and called in Rennenberg. Koevorden and Delfzyl opened their gates for him. Steenwyk was held thanks to a vigorous commander, and the States troops could also safeguard Friesland and the Ysel towns. But everywhere citizen stood over against citizen, exiles returned while other groups went into exile (as did almost the whole of the Ommeland nobility, which had ever been zealous in the cause of the revolt), and a wide area was exposed to raids from either side.

A man like Coornhert, the poet and philosopher, the friend of liberty, was alarmed to see how the Reformed, by their consciousness of constituting "by far the smallest band," were driven to ever sterner repression of the "wronged" Catholic majority. In the end, he feared

the town populations which have let in the Beggars, hoping for better from them and experiencing worse, will again help to drive them out and will open lands and towns to the enemy. So that they will, together with the oppressors of their consciences, see this delightful country once more subject to Spanish slavery.

How is it that events have not taken this course? How is it that in part of the Netherlands, at any rate, that "small band" has managed to maintain itself, and in the long run even to fashion the majority after its wish? At the moment when this chapter is closed no equilibrium has been established between the contending parties. But in the forces which will make themselves felt from now on the military factor is much more prominent than it was in those to which the enormous losses of the States in 1579 and 1580 were due. No doubt the religious divisions still remained a source of weakness to them; in the loss of Zutfen, Doesburg, and Nymwegen, for instance, and also in that of some of the Flemish and Brabant towns which Parma won in the coming years, the dissatisfaction of the Catholics was to play an important part. But the great moral issue had been decided. Netherlands liberty was to be anti-Romish. That was the doing, despite Orange, of the Calvinistic regime of Holland and Zealand through the Union of Utrecht, and of the Calvinistic regime of Ghent through the subjection of Flanders and the co-operation with Brussels.

It is undeniable that sentence of death had thereby been pronounced over Netherlands unity, but it should neverthe-less be observed that the line which we have now seen drawn by the Malcontents movement between Flanders and Wallonia, and between the extreme North-East and the neighbouring region, was not to be the final line of separation. The defection of the North-East represented little less clearly than did the defection of the Walloon provinces the spontaneous refusal of the Netherlands people to sacrifice its old religion to liberty. Nevertheless Groningen and Oldenzaal, like Zutfen, Doesburg, and Nymwegen, were in course of time to become free and Protestant; Flanders, and Ghent itself, not less Protestant than Holland and Zealand, were on the contrary destined to slide back under Spain as well as under Rome. How was it? Because, as has been said, the military factor now became paramount; and in the trial of strength between Spain, based on the wide perimeter of the Netherlands—from Grevelingen over Nivelles, Leuven, Maastricht, and Roermond to Groningen—and the revolt, based on the maritime provinces of Holland and Zealand, the geographical configuration of the country, in particular the inestimable strategic importance of the great rivers, was to be the determining factor.

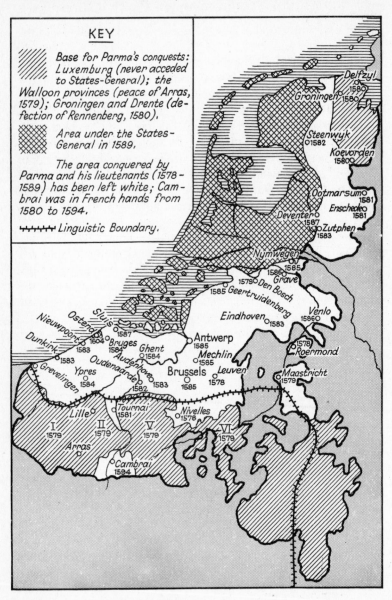

KEY

///// *Base for Parma's conquests: Luxemburg (never acceded to States-General); the Walloon provinces (peace of Arras, 1579); Groningen and Drente (defection of Rennenberg, 1580).*

XXXXX *Area under the States-General in 1589.*

The area conquered by Parma and his lieutenants (1578–1589) has been left white; Cambrai was in French hands from 1580 to 1594.

+++++ *Linguistic Boundary.*

Delfzyl 1580

Groningen 1580

Steenwyk 1582

Koevorden 1580

Ootmarsum 1581

Enschede 1581

Deventer 1587

Zutphen 1583

Nymwegen 1585

Grave 1586

1579 Den Bosch

1585 Geertruidenberg

Eindhoven 1583

Venlo 1586

Sluis 1587

Ostend 1604

Nieuwpoort 1583

Dunkirk 1583

Bruges 1584

Ghent 1584

Antwerp 1585

Mechlin 1585

Roermond 1578

Ypres 1584

Oudenaarde 1582

Audenhove 1583

Brussels 1585

Leuven 1578

Maastricht 1579

Grevelingen

Lille
I 1579

II 1579

Tournai 1581

V 1579

Nivelles 1578

VI 1579

Arras

Cambrai 1584

MAP IV THE CONQUESTS OF PARMA, 1578–89

IV

THE SPLIT

a. PARMA'S CONQUESTS, 1580–1589

Thanks to the energy displayed by Orange and the delegates of the Closer Union, together with their military commanders, the revolt had for the moment withstood the shock of Rennenberg's defection. Rennenberg died in 1581, in the bitter consciousness of failure, after having been forced to raise the siege of Steenwyk. Nevertheless the outlook for the States was indeed gloomy. On the land side their territory was now encircled by the revived power of Spain, although Venlo and Upper Gelderland, firmly secured by John of Nassau, still hampered the communications between Parma in the South and Verdugo, the successor of Rennenberg, in the North-East. In the South the enemy took Kortryk by surprise, but as against this Mechlin was recovered by a movement from Brussels and soon resumed its place in the States-General. Flanders and Brabant were threatened with continual attacks and raids from Kortryk and Leuven, while in the North-East not only was the greater part of Groningen, Drente, and Overysel either actually lost or in imminent danger of falling into enemy hands, but Friesland, Gelderland, and even Utrecht had to endure the intolerable vexation of troops, their own being scarcely less troublesome than those of the enemy.

Despite the scant good done in 1578 by Casimir or Anjou (both had departed somewhat ignominiously in the following year), more than ever the feeling asserted itself that without foreign help the revolt must collapse. Already early in 1580 Orange had prevailed on the States-General to draw up a new constitution which must serve as a basis of negotiations for conferring the sovereignty on the Duke of Anjou, and which, no less than the constitution of 1578 had done with respect to Matthew, met all the fears of the privileged class and of the provinces now grown accustomed to their independence,

lest in the new monarch they should give themselves a new
master.

Yet it still required endless patience to get the harassed
Netherlands to welcome their French deliverer. The great
objection was not to the revolutionary nature of the action
demanded of the States in disposing of the sovereignty which
had hitherto been considered as Philip's inalienable possession;
for, whatever the opinion of the nation, in the States there
now sat only men who had abandoned all thought of reconciliation with the King. It was about this time that Philip
issued against Orange the ban by which he armed all mur-
derers against him, promising huge rewards in case of success.
But to choose for sovereign a Catholic and a Valois, and one
with the personal reputation of Anjou! It was hard. No more
than anyone else did Orange cherish illusions about the ability
or reliability of this tainted scion of a despised house, but a
dispassionate contemplation of the state of Europe persuaded
him that there was no alternative, and he accepted the inevitable conclusion. From the German princes there was nothing
more to expect. It might seem even more surprising that
England was not more ready to help, for who could doubt
that the safety of her Protestant Queen was bound up with
the maintenance of Netherlands freedom? But evidence of
the understanding between her Catholic subjects and Philip II
frightened Elizabeth as much as it angered her, and she had
shaken all Orange's confidence in her by her jealous and
capricious policy. A royalist writer railed at the Prince thus:

> Of the English Jezebel you get no audience,
> She leaves you in need without any defence,
> She has turned her coat . .

Anjou, on the other hand, was personally full of zeal. And not
only should his position in France make it possible for him
to raise a host of adherents and adventurers for a private
campaign, but Orange could even hope (it was the old dream
of 1572) that his influence at the court of his royal brother
would enable him to provoke a war between France and Spain,
and that would have decided the issue. Thus the Prince defied

all the suspicion and opposition which he incurred as a result of his support of Anjou's candidature, and yet the affair progressed but slowly. The treaty was not concluded until the autumn of 1580, and in the spring of 1581 the Duke ratified the agreement; not even the most serious limitations on his power had sufficed to discourage him. Under that treaty Holland and Zealand retained their special status and their particular relationship to Orange.

A whole year had been wasted, and it was fortunate that Parma was hindered by the very conditions of his first great success, the Peace of Arras; for by that treaty, as we know, he had agreed to send the Spanish troops away again. But the Walloon provinces were now too deeply interested in the recovery of the King's territory not to let themselves speedily be persuaded to assent to their being recalled once more. Besides, after the occupation of Portugal, which had engaged much of his attention during 1580, Philip again had means at his disposal to carry out those designs in the Netherlands to which he clung so tenaciously. It was thus an excellent thing for the States that Parma was compelled in 1581, as Alva had been in 1572, first to turn southwards for fear of a French invasion. But Anjou's performance was disappointing from the start. With an army for which he demanded subsidies from the beggared States, while his brother would not be hustled out of his neutrality, the whole campaign was spent in the siege of Cambrai, in which France had a more direct interest than the Netherlands. Then, while Parma took Tournai, the last Walloon province remaining in the States-General, the Duke went off to England to court the elderly Elizabeth. There again he achieved nothing, and so in February 1582 he appeared with a brilliant retinue at Flushing and made a festive entry, first in Middelburg and afterwards in Antwerp.

The majority of the provinces now did homage to Anjou as ruler. To make this possible Matthew had departed, and the preceding summer the States-General, assembled at The Hague as it chanced on this occasion (though naturally there were delegates from Flanders and Brabant present), passed the famous resolution, whereby Philip, on account of his tyrannical

rule and his trampling underfoot of the privileges of the
country, was deposed from dominion over his Netherland
provinces. Following this resolution all authorities, officials,
military commanders, and the like, were required to take a new
oath, in the absence of Anjou, to the United Provinces. This
was obtained without much difficulty throughout the Dutch-
speaking Netherlands, while in the North as well as in the
South the Catholic population looked sullenly on. There were
those who argued that unconditional obedience to the King
was the duty of every Catholic, but it would be hard indeed
to square this view with the facts of medieval history. In
reality the "Placard of Dismissal," drawn up by the Brabander
Van Asseliers, was a brilliant, though late, expression of the
sturdy medieval tradition of freedom, which was everywhere
losing ground before the encroachments of modern absolutism,
rather than a manifestation of the specifically Calvinistic spirit.
No doubt Calvinism, with its strong consciousness of individual
rights, which in the Netherlands fell in quite naturally with
the old tradition of privilege, was responsible for much of the
energy which the carrying through of the principle demanded.
Moreover, the revolt was now so closely identified with the
Calvinist movement that the abjuration could not but be
obnoxious to the Catholics.

The Catholic Duke of Anjou entered indeed into a strange
position as lord of a land where the Catholics were suspected
and excluded from all influence. There were, it is true, among
the leading spirits in the States-General, besides Orange, still
some men, like the Fleming Van Meetkerke and the Geldersman Leoninus, who either from indifference or from a well-
understood patriotism put policy before religion, and were able
to co-operate wholeheartedly with Catholics. But this attitude
of mind was a rare one, at any rate outside the circle of
prominent magistrates and jurists. Wellnigh everywhere the
Religious Peace had now come to an end, and the Calvinist
ministers were working tirelessly at the organization of the
new religious community. It was a difficult matter always to
satisfy the demand for efficient ministers of the Word. Nevertheless, as early as 1581, there were ministers in the classis

of Brugge alone, besides in the town itself, at Sluis, Damme, Aardenburg, Oostburg, St. Kruis, Westkapelle, Oostkerke, Knokke, Heist, Wenduine, Groede, Meetkerke, Zoenkerke, Moerkerke, Dudzeele, Lissewege, St. Pieters op den Dyke. The support of the secular authority, which had appropriated ecclesiastical property, was indispensable. It was also expected to lend a strong hand for the expulsion of the old religion from its last hiding-places in the country-side. Thus we read in the minutes of a meeting of the classis of Ghent as early as November 3, 1578:

On those of Ghent asking how the Roman religion may best be impeded everywhere in the surrounding villages, answer was made that the notables of this town shall be requested in the name of the classis to prohibit by open letters all priests of the Mass from exercising their Roman religion.

This work, which was carried on no less zealously in Holland and Zealand and all the other provinces than in Flanders itself, was still far from finished a few years later, and under Anjou went merrily on, certainly not to his edification. It was with great difficulty that the Duke prevailed upon the magistrates to re-establish a church for his co-religionists even at Antwerp, which was, since 1578, virtually the capital, and Anjou's usual place of residence. How heartily the Netherlanders and their new ruler distrusted each other became apparent when an attempt was made at Antwerp on the life of Orange—the first-fruits of the ban—and the general impulse was to regard the French as the instigators of the crime, so that Anjou and his compatriots had to be protected against the popular fury.

It would have been impossible, even had there not been the treaty limitations on his power, for this man ever to establish that strong central authority of which the Netherlands people in their distress had so great a need. The tragedy of their history repeated itself. Once more a foreigner was sovereign. For his sake the Council, which the States-General placed beside him, had again to use French—Orange, too, no doubt preferred it—though in the now purely Dutch-speaking

States-General the vernacular ruled supreme. But this difference in language was merely symbolical of a divergence of interests and a complete lack of mutual confidence.

Despite the unfavourable circumstances—and this is a fact well worthy of note—the Netherlands provinces continued to manifest a feeling of solidarity. At the same time it can hardly be called surprising when this sentiment, forced into the old channels of provincialism by the very origin of the rebellion, exposed to the storms of war and under distrusted leadership, failed to give itself enduring forms. The Council of State just mentioned was at any rate an attempt to tighten the bonds of General Union, which had undoubtedly been loosened by the Union of Utrecht.

It is true that the Union of Utrecht now embraced almost the whole of the territory of the rebellion, and had furthered the Protestantization of the South as well as of the North. But so far as its original object, that of defence, was concerned, it remained mainly a North Netherlands grouping. Holland and Zealand supplied the driving-force behind it, and they took an interest first and foremost in the defence of the helpless eastern provinces, which were of such great importance for their own safety. The Committee of the Closer Union, which in its own territory virtually replaced the central authority, had, especially since the defection of Rennenberg, almost limited its activities to the theatre of war north of the great rivers, although Flemings and Brabanders continued to serve on it. In any case the administrative changes rendered necessary by the coming of Anjou were seized upon to put an end to this state of affairs. Now that the States-General no longer formed a battle-ground, as when the Union was concluded, between the Reformed and Catholic factions, but presented a homogeneous appearance as a result as well of the secession of the Walloon provinces and Groningen as of the triumph of Calvinism in the remainder, there was a desire to dissolve the Union of Utrecht in the General Union. Thus, simultaneously with the institution of this new Council of State, the Committee of the Closer Union was abolished; but the necessity for dealing separately with the problems of the war in the North was so keenly felt that there was established, under the Council of State, a new Council "East of the Maas" (north of the rivers). In practice nothing came of the subordination of this new Council to the Council of State, and actually it simply took the place of the Committee of the Closer Union, while the activities of the Council of State (and this remained so after the arrival of Anjou and his assumption of the government of the country) were limited to the southern provinces and the southern theatre of war.

The dual organization thus emerged again the moment after it had been suppressed. What does this signify? No more than that the duality of the strategic problem with which the provinces were faced dominated the situation. It was inevitable that the fighting on the southern and eastern fronts should be conducted as two distinct wars. In the first place, they were separately financed. The Union of Utrecht had prescribed uniform taxes—"general means"—for the Union treasury, but these could never be put into operation. The provinces continued to raise their own taxes, and they had to be spurred on severally for their contributions. In proportion as their exhaustion increased, it became more necessary in every single case to specify a definite object which touched each particularly. The central authorities—Anjou and the Council of State —who resided for the most part at Antwerp or even at Ghent, were almost overwhelmed by the cares of the war on their own side. Not only did they lack the power to assert themselves against Holland, the unassailable province which had pursued its own course since 1572, and entrenched itself more firmly in its own exceptional position with every change of government, but, indeed, they were not sorry when Holland took eastern affairs off their hands.

How inevitable such a development was can be understood only if this exhaustion and the consequent impotence—one may say the paralysis—of authority are clearly visualized. Holland and Zealand were the only provinces not directly exposed to the raids of the enemy, but they could no longer cope with the importunate appeals of their neighbours for assistance. The cosmopolitan soldiery, not very numerous, but too numerous to be paid regularly, became useless by reason of mutiny and disorder:

All mutineers, who cried out for money when they were ordered to fight.

Hohenlohe, the commander in the North, a fighter but no organizer, and a lover of women and wine, was not the man to maintain discipline. Following his example, throughout the army

virtue of life was derided and explained as lack of courage. [At the same time] the States everywhere lost their authority, no less over the soldiery whom they did not pay than over the townsman and farmer whom they did not protect.

It was inevitable that in these circumstances centrifugal forces should get free play, but this fact does not teach us anything about the desires or inclinations of the people. It was simply that in the difficult days of its birth the young Netherlands state had as little control over its limbs as a newborn babe. This naturally meant a considerable weakening of its ability to resist Parma, whose own leadership, for that matter, met in the subjected provinces with a resistance scarcely less unwieldy. But this is not to say that the split which in the ensuing years was to rend asunder the Dutch-speaking Netherlands proceeded from any internal urge or from any inherent failing of the people. The line which this split was ultimately to follow was determined by the interplay of force and counterforce, and these conformed, not to the disposition of the people, but to that of the soil. The Union of Utrecht had nothing, the great rivers everything, to do with it.

Anjou was unable to hold Parma in check. His brother Henry III persisted in his neutrality, while the few French troops, partly Huguenots, partly adventurers of all sorts and conditions, which Anjou had been able to lead into Flanders, played havoc with the people. In April 1582 Parma took Oudenaarde, in August treachery made him master of Lier, while in the East Verdugo took Steenwyk and other places.

But however ineffectual Anjou's help, the case was rendered

still worse when the helper suddenly turned against those he should have protected. Anjou's position was false and disagreeable. The oppression of his co-religionists, the ever recurring suspicions of the men of Antwerp and Ghent against himself and his entourage as Frenchmen and Catholics, the rigorous enforcement by the States of that clause in their agreement with him which debarred foreigners—that is, Frenchmen—from holding office in the Netherlands, all these things irritated him beyond measure. The French nobles at his court, whom the Netherlanders had wanted to exclude even from there, filled his ears with complaints and promptings. In January 1583 he made an effort at one blow to break the bonds of his agreement with the States, and to make himself indeed master of the land, just as in July 1577 Don John had tried to free himself from the Eternal Edict by a *coup d'état*.

The French troops made simultaneous attempts on several places. The Duke, who up to the last had shown a friendly countenance to Orange, himself took charge of the principal enterprise, namely, against Antwerp, but this miscarried badly. While the French nobles and soldiers were rushing through the streets with cries of "Vive la messe! Ville gagnée," the citizens organized a stout resistance and in the end drove them with heavy loss out of the town. Anjou had to retire with great difficulty to Vilvoorde, which his followers had succeeded in taking, and thence via Dendermonde to Dunkirk. Meanwhile a great fury possessed the people, not only at Antwerp but all over the Netherlands, especially in the South, against their treacherous protector and all his countrymen. He was suspected, not without reason, of an intention to come to an agreement with Parma, with the towns he occupied as the price of the bargain. Suspicion of the Catholics was stirred to new life. Meanwhile Anjou was no longer considered as sovereign, and the States urged Orange to put himself at their head. But the Prince, however deeply moved with indignation, held fast to the idea that only with the help of France could the revolt be saved and persuaded the States to open negotiations, which actually led to a provisional agreement. He had made play with the prospect that a French force would be available for the relief of Eindhoven, which was of importance as a strong place wedged between the power of Spain in the South and in the East. The French force, however, came too late and Eindhoven fell. Shortly afterwards Dunkirk was also lost; Anjou, discouraged and embittered, had recently left it and returned to France. And now the cry of treachery went up more fiercely than ever against the French. Orange, who continued stubbornly to advocate the necessity of continuing the negotiations with Anjou, did so at the cost of a good deal of his popularity. Thus writes an Antwerp rhetorician in a ballad—the customary opening of the final couplet "O Prince" here obviously levelled against Orange:

> O Prince, mark well God's Law. Beware
> Thou lead'st us not into the snare
> Of this French fellow.

Such was the prevailing temper that Orange left Antwerp for Middelburg, from where he soon moved on to Delft. The Hollanders disliked Anjou no less than did the Flemings or Brabanders, but the Prince's remonstrances and appeals to reason made more impression on their oligarchic town governments than on the democracies of the great towns in the South. In Flanders, where excitement reached the highest pitch—Nieuwpoort had been taken by a movement from Dunkirk, and thus Yper was almost cut off and Brugge directly threatened—the ministers admonished the people from the pulpit:

That they had to expect no help or blessings from the said Duke, seeing that he was of contrary religion, and that God promises His help to Kings and Lords who walk in fear of Him.

Thus there arose really fundamental dissensions to aggravate the confusion and to weaken powers of resistance. In their distress, and as if to give expression to their mistrust of Orange's collusion with Anjou, the Flemings chose as Stadtholder a man who had ingratiated himself with them by energetic professions of zeal for Calvinism and hatred for the French; this was the Prince of Chimay, Aerschot's only son, who in 1582 had ranged himself on the side of the States.

Whether he aimed at treachery from the beginning is not clear. What is certain is that he was soon involved in relations with Parma, and paved the way for the surrender of Brugge by the removal of men loyal to the States and the introduction of partisans of Spain. In Gelderland the Count Van den Bergh had got himself appointed Stadtholder in 1581 in succession to his brother-in-law, John of Nassau, and in his case there is no doubt that this had been arranged with Parma. The first-fruits of his treachery was Zutfen, which was tricked into the hands of the enemy in September 1583, but before he could do more mischief he was apprehended and sent to Holland by Leoninus, the Chancellor of the province.

The treachery of Chimay was scarcely less obvious, but while the Bailiff of the Free Land, and Casembroot, a burgomaster of Brugge, were urging Orange to render him harmless, Chimay got ahead of them and threw the leaders of the party of resistance into prison. At that moment, March 1584, Parma had already for a considerable time been besieging Yper, and shortly afterwards, threatened with starvation, that town surrendered. Now Chimay was free to proceed, and on May 22nd the agreement was concluded at Tournai whereby Brugge and the Free Land once more resigned themselves to the King of Spain. Three of the four "members" of Flanders were lost.

Parma took care that their example should make the desired impression on the rest of the province and of the Netherlands. With Alva's departure the system of barbarous severity had been discarded. Parma, it is true, could not tolerate Protestantism, and the exclusive reign of Catholicism was re-established by the terms of each capitulation. But the Inquisition did not return, and the Reformers were given the choice, either to realize on their possessions and depart or else to submit. An exodus of ministers and of the faithful followed each conquest, but the greater part of the citizens conformed to the new change without difficulty. They had after all merely undergone the Calvinistic Reformation, nor was this more the case at Brugge or Zutfen, which were now once again Spanish and Catholic, than at Dordt or Utrecht, which were still

"States" and Reformed. And, indeed, did not this new change bear the appearance of inescapable finality? The revolt seemed like a passing nightmare, and its watchword, the retrieval of the ancient welfare of the Netherlands, sounded a mockery in the midst of the miserable confusion which prevailed. With a sigh of relief the people could submit themselves again to the old authority, which seemed to have unlearned its excesses and to be ready to respect the privileges. Were not rest and peace to be found there, and there alone?

But however grave the doubts which assailed the spirits in the most exposed towns, the party of resistance was everywhere too firmly seated in the saddle to be lightly thrown out. It is true that Ghent, whose supplies Parma now obstructed on all sides and whose population, swelled by thousands of fugitive peasants, began in consequence to suffer privation, was seriously threatened by treachery; and it was none other than the old zealot Hembyze who, after having been carried to power on the tidal wave of anti-French Calvinism and with the aid of insinuations against Anjou's friend Orange, was now intriguing there with Parma. But he was seized just in time by his indignant fellow-citizens, and a few months later ended his life on the scaffold. Ghent prepared itself for defence. But the attack which followed was a formidable one, and did not aim at this town only.

Meanwhile the Reformed who would have none of Anjou met with another grievous disappointment. In Germany, where they had placed great hopes upon the Archbishop of Cologne, who had gone over to Protestantism, everything miscarried, and a staunch Catholic was installed in the archiepiscopal see. Orange saw in the event a vindication of his French policy. But the envoys who went for the third time to urge Anjou to make haste with his assistance no longer found him among the living. He had died on June 10, 1584. It was still an open question what would now be done with the sovereignty, which had thus reverted once again to the States-General, when just a month later, on July 10, the Prince of Orange was assassinated at Delft. Only a little while before, in a long exposition of the distressful situation, the defection of selfish noblemen,

the disproportion between the power of Spain and that of the
States, he had written that as for himself he

would take his stand unperturbed against those dangers. For no
dangers can for me and mine be compared with a base desertion
of such a noble cause—the honour of God, the peace of the provinces,
the freedom of the Fatherland—and the abandonment of the sacred
and honourable side which I have up till now followed.

"Faithful until death"—the *Wilhelmus* had prophesied it. But
at what a moment was William of Orange called away from
the people he had served, and how must the danger of Flanders
and Brabant have oppressed him in his last moments!

The enemy rejoiced. To them the revolt seemed personified
in the Prince, his ambition its mainspring, his guidance indispensable. That was the idea which had inspired the ban, and
so now it was hoped that the revolt would soon collapse. An
utter miscalculation! The rebellion had its own life. Invaluable
had been Orange's services in animating and giving direction
to the national feeling, even though the passions of the time
had, alas, only too frequently paid little heed to his admonitions.
Certainly his position had been in no sense that of a dictator.
His death interrupted plans for investing him with the Countship of Holland, but the conditions on which this was to be
done placed the sovereign authority no less effectually under
the surveillance of the States than had the treaty with Anjou;
reference was indeed expressly made to that treaty and to
the "Joyous Entry" of Brabant. In a crisis occasioned by the
abuse of monarchical authority, Orange's greatness as a leader
of the Netherlands people lay precisely in his unsurpassed
talent for co-operating with the States assemblies which, by
the former misgovernment, had been impelled to go beyond
their appointed places in that people's ancient constitutions.
Persuasion was what he excelled in. Many were the long
memoranda which he wrote to refute objections to his views;
in the council-chamber he was clear and firm, but also resource-
ful and patient. Thus it was that under his auspices the new
oligarchy had been able to form itself into a real ruling class,
in which, owing to the defection of so many nobles, the town

element had become predominant. Several who were too firmly fixed in the government of their provinces not to see everything primarily from a provincial standpoint had yet, by the circumstances which demanded the weightiest decisions from both provincial States and town governments, been taught to grapple with problems of general policy. Moreover, in close intercourse with Orange, there had arisen from out their midst, in the States-General and in the Councils, a group of truly national statesmen of a different character from the official, noble, mostly non-Dutch class which the monarchy had reared.

When their leader fell, these were the men who at once did what they could to prevent the courage of the provinces from failing. On the same day letters were sent out in every direction by the States-General giving, together with the dreadful tidings, the assurance that determination remained unshaken, and that the enemy would reap no advantage from the crime; the Fleming Van Meetkerke presided over the assembly, where among others Aerssens represented Brabant; Mechlin, too, was present. Shortly afterwards, in consultation with the provinces, a new attempt was made to put the government in the united provinces on "a uniform basis," as it was expressed, and a solemn resolution was taken to remain united "according to the Union of Utrecht," notwithstanding the death of His Excellency the Prince. This resolution, in which Brabant and Mechlin participated, was, so far as Brussels and Mechlin were concerned, like an accession *in articulo mortis* to the Union of Utrecht, and the dual character of the Government was still further reduced by the abolition of the Council East of the Maas and the institution of yet another Council of State, which, under the presidency of the young Maurice of Nassau, Orange's son, was to exercise the government until a new ruler should be found abroad.

For now Parma was straining his energies to the utmost to possess himself at one blow of the South: the siege of Antwerp began in August 1584, at the same time Brussels and Mechlin were invested and communication between them hindered by the capture of Dendermonde: Ghent was completely cut off, and while the whole of Flanders and Brabant was thus beset by the most imminent danger, the States-General had once more to attempt to interest a foreign Power in their cause. They addressed themselves first to the brother of Anjou, Henry III, King of France. Especially the threatened towns of the South pressed for the removal of all hindrances to these negotiations, which, after the fashion of the time, dragged on through many months. Necessity alone drove them to it, for how vigorously had they themselves censured Orange for his partiality to the French! Out of Holland there now came another voice, harbinger of many miseries for the Netherlands people.

Even if they of Brabant and Flanders, through impatience of their sufferings (whereby all good counsels are hindered) would desperately adventure a lost cause, are we bound to plunge ourselves and so many thousands of brave men into sure ruin and decay along with them? . . . Was it for this that the noble defences of Antwerp were raised up, and is not the finest town in Europe worthy of some suffering? Let them come and take courage from Holland, where the little town of Alkmaar engaged the whole might of Spain, and where nearly half the brave citizens of Leyden perished of hunger for the sake of their freedom. Did we rely on any princely power then? or have we suffered all this in order to be delivered up in the end to the French? Then we may well bewail to God that the noble Prince of Orange and so many brave men have died for us and for a cause which we are not resolved to maintain to the end. . . . And however great the evil which afflicts them of Flanders and Brabant (especially do we pity the great city of Brussels), nevertheless the enemy does not rejoice so greatly over what he has conquered there, that he would not willingly yield it all provided he could have for it the one island of Walcheren.

The remonstrance of the town of Gouda, drawn up by her pensionary François Vrancken, from which the above passage is taken, is without doubt a spirited document, and there is only too much truth in its argument that no reliance was to be placed on French help, and that the menace to religion and freedom from France was scarcely less dangerous than that from Spain. And this quite apart from the fact that a separate national existence, based on a specifically Netherlandish culture, would have been under no ruler so difficult to achieve as under the King of France. Nevertheless, how

strongly does one feel here that their exceptional strategic
position not only gave the Hollanders confidence, but, aided
by the legend which had already grown up around the events
of 1572 to 1576, created a self-righteous feeling that could be
dangerous to the cause of unity! It is true that this attitude
produced its most harmful consequences only after the split
had become a fact, since for the time being the arguments
of Holland particularism found no acceptance, and the States
of Holland and Zealand both did what lay in their power to
prevent the cleavage. To begin with they let themselves be
prevailed upon to relinquish, in conformity with the demand
of the French King, the special position they had maintained
as against Anjou—no mean sacrifice—and thus the offer of
the sovereignty could be made in due form by an embassy
of all the provinces. By that time the starving population of
Ghent had already compelled the town government to make
peace with Parma on the usual favourable terms—a serious loss,
also on account of the war-material which fell into the captor's
hands. And when finally the embassy executed its commission,
Henry III, who was now himself hard pressed by the ultra-
Catholics and their League in his own kingdom, declined the
offer which at first he had striven so hard to obtain.

The entire winter was thus wasted, and now the whole thing
had to be done all over again with England, for Elizabeth,
disturbed at the prospect of seeing the full might of Spain
restored on the other side of the water, had for some time
given to understand that she might now be found ready to
do something. Not before June 18 could an embassy sail for
England, whereupon it quickly appeared that the Queen still
shrank from a complete break with Spain, such as would be
the inevitable consequence of an acceptance of the sovereignty.
Then negotiations for simple assistance began, and it was
August 20th before the treaty was signed whereby the States
were promised 4,000 infantry and 400 cavalry, against the
cession to England of The Brill and Flushing as cautionary
towns for the repayment of the expenses incurred. The commander of this force (the Earl of Leicester obtained the
appointment), arrayed with the ambiguous title of "Governor-

General," was to have access, along with two other Englishmen, to the Council of State. A most onerous agreement! The English commander who entered Flushing in 1572 had been instructed from home to make himself master of that town, and to prevent the French auxiliaries from doing so, rather than to fight the Spaniards. Now the English were laying hands on the mouths of the Maas and the Scheldt in exchange for very niggardly promises, and without Elizabeth's being willing to make herself answerable for the country's future. What would she do in course of time with the strategic position afforded her by these cautionary towns?

Sadly, indeed, had the States' affairs deteriorated during these procrastinations. In March Brussels, suffering no less from hunger than had Ghent, and after making one last pitiful appeal to Holland for relief, surrendered to Parma. Mechlin followed in July. It was easy for François Vrancken to talk: the fact was that the sieges in Holland and Zealand which he recalled with such pride had been rendered difficult for the Spaniards by nothing so much as by the inundations, and by the lakes, canals, and rivers which gave free play to the naval power of the Beggars. To strike a blow which would have forced Parma to let go his prey in Brabant, Hohenlohe would have had to move outside the river-area, and that he was incapable of doing. All the more serious, therefore, was the loss of a town inside that river-area. Nymwegen was not pressed overmuch by the enemy, but in April 1585 the Catholic citizens broke with the Count of Nieuwenaer, the new Stadtholder of Gelderland, a Calvinist just as intolerant as John of Nassau, and, after making themselves masters of the town government, thrust the States' garrison out of the gates. The same thing happened at Doesburg, while Arnhem had to be secured for the States by surprise. The worst blow was nevertheless inflicted by the arms of Parma: just before the envoys in England signed the treaty with Elizabeth, Antwerp had surrendered.

The siege of Antwerp was a long drawn out tragedy. At the end of 1583 Orange had sent Marnix there as "External Burgomaster" in preparation for the expected siege; subse-

quently he had urged the necessity for cutting the Kouwenstein cross-dyke and the Blauwgaren Scheldt-dyke. Antwerp
lay on the edge of the Netherlands water-area, and had to be
victualled and relieved from Zealand. To that end, however,
it would be useful to submerge the broad border-land north
of the Scheldt which these dykes protected; otherwise everything would have to come along the river itself. Private interests,
which found unrestrained expression in the democratic town
government (for Marnix wielded only a very limited authority),
had prevented the cutting of these dykes. So Parma, who
sought to invest the town (since an assault was out of the
question), promptly seized them, and when, to the astonishment of the Antwerpers, he subsequently succeeded in driving
a strong bridge over the river just below Calloo, the unwisdom
of neglecting Orange's advice was made clear. All attempts to
reach the town must now involve the forcing either of this
bridge or of the Kouwenstein dyke, and on them they all spent
themselves in vain.

The Hollanders and Zealanders did their best. Everyone
recognized what a disaster the fall of Antwerp would be. But
reverse followed reverse. Early in 1585 the power of the
Zealand fleet was crippled by a vehement dispute between
Treslong, now admiral of the province, and the regents deputed
to deal with naval matters. After that an enterprise against the
bridge, broken through by Gianibelli's famous fire-ship drift-
ing down from Antwerp, failed owing to a misunderstanding
of signals. Finally, in May a new attempt was carefully prepared. The States of Holland sent some of their own number
to supervise everything—among them was the pensionary of
Rotterdam, Oldenbarnevelt, a rising man. The Kouwenstein
dyke was taken by hard fighting; Hohenlohe from Zealand met
Marnix from Antwerp, and together the two were rowed over
the flooded land to the town to announce the glad tidings.
Their rejoicings were cut short by the news that the Spaniards
had recaptured the dyke and made it fast again. Never was
victory more recklessly thrown away. Elizabeth, too, bore a
heavy responsibility. Had she, in anticipation of a treaty, sent
over a couple of thousand men, Parma, who had barely suffi-

cient troops, would certainly not have been able to make good the losses he suffered.

Now Marnix threw up the game as lost. The poorer classes in the town had long been suffering privation, and the fresh disappointment at the failure of relief led to rioting. The Broad Council resolved to negotiate, but for weeks they maintained a demand for the freedom of the Reformed religion. Parma received the envoys, and particularly Marnix, with every mark of honour, but on that point he was inflexible. In spite of this the impressionable and vacillating Marnix let himself be so captivated by the Duke that to the fury of the Reformed, who already disliked his French leanings, he became at Antwerp the great advocate of surrender.

There was not one assistant in the said assembly of Great Council but gave attentive ear unto the relation Monsieur de St. Aldegonde made, and not a little marvelled to see and hear him in that sort vehemently exalt the virtues of that Prince, naming him to be full of benignity, clemency, and void of all dissimulation, adding for his opinion, that he did believe all that the said Prince had told him. . . . As these persuasions to a reconciliation with the King of Spain, through the good opinion he hath conceived of the Prince of Parma, did not greatly please the ear of those in the Great Council, much less it did unto these Colonels and Captains [of the citizens], the most part thinking it was a dream unto them to see and hear Monsieur de St. Aldegonde speak in that sort. . . .

For a year Marnix had succeeded in checking all sedition and in making all the well-disposed co-operate. What was it that now caused him to despair? Like Orange he had placed his hopes on France, and thus the success of the Catholic League in that country was a grievous blow to him. From England he expected nothing. Moreover, throughout that disastrous year, as town after town fell, the Flemings and Brabanders had been complaining bitterly that Holland and Zealand were leaving them to their fate. Van den Tympel, the governor of Brussels, for instance, after the capitulation of that town, had spoken vehemently in this strain to the deputies of Brabant assembled at Antwerp. Doubtless Marnix was affected by this bitter feeling. The tragedy was that the Hollanders and Zealanders were doing what they could. Certainly, had the

Prince of Orange still been there to compose disputes as to
competence and quarrels between individuals, they might have
done more. The Council of State, under the young Maurice,
was powerless; everything devolved upon the provincial States.
Nevertheless, the complaints of the Southerners were only
an expression of that universal human disposition to cast on
to friends and supporters the blame for an overwhelming
flood of misfortunes. Here, too, Orange's death proved a
disaster: he might have preserved Marnix from this weakness.
A man of determination in the position of the "External
Burgomaster" could have postponed the surrender for weeks.
And the Hollanders were only waiting for a favourable wind
in order to make a new attempt at relief, nor would the tardy
English troops have tarried for ever. But the Broad Council,
thrown into confusion by the attitude of its appointed head,
let itself be intimidated by the cry of "Peace" from the starving
multitude gathered in the square before the town-hall, and on
August 17, 1585, was signed the treaty by which the town
resumed obedience to Philip. Catholicism was re-established,
but the Reformed were granted four years before they had
to depart. All privileges were restored, no Spanish garrison
was to be placed in the town, and the citadel, which was
rebuilt, would be pulled down as soon as Holland and Zealand
were likewise subdued. Marnix betook himself back to Zealand;
it is, indeed, not to be wondered at that he was overwhelmed
with reproaches and accusations from Holland and Zealand.

Antwerp, still, in spite of the many shocks it had suffered
since 1566, by far the largest and wealthiest town of the Netherlands, from 1578 to 1583 the capital of the rebellion—Antwerp
had fallen! It was everywhere expected that the subjugation
of Holland and Zealand would soon follow. But, behind the
rivers, these provinces lay sheltered from a direct attack. They
were themselves masters of these waters, and Parma was at
once made to feel the importance of naval power. The Beggars
of Zealand had not been able to force his bridge, but now that
Antwerp was once again in Spanish hands they could cut her
off inexorably from the sea. The town which Parma, thanks
to his indomitable spirit, his military genius, and his knowledge

of human nature, had succeeded in conquering, now withered, as it were, beneath his hand. Thousands left Antwerp, not only for the sake of their religion, but because the stoppage of all trade struck at their means of livelihood (just as thousands had left Brugge, Ghent, Brussels, Mechlin, and all the other towns which had fallen into Spanish hands), and the majority of them came to Holland and Zealand, where they strengthened the Reformed element and at the same time brought a wealth of capital, knowledge, and enterprise. The peace and order which Parma gave to Flanders and Brabant very much resembled the stiffening of death. On the other hand all the best vital forces of the Netherlands people drew together in the small area north of the rivers.

Holland, Zealand, and Utrecht, Gelderland within the Waal and Ysel, the Ysel-towns of Overysel and Friesland, a couple of coastal towns in Flanders and Brabant, a single isolated place, Venlo, that was all the territory which now remained to the States. In the beginning of October 1585 the English troops arrived, and the Earl of Leicester followed in December. During the two years of his governor-generalship there was never any question of his being able to recover the lost territory. He could not even keep intact the little that remained. In 1586 Grave and Venlo were lost. During his absence in England in 1587 two of his lieutenants (Yorke and Stanley) betrayed Deventer and the entrenchments by means of which the States had controlled Zutfen since it had become Spanish. When he returned he failed to relieve Sluis, which gave the Spaniards a foothold on the Scheldt estuary; after his second departure mutinous English troops sold Geertruidenberg to the enemy. Nevertheless there can be no doubt that the slackening of Parma's advance during Leicester's unquiet governorship—we shall presently consider its importance for the establishment of a North Netherlands state—was partly due to the strengthening afforded by the English auxiliaries. The first explanation must, however, be sought in the fact that Parma's conquest had reached the rebellion's last natural line of defence. On all sides he was confronted by water, as far as Friesland, where lakes and morasses took the place of rivers. It is true that the States held several places on the other side of this natural line, Ostend and Bergen-op-Zoom, for example, but, thanks to the water, these too were within immediate reach of their forces, whose wide arc now more than ever reposed on the unassailable and sea-faring province of Holland.

But the position was not one of equilibrium. The North-East had not been conquered by force of arms; situated on the farther side of Maas and Rhine, it was too far from Parma's base for that; it had fallen to him by Rennenberg's defection and the disposition of its inhabitants. Nymwegen had since afforded him a better line of communication with that distant region, yet his hold on it remained uncertain. Nevertheless contemporaries can hardly have expected its reconquest from the North-West that was soon to take place. To them it must have seemed much more probable that the country east of the Ysel would serve Parma as a base for an attack on the last refuge of the revolt. Sluis and Geertruidenberg also seemed the prelude to a thrust at the heart, for the two places respectively threatened Zealand and Holland. But there the friendly element was of greater help to the rebels than anywhere else, and a break-through from the East seemed the more imminent danger. With Zutfen and Deventer the enemy impinged on the line of the Ysel, and the Spanish cavalry raided over all the Veluwe as far as Utrecht. Friesland, too, was threatened from Steenwyk and Groningen.

The position which Parma had won by 1589 was a position for further attack. How came it that he was unable to use it, and that on the contrary the Northerners, leaning on their Holland base, could wrench it from him, soon even pressing across the inmost and uncertain line of defence, and not content with the outermost strategic boundary, that of the great rivers, managed to secure it by the capture of the fortresses to the south of it? The amazing economic development, which along with political consolidation took place in that north-western sea-territory, was an important factor. But without the opportunity which Philip's unwisdom offered, when he first exhausted his resources in a mad enterprise against England, and then instructed Parma to divide his forces in order to intervene in the French civil war, the success of the northern provinces would be inexplicable.

b. THE ESTABLISHMENT OF A NORTH NETHERLANDS STATE

When the Earl of Leicester came to the Netherlands he had not only a military task to perform. The treaty gave him a vague political position, and Elizabeth had urged him to effect certain modifications in the constitution of the nascent state, as, for instance, a strengthening of the position of the States-General as against the provinces. Indeed, an excellent instruction, but one difficult to carry out if, as she also wished, he was at the same time to abstain from assuming greater political power. Hardly had he landed in Holland, however, when Leicester saw this power thrust upon him by the hard-pressed States. His governor-generalship was made a reality; early in February 1586 he was invested with a truly sovereign position, with less restrictions than those which had irked Don John or Anjou. He, too, was a foreigner (knowing neither Dutch nor French), but he was at least a Protestant. Moreover, he stood high in Elizabeth's favour, and the States, notwithstanding all their experience of this woman, as self-opinionated as she was incalculable, made the mistake of thinking that by exalting Leicester they could involve his Queen in the war more deeply than she intended. Above all, confusion had become worse confounded, and everyone was ready to believe that only a strong personal government could save the country.

But that is not to say that everyone was prepared to submit to whatever the new Governor might dictate. There existed at that moment markedly divergent and well-defined ideas as to the policy to be pursued, different parties, each of which expected support from Leicester. The revolution had done much more than remove the royal government or even overset the Catholic Church. It had thrown the whole of Society, as well as the State, into confusion. All the bonds which the monarchy had forged between province and province were broken. The leading classes in the towns, in each province, in the whole of the Netherlands, had been partially swept aside, and the remainder had to strengthen itself with "new men." That, following these shocks, all kinds of new problems arose and were approached in an impassioned and contentious spirit is less wonder than that the main lines of the social and political structure resisted the convulsion, and that what was new for the most part masqueraded in old dress. Although the States arrogated to themselves an authority which by no means appertained to them historically, they were—especially those of Holland—in the main a conservative force, and they proved well able to hold out against the attack that was directed against them.

This attack did not come from the mass of the Catholics who had been robbed of their rights. In fact the States of Holland stood in the breach to defend what position still remained to them; but they themselves remained passive in the midst of all this agitation. The attack came from the zealous Reformers, who were especially strong among the urban lower middle class, led by the ministers. These people looked upon themselves as the true exponents of the rebellion, even of the national idea; the State was their State, dissenters must be kept down as much as possible. Their own religious zeal seemed to them the only effective patriotism; in no other way could the enemy be held at bay. We have seen how deeply this idea had influenced the course of events, but it is now time to notice that it was nevertheless continually and strenuously resisted from within the circle of those who accepted and led the revolt, and that it was only very imperfectly realized.

Orange, as we know, had never submitted to it. But the town oligarchies of Holland, which remained oligarchies, in spite of the sudden change of personnel brought about by the revolution, looked on it with no more favour. They had, it is true, accepted the Reformation and suppressed Catholic worship, but they viewed things very differently from the true zealots of the new creed. Some had themselves been swept into office on the flood-tide of the Reformation; the majority had done no more than adapt themselves to the new circumstances, or had hardly even done that. On the whole they felt themselves much more, as of old, the representatives and protectors of the whole body of the citizens, the guardians of the privileges and welfare of town and country, than the champions of a particular new religious faith. In other words, they regarded matters from a secular standpoint, and, while the new Church had in their scheme of things its indispensable place, they felt it incumbent on them carefully to circumscribe this place. From one point of view—especially in Germany and England can this be clearly seen—the great European movement of the Reformation was a revolt of the lay community under the leadership of their rulers—a revolt, that is to say, of the State against priestly influence. When they required theories to justify secular supervision over the new Church, of which for a long time to come not even all of them were members, the Netherlands "regents" did not therefore have far to seek.

But indeed, in Holland, though the political tendency of the revolt had in 1572 been temporarily overlaid by the religious tendency, it had preserved its identity and maintained its ideology. William of Orange had greatly assisted it in doing so, but the town governments and the States also gladly appealed to liberty as well as to religion as the issue in the great struggle. *Haec libertatis ergo* inscribed on the emergency money which was issued at Leyden during the siege epitomized a political programme. Two kinds of patriots were distinguished:

those who are attached to our cause through love either of freedom or religion.

And these "Libertinists," as the former were called, were not merely "Politiques" (the name of the party in France which wanted to keep peace between the two warring religious parties); they could meet the zealous Reformers on their own ground and clothe their ideas in religious garb. An anti-confessional theology came naturally to the land of Erasmus, and in the North, amidst stress and conflict, it was now formulated and developed.

The outstanding figure among the "Libertinists" of these

years was Coornhert, who had returned to Holland in 1576, and whose utterances on religion attracted attention if only on account of his political relations. Coornhert refused to join any religious community. He frankly declared, both in his numerous pamphlets and in public disputations held under the eye of authority, at Leyden in 1578 and at The Hague some years later, that knowledge of the truth was withheld from man. He inveighed vehemently against the ministers who demanded precise assent to the dogmas laid down in the professions of faith. Such words certainly echoed the sentiments of many, and the regents listened the more readily to Coornhert since, despite his aversion from all forms of coercion, his fear of the tyranny of the ministers made him willing to call on the secular power for assistance. At the request of the government of Leyden he wrote a couple of vigorous remonstrances to prove the justice of their case in a dispute with one of their ministers over the appointment of the consistory, and in them he hurled bold defiance at the Synod, which had presented to town and States a vindication of the Church's right to govern itself.

The Synod attempts to make itself the head of the Government.

That was the conclusion he drew from its demand that magistrates should be of the Reformed religion; for the Synod claimed the right to determine what was meant by "Reformed." At the same time the supervision of the ministers over education would result in their becoming "the hereditary masters" of all the people. The secretary of Leyden, Jan van Hout, was himself a good "Libertinist," and under his influence and that of Coolhaes, a minister whom the Synod excommunicated on account of his unorthodoxy, the Leyden government pursued the quarrel with astonishing acerbity and high-handedness.

It was apparent that no agreement existed on the elementary principles which should govern the relations of Church and State. The Church wanted to keep her doctrine undefiled; she wanted to be able to censure, and, if necessary, expel those who were lax, careless, or unorthodox, even when they sat in the seats of the mighty. She regarded it as the godly duty of the secular authorities, under her direction, to give effect to the precepts of Calvinism in the life of society and to suppress dissenting groups. Naturally the State was no longer wholly free with regard to a Church with which it had struck an alliance against Spanish domination. At Leyden, for example, Van Hout was unable to carry through a project to put the care of the poor wholly in secular hands; town governments and consistories jointly administered this potent means of gaining over the mass of the poor to the new religion. But, as far as they were able, the oligarchy wanted to protect their own freedom and that of the people, whether or no they belonged to the Church, and so while they never applied very stringently the repressive measures against dissenters, they hindered the Church as much as possible in the use of corrective measures against its own members. This, together with the whole supervisory power exercised for the purpose by the State, seemed to the Church party an intolerable infraction of its independence. Is it to be wondered at, however, that the secular power, whose help had been as indispensable to the formation of the Church as it was to her continued welfare, and which had, moreover, laid hands on the ecclesiastical property from which the new organization was maintained, did not suffer itself to be used as an inanimate tool?

This conflict, whose last echoes, despite the profound change of circumstances, have not yet died away in North Netherland, has had an inestimable importance for the spiritual life of that country. Each of the parties concerned stood for something of value, and the conflict between them, which sometimes assumed heroic forms, strained mind and soul of the contending sides to the utmost of their power. There lay a mighty strength in the stiff-necked conviction of the Precisians, but, had they been able to enforce their programme, North Netherlandish civilization, which was soon to exhibit so fresh and vigorous a diversity, would have been narrowed down to something very rigid and monotonous. As against that, the protection afforded by the "Libertinist" oligarchy to the multiplicity of forces still springing out of the old cultural traditions was an invaluable asset. But in its turn the power of that oligarchy itself threatened at times to become a stifling bond, and then the stubbornness of the strong Calvinist, who had no conception of conscience in general, but to whom his own conscience was an inviolable sanctuary, was an unqualified gain for the independence of spiritual life.

The States of Holland, indeed, were not inspired by a pure zeal for the freedom and rights of dissenters; they feared the Church as a potential organization of the people, whose last remaining political organizations they had themselves reduced to impotence; since 1581 they had forbidden town governments (it was certainly no longer necessary for most of them) to consult on provincial matters with guilds or corps of civic guards. One of their objects in keeping the Church under their supervision and control was to bolster up their own new political authority; the struggle between Church and State coincided with a struggle between democracy and oligarchy. Other factors added their weight to these. The States of Holland were not only at variance with their own "commonalty"; in most of the smaller provinces too there prevailed a feeling of intense irritation against them.

Holland was rich, strong, inviolate. It pursued trade in the midst of the war. Its harbours gave access to all seas. Indeed, so dependent were the inland provinces on the imports which came through these harbours that Parma had to connive at them in the areas which he recovered; even in Spain itself Philip could not do without the ships of his rebellious subjects. Now that Antwerp was shut off from the sea, the towns of Holland and Zealand—and in the long run particularly Amsterdam—assumed the rôle which the great city of the Scheldt had hitherto played in the economic life of Europe. After the loss of Brabant and Flanders the expenses of the war fell largely on Holland and Zealand. With Groningen, Overysel, and Gelderland wholly or in part occupied by the enemy, and Friesland exposed to predatory incursions, Holland alone contributed nearly two-thirds towards them. No wonder that at times it acted somewhat independently. In 1585, for instance, it had invested the young Maurice with the Stadtholderate, the appointment to which hitherto the States-General, as having stepped into the King's place, had always kept in their own hands. The States of Holland now made this office, which carried with it traditions of supreme power, subordinate to themselves. In the circumstances it was a quite natural development. In other matters, too, Holland felt that it had no need to let its needy allies in the States-General dictate to it. But the provinces which, without the assistance of Holland, would not have been able to continue the struggle for another month, complained bitterly that Holland was not doing enough.

The Flemish and Brabant refugees swelled this chorus. They belonged to the most zealous section of the Reformed; moreover, they were full of bitterness, and apt to detect cowardice and treachery everywhere—the true exile mentality:

before they had quite settled down,

as a shrewd Zealander, who had had much to do with them at Middelburg, remarked, as it were in extenuation. In the Generality Colleges (from which, as their provinces fell, the Brabanders and most of the Flemings had nevertheless been compelled to resign, though Van Meetkerke still sat on the Council of State) every reverse was attributed, with all too much readiness, not merely to the lack of a powerful central authority, but definitely to the indolence and selfishness of Holland.

The orthodox, the democrats, the inland provinces, the exiles, the politicians and officials of the Generality—all were agreed that salvation would only come with a ruler who could ride the States of Holland on the curb, and such a man they thought had been vouchsafed to them in Leicester. His religious inclinations as well as his dislike of a burgher-administration indeed disposed him towards this ambitious plan. Yet the haters of Holland mistook their man, while he for his part was similarly at fault in his estimation of the forces which contended for the mastery in the foreign land he came to govern.

Received at first without suspicion by the States of Holland, Leicester quickly plunged into the party-struggle, and fell into the hands of a faction who wished to overthrow the provincial oligarchies and set up in his person a National Reformed dictatorship. In the Council of State the Governor placed faith only in the Fleming Van Meetkerke and the English members, besides the Secretary De Borchgrave, who was also Flemish. Further, he relied on the ministers of religion and the democratic party.

The latter succeeded in making themselves masters of Utrecht, which became Leicester's centre of action. The burgher captains of this town, now no longer concerned for "the Catholic Apostolic Roman religion,"[1] but zealously Reformed, and spurred on by a crowd of Brabant refugees, of whom Prouninck, of 's Hertogenbosch, was the leader, stood strongly in opposition to the magistrate and the provincial States, who were no less "Libertinist" than in Holland. For years the "regents" had maintained a minister, one Duifhuis, who remained outside the establishment of the Reformed Church. But in 1584 the democrats had managed to raise by force the Stadtholder of Gelderland, the Count of Nieuwenaer, to the Stadtholderate of Utrecht, and with his assistance, now reinforced by that of Leicester and his English troops, they held in check the aristocratic and Libertinist party, with which the Prince of Orange used to work, and subjected Utrecht to an intensive Calvinizing process. How bitter were the feelings of these men against the Hollanders was made clear, before the coming of Leicester, by a remonstrance which they had presented to the States-General against what they described as the "shameless" violation by Amsterdam of an edict prohibiting trade with the enemy, which could only proceed (so they asserted) from the subordination of the common interest to that of individuals, from self-righteous contempt for the authority of the States-General, perhaps even from secret leanings towards Spain.

This question was the first in which Leicester openly showed his hand. In April 1586 a stern edict against this trade was promulgated, and confiscations and penalties followed. The Holland merchants protested, and the Holland oligarchy put its back to the wall in defence of this protest. Did it do so

[1] See p. 155.

merely because it was so intimately linked with the mercantile class, because its own particular interests were at stake? Were its motives purely selfish? The Utrechters, and the Flemings and Brabanders who had thrown in their lot with them, seeing how bad was the condition into which the provinces subdued by Parma had fallen—in Flanders and Brabant in 1586 the farmers could not be got to sow the land—thought that it needed only a few more turns of the screw of starvation to compel the Spaniards to negotiate. The Hollanders maintained that the only people to benefit would be their foreign competitors, that Flanders and Brabant could easily be victualled from elsewhere, but that in that case *their* trading towns would lose the revenues without which the war could not be carried on. Out of the licence-money raised from this trade, moreover, were defrayed the expenses of the naval force which commanded the rivers and coastal waters. Although the war-contractors were undoubtedly far from scrupulous in their methods, and private interests sometimes exerted far too great an influence in the States, the Holland case was not lacking in strength. Yet the zealots who had Leicester's ear only replied with wild accusations of treachery, popery, even atheism. Leicester arbitrarily instituted a General Audit Office, whose chief function would be to inflict fines on smugglers; a Brabant adventurer with a very suspicious past, one Reingout, had held out to him the prospect of treasure from the activities of such a body, and this man was the leading spirit in it. A strengthening of the Central Government was precisely what the Union needed, but by associating this College with a policy which appeared ruinous to the welfare of the most powerful province, Leicester dealt a blow at the idea of unity, and drove Holland into defending itself with the help of its provincial rights and its actual superiority of power.

Thus there originated an antagonism so sharp that it threatened to lead to a split, if one party did not get the better of the other. But that was exactly what Leicester and his supporters wanted to put to the test. In June they gained complete mastery of the government of Utrecht: Prouninck became burgomaster, another Brabander sheriff, while Floris Thin and sixty other members of the States party were exiled; Paul Buys, the foremost representative of Holland's point of view in the Council of State, was imprisoned—although he had worked harder than most men for the treaty with England, he was now generally referred to by some such word as traitor, papist, and atheist in Leicester's correspondence. The moment had come when the people in Holland were to be called upon to rise against the oligarchy, and when the English troops were to take a hand in the business.

Had Leicester's supporters been able to look into his confidential correspondence with the Queen, they would have seen what a dangerous game it was for Netherlands independence. The favourite, who when he accepted the title of Governor-General had presumed too much on his favour, now made it up by slavish submission to the will of his mistress. He advocated the possession of a couple of towns in North Holland,

which [together with The Brill] will be such a strength to you that you may rule these men, make war or peace as you list . . . peace with the King of Spain so as to restore his authority here again.

Leicester does not indeed commend such a peace, but leaves everything to the wise disposition of Elizabeth.

Few or none but yourself may be privy to your full mind, especially if you shall not mean to go through with these people.

The position of power into which he was to be placed by the most zealous Calvinists must only serve to make the unreliable Elizabeth the judge of their cause! But when the moment came to act, he shrank back. He was not, after all, the true Gideon to redeem Israel. Did he already perceive that the States of Holland were more firmly seated in the saddle than he had thought? In any case it was his own mistakes of judgment which had enabled them to take their stand not only as the champions of the oligarchic system but as the guardians of the commercial prosperity of the whole nation. A strong hand had grasped the control of their affairs; Oldenbarnevelt, the first great statesman to spring from the North Netherlands people, had become Advocate of the province of Holland. What further strengthened the position of the States not a little was the fact that Maurice and Hohenlohe, together with William Louis of Nassau, now Stadtholder of Friesland, took their part; that gave them the control over the greater part of the army. Leicester in any case did not dare to push matters farther; and when in November 1586 he sailed for England, delegating his authority to the Council of State, he left behind him an unsolved crisis and complete confusion.

He had not been gone long when the English governors of Deventer and of the trenches at Zutfen betrayed their posts to the Spaniards; the most alarming reports came in about the attitude of the badly paid English garrisons in several other places. The States of Holland now felt themselves borne along on the strong tide of anxious and indignant public opinion. Oldenbarnevelt acted. Setting aside the authority of the absent Governor and of his distressed Council of State, Holland entrusted its Stadtholder, Maurice, with special powers and demanded a new oath of the soldiery. In vain did the English member of the Council, Wilkes, protest, denying to the States of Holland the right to act as they were doing:

The sovereignty, or supreme authority, in default of legitimate prince, does not belong to you, gentlemen, but to the commonalty.

It was easy to match theory with theory, and Vrancken's ready pen now formulated for the first time the thesis of the absolute and independent sovereign right of the States of Holland. His historical arguments only reveal the complete ignorance of the Middle Ages characteristic of his time, but however wrong he was about the past, the States of Holland, led by Oldenbarnevelt, were undeniably the only purposeful force in the Union at the present, the only one able to save the country from complete anarchy in the face of the enemy. The States-General were persuaded by the States of Holland to give, out of the fullness of their sovereign power, a new composition to the Council of State, by which Van Meetkerke and De Borchgrave were barred. This was a serious encroachment upon Leicester's supreme authority, and yet the need of foreign assistance was still felt so keenly that negotiations were opened at once to obtain his return. The popular party of Utrecht, too, which had not yet given up the game for lost, implored him to come and restore his authority.

He came in the summer of 1587 with some fresh troops; Sluis, as mentioned before, he could not save. And now he was forced into the execution of the *coup d'état* he had shirked the year before. Utrecht was still devoted to him, and so were the ministers, who never hesitated to impute to the States all blame for the loss of the important fortress on the mouth of the Scheldt. Yet Leicester was approaching his great enterprise in most unfavourable circumstances. His Queen, for ever hesitating, was busy negotiating with Parma, and Leicester, after having stoutly denied the fact when taxed with it by the States, had now not only to admit it, but was also compelled to invite them to take part in those negotiations on an entirely unsatisfactory basis. This exhibition cost the hero of the exiles and of the ministers most of his prestige. The commonalty, whose rights his henchman Wilkes had advocated so eloquently and whom he wanted to lead against the States, were bewildered when he spoke of compromise with Spain. The attempt against the States had nevertheless to be made, and in September Leicester came from Utrecht to Holland, where he tried to possess himself of a number of towns. Sonoy, at Medemblik, was his faithful supporter, and refused to obey the orders given by Maurice in his capacity of Stadtholder, but nowhere did the people stir. At Leyden some South Netherlanders, Van Meetkerke and the professor of theology Saravia, with part of the garrison, undertook in consultation with Leicester an attempt, which was, however, discovered in time. Van Meetkerke and Saravia escaped, but a few others from amongst the principal plotters were punished with death by the Libertinist town government acting in concert with the States of Holland and with Maurice. Leicester, humiliated and embittered, soon left the country for ever.

Confusion was even worse confounded now than after his first departure. With Utrecht and Medemblik and the places garrisoned by English troops recalcitrant to the States' authority, the situation hardly differed from civil war. Only when Leicester's letter of resignation arrived early in 1588 were the States able, with the help of Maurice, William Louis, and Hohenlohe, to break that opposition. Sonoy submitted. For Van Meetkerke and De Borchgrave there was no political future left. At Utrecht the popular party was brought down, Prouninck had to leave the town, and the aristocratic States regime was restored there too. The ministers of religion were defeated along with the Flemings and Brabanders and the popular party. In 1586 a Synod had drafted an ecclesiastical constitution after their own hearts, but although Leicester had confirmed it, on the strength of his authority, it was now shelved. When a number of ministers presumed to offer to the States an admonition calling for unity, Oldenbarnevelt, with insulting hauteur, begged them not to meddle with affairs of state. In Utrecht the restored States rudely interfered in the administration of the Church, which had threatened them in their authority, and held it under vigorous control. Leicester had hopelessly compromised all the causes which he had advocated.

Thus there emerged out of all this strife the oligarchic, erastian, decentralized Republic of the Seven United Provinces. The treaty with England was preserved, English troops still remained in the country, and their commander with two more Englishmen had still access to the Council of State. But the idea of delegating supreme authority to some foreign ruler went under with the popular party. The States were now sovereign in reality. They had learnt the lesson that if the old liberties of Netherlands society were to be saved, the country would have to stand upon its own feet. Following the States of Holland, themselves led by Oldenbarnevelt, the States-General set out on their independent course.

For by the course of events we have described yet another matter had been decided, namely, that Holland was to occupy a preponderant position in the Union, and that therein was to reside the strongest unifying force. Oldenbarnevelt, who owed to his courageous lead against Leicester an uncommon prestige in his province, inspired the States of Holland and through them the States-General. But in the inland provinces the Stadtholder's authority still counted for much beside that of the oligarchy represented in their various States, and here the death of Nieuwenaer in 1589 gave Oldenbarnevelt the opportunity for a great stroke of policy. He persuaded the States of Utrecht, Gelderland, and Overysel, to offer Maurice the Stadtholderate over their provinces. Thus, he pointed out to them, military affairs would be better co-ordinated, and Holland assistance more easily obtainable for the conquests required for the restoration or safeguarding of their territory. Just as he had used Maurice against Leicester, so he used him now for the purpose of guarding under Holland leadership against the worst weaknesses of federation. It was a fortunate circumstance that the only other Stadtholder now remaining in the Union, William Louis in Friesland, was bound to his cousin and brother-in-law Maurice by a firm tie of friendship, and was animated by too high a sense of duty to let jealousy of the younger man's greater position inspire his actions.

Constitutionally speaking, the influence exercised by Holland through its great Advocate and through the authority of Maurice as Stadtholder of a number of provinces was no more than a palliative for a disease the effects of which would none the less one day make themselves felt. An organ of government like the Council of State, through which unity might have found a more regular expression, was thrust into the background. The States-General, in which the provinces sat side by side as free equals, became not only the bearer of the collective sovereignty, but the actual and daily government of the Union. Later, when the national vigour which now kept the cumbrous machinery going began to relax, it was to appear only too clearly how woefully unfit they were for that task. It is, moreover, difficult not to feel some sympathy with the cheated democrats and the disillusioned exiles. But they had had in Leicester an impossible champion for their ideals, while on the other hand the Holland regime was in the immediate future to prove equal to the demands of the war. Can one expect of a statesman, confronted with so urgent a crisis as Oldenbarnevelt was in these years, that he should build his system for a distant future? Flanders and Brabant were not regained. But would Prouninck and Van Meetkerke have had better success in that respect than Oldenbarnevelt?

c. THE CONQUESTS OF MAURICE

We have indicated the lines along which the independent North Netherlandish state was to develop in the future. On Leicester's departure, however, the first question still was whether that state had a future at all.

It was not only the internal divisions which made this appear uncertain, but danger threatened also from the English auxiliary troops which by their possession of the cautionary towns of Flushing and The Brill, added to their positions on the land-side frontiers, commanded the entries to the country. If Elizabeth came to an agreement with Spain, the Netherlands revolt was lost. And even if the English continued to assist, so far their help had proved insufficient to check Parma's advance, and now, with the Ysel-line broken into, and Sluis in Spanish hands, the main stronghold of Netherlands independence, Holland-Zealand itself, seemed threatened.

It was great events outside the Netherlands which caused the Spanish attack to waver at this very moment, and Parma's progress not only to be checked midway, but to be converted into a retreat. When in 1589 Geertruidenberg was given up to him by English mutineers—a gate of attack straight against Holland—the worst danger that had threatened from the English side had nevertheless subsided: Elizabeth no longer hesitated, but was engaged in open war with Spain In 1588 Philip had thrown off the mask, and while the Pope deposed the heretical Queen, the King undertook the long-prepared expedition of conquest by sending the Armada against England. Much against his inclination Parma had had to waste the campaigning season by concentrating his army at Dunkirk and Nieuwpoort; the Holland and English fleets prevented its crossing, while the cumbersome Armada could not come near the shore. The disaster which finally overtook the Spanish fleet was a formidable blow to Spanish prestige. The scheme, for the sake of which Philip had withdrawn his attention from the Netherlands, had proved a chimera, and as for Elizabeth, she was cured for good of the illusion that peace with him was possible. For the Netherlands, this was an important consequence of the affair, even though it did not mean that she now became free with her money or even carried out the treaty of 1585 to the letter.

Events in France exercised an even more profound influence on affairs in the Low Countries. We saw how in 1585 Henry III had been compelled to refuse the sovereignty offered him by the States-General out of fear of the growing power of the Catholic movement in his kingdom. Since then the League, under the Duke of Guise, had become master of Paris. In 1588 the King had Guise murdered, a deed by which the Catholic party was even more intensely embittered. In 1589 the King himself was murdered, and a situation developed which was serious indeed, for Henry III's successor was Henry of Bourbon, King of Navarre, a Huguenot, nay more, the leader of the Huguenots. The League, which controlled a large part of France, refused to recognize the heretic as King, and it was inevitable that they should seek the support of Spain.

It is clear that Philip's interests were vitally concerned in that crisis. A victory for Henry IV would create the situation which William of Orange had always hoped for: it would mobilize the power of France against Spain's position in the Netherlands. No matter, therefore, how keenly Parma felt that the whole issue in the Netherlands remained uncertain so long as Holland and Zealand held out; no matter how fervently he wished to complete his task there, he had to obey Philip's positive orders and turn southward. For some time already he had been supporting the League with money and troops which he could ill spare. Now in 1590 he marched into France himself with his main army in order to protect Paris against Henry IV. Finally, in the winter of 1591 to 1592, he had to go south once more in order to secure the election to the French throne of Isabella, Philip's daughter by his first wife, who had been a French princess. No less a stake was now gambled for, and at last there seemed to be a prospect of fulfilment for the scheme that Philip, as long ago as 1558, had arranged with Henry II, of France side by side with Spain beginning to work for the suppression of heresy in Europe. Only, time and again the hopes of a decisive defeat of Henry IV were dashed to the ground. Thus the Spanish interference in France offered a splendid opportunity to the North Netherlandish provinces, and the vigour with which they availed themselves of it, compelling Parma in spite of the policy imposed upon him to turn his attention northward again, in its turn benefited Henry IV. In the course of a few years the Spanish cause was sadly impaired in the Netherlands as well as in France, and Parma, triumphant for so long, at the end of 1592 died in disgrace and despair, like Don John before him.

International circumstances thus became in 1588, and especially in 1590, favourable for the revolt as they had not been since the deceptive spring of 1572. Yet the young Republic might not have been able to make use of them but for the internal developments which had just carried the vigorous personality of Oldenbarnevelt, supported by the whole weight of Holland, into a position of real power; and no less important was his happy co-operation with the high-born Stadtholders, Maurice and William Louis. The moving force behind everything that was done in those years was the powerful mind of the Advocate of Holland, but the two Stadtholders were far more than convenient tools through which he could impart unity of policy to the entire body of the Northern Netherlands. Their great merit lay in what they did together for the improvement of the army, while, moreover, Maurice handled with masterly skill the weapon they created for themselves. After the Hohenlohe regime the mere fact that the young commanders had a sense of order and discipline was a boon. The greater regularity in public finance and the wise self-restriction of the States, who reduced the size of the army so as to be better able to pay what remained, created a favourable atmosphere for their work of reorganization. But they also introduced all sorts of novelties which at first gave rise to mockery, but soon were imitated all over Europe. In the classical authors they read of military movements in which they strenuously trained their troops. They improved the armament, and with a just sense of the nature of the land where their services were required, they accustomed the soldiers to do the digging which until then the military had considered beneath them, and which used to be carried out by peasants hired for the purpose. Maurice had followed at Leyden the lectures on mathematics of Simon Stevin of Brugge, and he was profoundly aware of the importance of a scientific study of engineering. The commissariat, the means of transport on land but especially on water—everything had their attention, so that when the moment came to strike they could strike home.

In 1590 everyone felt that the moment had come. The Council of State, whose activities were now practically limited to military matters, pointed out to the States-General

the good occasion and opportunity which present themselves for doing the enemy an injury, and for carrying out successfully some attempts, caused by the present diversion of the enemy's armed forces.

The States-General decided to levy additional troops. After so long a period of defensive warfare, after years of giving ground, men longed for an offensive. A successful attempt on Breda had a stimulating effect. Maurice was less fortunate with respect to Nymwegen, but in September 1590, while Parma was in France, he took in addition to Steenbergen a number of small places and fortresses on the Maas near Den Bosch. The next year witnessed the real beginning, although Parma remained in the Netherlands, with half his attention riveted on France it is true. Zutfen and Deventer were unexpectedly surrounded by the Dutch forces and quickly surrendered, and although an attempt on Groningen failed, Delfzyl and other strong places in the North were taken. The army then hurried southward to prevent Parma from taking the entrenchment of Knodsenburg opposite Nymwegen. With this the campaign seemed at an end, and the troops went into winter quarters. To the enemy's complete surprise, however, Maurice sud-

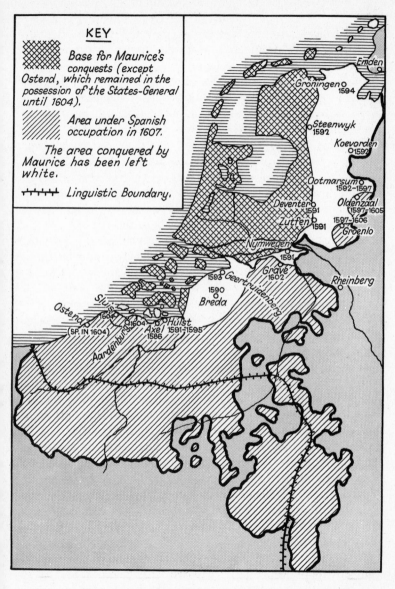

KEY

Base for Maurice's conquests (except Ostend, which remained in the possession of the States-General until 1604).

Area under Spanish occupation in 1607.

The area conquered by Maurice has been left white.

+++++ Linguistic Boundary.

Emden

Groningen ○ 1594

Steenwyk 1592

Koevorden ○ 1592

Ootmarsum 1592-1597

Deventer ○ 1591

Oldenzaal 1597-1605

Zutfen 1591

1597-1606

Groenlo

Nymwegen 1591

Gravé 1602

Rheinberg

1593

Geertruidenberg

1590 ○ Breda

Ostend 1604 (SP. IN 1604)

Sluis 1604

Aardenburg

Hulst 1591-1595

Axel 1586

MAP V THE CONQUESTS OF MAURICE, 1590–1606

H

denly collected a little army and appeared before Hulst in
Flanders, which capitulated. Nor was even this the end. As
unexpectedly he laid siege to Nymwegen and took that town
as well. It was only an effective use of the waterways that had
made possible those disconcertingly quick movements.

In 1592 Parma had again to go to France, and the Spanish
commander in the North-East was, in spite of his warnings,
left to his own devices. Steenwyk and Koevorden, however
strongly fortified, proved impossible to hold. Here Maurice's
scientific methods of siege warfare first showed themselves in
their full glory. The possession of those two places not only
safeguarded southern Friesland from marauding raids, but cut
Groningen off completely from its base in the South.

In 1593 Maurice, to the great resentment of the Frisians,
who wanted all forces concentrated against Groningen first,
besieged Geertruidenberg, by which the Hollanders felt themselves to be threatened, and which he took in spite of all
attempts at relief. The irritation of the Frisians assumed such
violent forms, and without heeding William Louis' efforts to
calm them down they protested so passionately against "Holland tyranny" that one can plainly see there were as sharp
particularist contrasts left in the area which still belonged to
the revolt as there had formerly been in the greater area of
all the Netherlands. Only, within the northern state success
was to compose them. In the winter of 1593 attempts were
undertaken against Brugge, Den Bosch, and Maastricht, all of
which failed, but Groningen, whose turn came in 1594, had
to capitulate after a siege of two months; Friesland could be
easy in its mind. Joyful homage was paid to Maurice on his
return; in the Holland towns through which he passed the
Rhetoricians performed symbolic shows in his honour. It was
in vain that the citizens of Groningen, on whom the defence
of their town had mainly fallen, had sent urgent petitions to
Brussels for an expedition of relief. Renewed mutinies of
unpaid troops, which again exposed large tracts of country in
the South to the excesses of the soldiers, had kept the Government paralysed.

After Parma's death in December 1592 the government

had been temporarily in the hands of Mansfeldt. A Netherlands magnate, no doubt, but under the cover of his name the real ruler was Fuentes, a Spaniard, brother-in-law of Alva, and a man of his school. He had been sent by Philip to replace Parma (who had died just in time to be spared that indignity); and yet another Spaniard, Ibarra, was, to the intense displeasure of the native nobility, and indeed against the provisions of the Treaty of Arras, placed on the Council of State. It was Parma's reluctance to use the forces at his disposal for interference in the French civil war, a reluctance shared to the full by the unhappy people of the Southern Netherlands, which explains Philip's decision to restore Spanish control. At the same time, however, the country had to be used as a means for the tightening of his relations with the German Habsburgs, required by the interests of the King's world policy. His cousin, the Archduke Ernest therefore, a brother of the new Emperor Rudolph (as also of Matthew, who nearly twenty years ago had come to Brussels in rather different circumstances), was made Governor, while the prospect was opened to him of one day obtaining the hand of Philip's daughter Isabella, and with it the sovereignty over the Netherlands. The new ruler's attention, however, was at the same time directed to France more insistently than ever, for although Henry IV had now embraced Catholicism, Isabella's claims were by no means given up. The subjected Netherlands none the less heartily acclaimed Ernest when he arrived in 1594: in their helpless state they expected every new master to save them. At his entry into Antwerp there were staged on "scaffoldings" dumb shows which brought the people's hopes in visible form before his eyes:

Seventeen maidens representing the seventeen provinces, of which the United ones were made fast apart at one string, and the others which are still under the King at another string, both groups being introduced to him, Ernest, by the *Nimpha Belgica* (the Netherlands Virgin), so that they might once more be joined together.

And indeed Ernest soon wrote to the States-General at The Hague a smooth letter inviting them to enter into negotiations.

The States, however, or rather Oldenbarnevelt—for he was the author of the striking document—replying with a plain refusal, pushed aside the well-meaning Archduke to discover behind him the old enemy of the entire Netherlands people—Spain.

Unhappily the southern half of the Netherlands people, kept down by the Spanish armies, robbed of all its most vigorous elements, and by the difference in religion separated from the ruling class in the North, was no longer able to raise its head against that old enemy. No doubt the unending misery of the war and the prospect of an open rupture with France were again causing bitter dissatisfaction. Ernest did not dare to call together a complete assembly of the States-General, but a meeting which he summoned of none but nobility and clergy voiced the grievances with sufficient vehemence, exclaiming against the foreigners in the administration, against the mutinies, against the unnational foreign policy. Aerschot, the hero of 1576, the deserter of three years later, was again the leader. The people of the South had got him back with the conquest. But his aristocratic love of opposition indeed benefited them but little. When Ernest died early in 1595, in the midst of confusion and discouragement, Fuentes himself emerged from his obscurity to take the government into his own hands until a new Archduke should come to play to the finish the part of the deceased. There was no thought of resistance to the hated Spaniard, and soon it became strikingly apparent that the Spanish military forces, if only led by a firm hand, still disposed of great reserves of strength.

The States had hopes of turning the dissatisfaction in the South to their advantage by undertaking military operations in the region of the Maas, in the direction of Liège. The plan was to establish communications with Bouillon in France, whither they had just sent an auxiliary corps for Henry IV, but also to open a breach in Brabant and Limburg. In enterprises of this kind, far from his base, Maurice, cautious and methodical, did not excel, and Fuentes easily frustrated the scheme. But more than that, exhausted as the subjected Netherlands were, pushed back on all sides from their natural fron-

tiers, and secured against the unrest of their own people and
the attacks of the Northerners solely by their numerous fortresses, the Spanish Governor, quite in accordance with his
master's wishes, still managed to use them as the starting-point
for an offensive against France. Henry IV, at last sufficiently
in control of his kingdom, in this year 1595 had declared
open war. In the next year an alliance was concluded between
France, England, and the States-General. Those same States-
General, who only a few years ago had come as supplicants
first to the Crown of France, then to that of England, to offer
the sovereignty over themselves, were now admitted on a
footing of equality. It is true that Elizabeth had at first objected on the ground of the special position which the treaty
of 1585 secured to her in the Netherlands. With so much the
greater earnestness had the King of France favoured the
Netherlands statesmen's ambitions towards recognition. Once
more the mutual jealousies of France and England where the
Low Countries were concerned proved a benefit.

Much direct advantage certainly this alliance did not yield.
The States made such an effort to assist Henry IV on his war
front that their power of attack on their own side was paralysed.
And yet Fuentes succeeded in taking Cambrai, and in 1596
the new Archduke, Albert, just come to assume the government, even captured the still more important town of Calais,
which, with Nieuwpoort, Dunkirk, and Sluis (Ostend being
still in the hands of the States), formed a serious menace to
the shipping of England as well as of the Northern provinces.
After this success Albert turned north and retook Hulst, but
the losses suffered there exhausted him for the time being.
A new bankruptcy of Philip II's exchequer made his situation
still more difficult.

So in 1597 it was Maurice's turn again, and while the Spanish
army was fighting in France he, after a famous cavalry skirmish
near Turnhout, completed the conquest of the Eastern provinces. He first took possession of Rheinberg, which commanded
the crossing of the Rhine for an attack on the Eastern frontiers.
It belonged to the archbishop of Köln, who had now to
acquiesce in an occupation by the States substituted for one

by the Spaniards. Marching north from thence, Maurice captured without much difficulty Grol, Enschedé, Oldenzaal, and all the other places from which the enemy could still lay Gelderland and Overysel under contribution. There was great rejoicing in the North. "The fence of the Netherlands is closed," so ran the phrase in which the situation was summed up. It meant that the entire territory north of the natural line of defence of the seven provinces still represented on the States-General was now cleared of the enemy. The Upper Quarter of Gelderland, which was situated south of that line, remained in his hands.

The success came none too soon. In 1598 Henry IV concluded peace with Philip. Elizabeth's close-fisted policy had discouraged him, and in any case, after a generation of wars of religion, France stood in need of rest. Philip, on his part, realized at last that it was beyond his power to dispute the succession of the former heretic, and he even restored Calais in his eagerness to get his hands free against the seven provinces once more. For the first time since 1590, therefore, the Spanish commanders in the Netherlands were able to turn their undivided attention to affairs in the North, but the strategic position which Parma in his happier years had prepared as a jumping-off ground for an attack on the main stronghold of the rebellion now lay in ruins. Even so the eastern frontier was still the weak point in the Republic's armour, and the first vigorous onrush, which the Spanish forces made in that same year 1598, was again directed to break through there. The attempt almost resulted in serious trouble with the neighbouring German princes, whose territory the attackers had to cross. It was nevertheless, as we shall see, repeated in 1605 and again in 1606, and each time, in spite of the enemy's remoteness from his base, which inevitably weakened the force of his thrust, people in Holland itself were alarmed as though the very existence of the young state had been at stake. The Reformed "regents" in Gelderland, Overysel, Groningen, felt their authority over their still so largely Catholic populations tottering.

The plans originally formed for Ernest had after his death

been carried out for the benefit of Albert. He had married Isabella, and Philip, who died in 1598, left to them the Netherlands in sovereign possession. In reality they were by no means cut free from Spain, but the nominal independence of "the Archdukes" nevertheless removed, in the eyes of Catholics in the North as well as in the South, some of the hateful character which with the Spanish name had so far clung to the champions of Catholicism in the Netherlands. The Archdukes soon became popular in the South in spite of all the misfortunes of the war, and in the North the Catholic clergy at least felt no aversion from regarding them as the legitimate rulers of the country. This is not to say that they always actively worked for them, or that even in their feelings they were always consistent.

The Catholic clergy in the North were again exercising some influence. A revival had followed the bewilderment and disorganization caused at first by the overthrow of the domination of the Catholic Church. In 1583 Sasbout Vosmeer was appointed Vicar of Utrecht, the first Archbishop under the reorganization of 1561 having died in 1580. Vosmeer, who became Apostolic Vicar in 1592, and in 1602 Archbishop *in partibus infidelium*, worked indefatigably at the re-establishment of the ecclesiastical organization. The spirit of Netherlands society was so much averse from persecution for the sake of religion that Catholic priests, even though they were suspect as enemies of the State, could move about fairly freely so long as they took some elementary precautions. The scope of their labours was nevertheless confined within narrow limits. All that Vosmeer and his helpers could do was to inspire with new courage a little band of faithful souls and keep them together as a nucleus. They could not prevent the indifferent majority from gradually slipping away to where the active Reformed organization, supported by the State, could catch them up. Especially in the country-side, where their movements could more easily be watched, the Catholic priests were unable to achieve much. A further great difficulty was created by the bad relations, soon leading to open quarrel, between the secular and the regular clergy. Of these latter especially the fiery Jesuits were detested by the States as the instigators of political assassination, and were persecuted more bitterly than the others. Vosmeer's activities were seriously hampered when in 1602 the States got hold of evidence showing that he had been received by the Archdukes, and had appealed to them for support in order to have the Archbishopric of Utrecht restored. This was, not unnaturally, considered an act of high treason. Vosmeer had to fly, and thenceforward he led Catholic mission work in the United Netherlands from Köln. His principal helper, Elbertus Eggius, was kept imprisoned in the Gevangenpoort at The Hague for a couple of years.

While the Catholics were thus able to save a few small remnants, the Reformed Church, with the support of public authority, went through a period of rapid expansion. In all conquered towns and districts the Reformed Church organization was introduced without delay. The Protestantization of the people was considered as an indispensable guarantee of their loyalty to the States regime. Small wonder when one remembers the way in which Nymwegen had gone over to the other side in 1585, or when one has observed the zeal with which during the siege of Groningen the Catholic population of that town supported their magistrates in the resistance against the States' army; they had been greatly influenced by the exhortations of some Jesuits who had come to Groningen a few years before. Groningen remained for years a weak member of the body politic. Reunited with its old partner and enemy the Ommelands, it had been admitted to the Union under William Louis as Stadtholder. But the town remained so unmanageable that the States-General had a citadel built to control it, to the consternation of the citizens, who had gone through the same experience under Alva. The Reformed organization was similarly a means for the safeguarding of the State.

In all towns that fell into the power of the States the exercise of the Catholic religion was at once suppressed, and the churches were seized for the Reformed and "purged" in accordance with their ideas. In the country-side, even in

Utrecht and in those parts of Gelderland which had long been freed from the Spaniards, the Reformed Church was in the nineties hardly yet in being. As late as 1599, for instance, the Court at Arnhem had to order that "in the districts of Veluwe and Veluwezoom the altars, images, holy water basins, etc., shall be removed from the churches, as also the crucifixes and chapels, standing in forests or along roads, shall be pulled down." In the town itself, indeed, even in the following year the magistrates had to prohibit the use of pictures or crosses on palls at funerals. The slow progress in the country districts was partly caused by fear for enemy raids, partly by a more general difficulty, namely, the shortage of suitable ministers. In wide tracts of the country the peasant population had to manage for the time being without any spiritual guides at all.

A shift was generally made with the old priests, who were placed before the choice of either "holding their peace" on a small pittance, or submitting to an examination before being admitted as Reformed minister. In Groningen Province this plan worked very well; less so in Drente.[1] Here, in 1598, the Stadtholder, William Louis, having been authorized thereto by the States-General, summoned all parish priests and other secular clergy before a committee of ministers and representatives of the Stadtholder's authority. "They were solemnly asked whether they had embraced the Reformed religion in their hearts, and if so, whether they were willing to give proof of their knowledge of the pure evangelical doctrine. Many gave insufficient answers, others submitted to a theological examination, a few were even ready to be tested on the spot." Only three, however, were admitted, and not without important reservations being made. Two years afterwards a few more were passed.

In 1593 a committee instituted by the States of Utrecht made a tour of that province in order to examine the ministers and former priests. It consisted of a nobleman with two ministers and an elder of the town of Utrecht. Its report gives

---

[1] Drente, which was really the eighth province, had its own States assembly, but no session in the States-General, being too poor and sparsely inhabited. It contributed one above every hundred paid by the seven provinces.

a vivid picture of the varied and frequently very peculiar conditions prevailing. In the large majority of villages the old rectors were still living. Many of these expressed their willingness to conform, but some were obviously still hankering after the old practices, others had come over half-way and failed, either through ignorance or obstinacy, on some particular point. Of one priest, whom the committee consider to be

an honourable man, having small children, whose mother has died,

the report says:

In baptizing and marrying this rector does not follow one way, but still accommodates himself according to people's inclinations.

Several boldly refused to submit and still used to administer "the popish sacrament" at Easter, or at least manifested a suspicious reluctance to marry their "housewives." One declared that

he did not wish to have violence done to his conscience either by the States or by anybody else.

The report continues:

He has not yet married his housewife, notwithstanding our Noble Lordships the States have ordered him to do so. He even said expressly that he will not publicly marry her, adding that he was willing to give her up, as he could easily live without her, nay, he offered derisively to make a present of her to anybody who had a use for her.

To remedy all these and suchlike deplorable conditions the committee looked to the intervention of public authority, just as fifteen years earlier we saw the Ghent Synod ask the magistrates of the town to take measures against "the priests of the Mass," just as in all the seven provinces Reformed Synods were now exhorting States and town governments to proceed more vigorously against "superstitions, idolatries, abuses, and profanations."

It would be especially serviceable to this purpose [thus concluded the Utrecht commission] if all church masters were ordered by edict or in any other way to have their churches purged immediately and within a certain fixed time of the remaining altars and other relics and filth of popery. Also, the superstitious bell-ringing at noon and in the evening should equally be abolished. Etc., etc.

It is evident that, after the first spontaneous period under the oppression, the progress of the Reformation had become an essentially different movement. It is evident that the majority of the North Netherlandish people have only abandoned Catholicism under the pressure of public authority. This is not to say that there was no longer any moral force at work in the Reformed Church. The ministers' zeal for education is noticeable. No doubt they saw in education, first of all, a means for driving the old religion out of people's minds. Papist schools must be rooted out as much as possible. In the village the beadle of the new Reformed Church appeared to be the man indicated to keep school. At any rate classis-meetings and synods never tired of urging the authorities to make better provision for public instruction, and their efforts helped to form a generation which was able to follow the sermon and to read the Bible. Without a doubt they represented a higher intellectual and moral standard than that of the priests they ousted.

But that was so only because in the Northern provinces the Counter-Reformation had had no time to make its influence felt. Shaken by the attack that was directed against it, the Catholic Church had pulled itself together. The foundation of the Society of Jesus, the decrees of the Council of Trent, the organization of the new bishoprics in the Netherlands—all these were so many attempts to strengthen by a friendly reformation the powers of resistance against the hostile one. The opposition to the new bishoprics, which had so greatly retarded their actual institution; next Alva's regime of terror, which had created an atmosphere in which no religious revival could flourish; finally, the revolt—these interruptions had long hampered the effect of the Counter-Reformation on the Netherlands people. It was only in the train of Parma's conquests that this great movement made its entry in full strength. Consequently, while the North was being Protestantized under the protection of Maurice's sword, the reverse process was carried on in the South. It was by no means completed with the expulsion, immediately after the conquest, of the most convinced Protestants. Great energy was spent, under Parma, under the Archdukes, on the rebuilding of the Catholic Church. Materially and spiritually, everything lay in ruins. No matter how much impoverished the country was, keen rivalry was shown in the restoration of buildings and works of art; architects, painters, sculptors were flooded with commissions. The great abbeys had suffered heavily under the revolt, in which at first they had taken part so whole-heartedly, and had to be reorganized from the bottom. Capable and devoted men were placed in the episcopal sees. Strict supervision was given to the fitness and conduct of priests. The Jesuits, protected by the Court, established themselves in all the principal towns and obtained great influence over the well-to-do middle class as confessors and teachers. Besides the thousands who emigrated, there naturally remained behind other thousands who submitted out of mere worldly considerations. The majority, however, settled down to the restoration of the old conditions quite comfortably. Fatigued by the years of distress and weakened by the departure of so many vigorous characters as had gone to strengthen the new civilization and society in the North, they were eager to seek rest and comfort in an order of things in which Roman Church and absolute monarchy supported each other.

Under those auspices a much more complete unity could be attained than was possible in the independent provinces. Here as well as there, it should not be forgotten, the substratum of the people's life was still in the main Catholic. But, moreover, compulsion on the part of public authority could make itself felt much more severely (even though the Inquisition and the stake belonged to the past) in a monarchical and Catholic country than in a Republic which, however closely bound to Calvinism, yet recognized liberty of conscience expressly as a basic principle of its constitutional law. The difference nevertheless was one of degree only. In the last resort the position of the Reformed ascendancy in the seven provinces was based on power, just as power was the foundation of Catholicism in the South. Power not only preserved the state of the free Netherlands north of the rivers; power not only kept the southern provinces under Spain. It was power no less that brought about along the rivers, by which the course of the war had been determined, this profound moral cleavage within the Netherlands people, for which native traditions had in no sense prepared the way.

For now a stalemate had come into being. Maurice had fenced round the territory of the new Republic with a tenable strategic frontier. To push forward much beyond the rivers was as hard for him as it was for the enemy to force them. But it was to take a few years more before both sides were ready to acquiesce in the accomplished fact of the split.

d. STALEMATE

It was not only to Maurice's conquests that the North Netherlandish Republic owed its power of resistance. If the States regime had been able to check the decline to which it seemed to be succumbing at the time of Leicester's arrival, it was due, in addition to them and to Oldenbarnevelt's vigorous leadership, to the wonderful economic development that took place.

It is known to all the world [so the Amsterdam burgomaster C. P. Hooft wrote a little later] that whereas it is generally the nature of war to ruin land and people, these countries on the contrary have been noticeably improved thereby.

Behind the "fence" Holland and Zealand had been enjoying an absolute immunity ever since 1576, and while the mercenaries were garrisoned in the frontier towns or lay in camps and manœuvred on the other side of the rivers; while the sailors kept watch off Flemish ports from which privateers used to sail—Dunkirk, Nieuwpoort, Sluis—the whole of Holland and Zealand was humming with activity, and the merchant fleets, finding access to Antwerp barred, were sailing to and fro in steadily growing numbers. Communications with Germany were restored by the conquests of the Ysel towns

and of Nymwegen. But trade still mainly hinged on the exchange between the Baltic countries on the one side, and
France, Spain, and Portugal on the other. In 1590 for the
first time Holland merchantmen ventured to pass through
the Straits of Gibraltar and to enter the Mediterranean. This
was the beginning of an enormous expansion. Stimulated by
the overseas trade and by the money it brought into the
country, activity and prosperity increased by leaps and bounds
on all sides. The towns were enlarged, new harbours were
dug, in North Holland there began the reclamations which in
a few decades, by the removal of the lakes, were to change the
face of the land. In the Zaan region thousands found work
in the shipbuilding yards. Haarlem and Leyden became
centres for the linen and woollen industries which had to
leave Flanders when life grew insecure there and access to the
sea was barred.

The sea was a great factor in this amazing development.
It was in their traffic with the sea that the Hollanders could
make the most of the possibilities of their new condition. It
was the sea that opened them the way to wealth and to power,
to adventure and to greatness. They were conscious of it.

In the command of the sea and in the conduct of the war on the water
resides the entire prosperity of the country.

Thus averred the States of Holland in 1596. It does not follow
that naval matters were in a satisfactory condition. There were
no fewer than five Admiralty Colleges, a striking instance of
the harm done to sound administration by the jealousies
between provinces and towns, each of which must have its
particular interests satisfied. Three of these Colleges were in
Holland (North Holland, Amsterdam, and Maas), one in
Zealand, and one in Friesland. They had powers delegated
to them by the States-General, and only too frequently
hindered each other's work in the fitting-out of men-of-war.
They obtained their incomes out of the duties levied on trade,
and particularly on trade with the obedient provinces, the
so-called "convoy and licence" duties, in the management of
which a great deal of corruption took place. The great and

permanent problem before them was created by Dunkirk. Never did more courageous sailors go out to sea than the Flemish privateers belonging to that port. Fate disposed that their courage should not, like the zest for the sea of the Hollanders and Zealanders, contribute towards the building up of a national system for their compatriots. It was Parma who, after the capture in 1583, had transformed Dunkirk from a peaceful little fishers' town into a veritable robbers' den. The war between the Dunkirk privateers and their fellow-Dutchmen of the North was waged with fierce inhumanity. The permanent blockade of the port laid a heavy burden on the navy of the Republic, nor was it very effective. The States-General themselves made liberal issue of letters of marque, and the North Netherlands privateers, who mostly belonged to Zealand ports, were often indistinguishable from pirates. In a few cases they even joined the Barbary pirates who were infesting the Mediterranean.

More edifying than these savage doings, which demoralized the skipper class, were the expeditions sent out by the States against Spain herself, and which had more success than fell to the share of Philip's Armada in 1588. The first of these was undertaken in concert with the English in 1596. The most famous is that of 1607, when the States' fleet, under the command of Jacob van Heemskerck, attacked and destroyed the Spanish fleet on the roadstead of Gibraltar and under the batteries of the castle. While the warfare on land, with the foreign auxiliaries, the innumerable foreigners even in the States' pay, the foreign noblemen surrounding the princely commander, could never create a really national tradition—not during the whole period of the Republic's existence—these activities at sea were the beginnings of a great story in which the people would see their own kindred glorified. Wealthy Holland was beginning to attract mercenaries and adventurers from all sides, and many Germans and Scandinavians served in the navy too, but the leading positions—in striking contrast to conditions prevailing in the army—were always occupied by Netherlanders, generally promoted from before the mast.

The same is true of the colonial enterprises which began

about this time, and which were of course intimately connected with the merchant service as well as with the navy. A man like Heemskerck, for instance, had graduated in that school. These expeditions were the beginnings of a splendid adventure, which was to demand of the Netherlands people, in so far as they had escaped from the stifling embrace of the foreign monarchy with its bureaucratic and aristocratic regime, the highest tests of enterprise and organizing ability, of war and of statecraft. Quite apart from the material advantages, the heavy task, of which even to-day has not seen the completion, was to call forth a wealth of personalities out of all classes of the Netherlands people; it added treasures to the store of national legend; it broadened the national horizon.

The navigation to America and the Indies sprang in the most natural fashion from the trade in Europe. While Castile maintained a monopoly for the intercourse with America, Portugal, which since 1580 also owed allegiance to Philip, barred the Indian Ocean to all would-be intruders. The Hollanders, however, were indispensable to both, so much so that although the Spanish Government once or twice yielded to the temptation to strike at the rebels by seizing their ships in the Spanish and Portuguese ports, it could not long maintain the embargo. These measures nevertheless whetted the desire of the Holland and Zealand merchants to establish direct communications. The Atlantic Ocean was soon crossed for the profitable smuggling trade in Brazil. The route to the Indies, however, ran right through the Portuguese sphere of influence, and seemed so beset with perils that between 1590 and 1595 the States of Zealand, the States-General, the town of Amsterdam financed several expeditions for the purpose of discovering a navigable way round the north of Asia. Maurice took a keen personal interest in these ventures. But in 1595 a consortium of Amsterdam merchants sent four vessels south under the command of Cornelis Houtman. Jan Huigen van Linschoten and Petrus Plancius assisted in preparing for the voyage; the former had been at Goa in Portuguese employment, and had just written his famous description of the Portuguese Empire; the latter, a Reformed Minister, driven out of Flanders by Parma's conquests, had made profound studies of geography and navigation. In 1597 three of Hout-man's four ships returned with a cargo of pepper and other spices obtained in the Malay Archipelago. Proof had been furnished that the thing could be done. Forces of energy and capital, long contained, immediately burst forth. Several "Companies of Afar" sprang up overnight. In 1598 no fewer than twenty-two ships sailed to the Indies from the Texel, the Maas, and the Scheldt. A new world opened for sailors, traders, adventurers—a wonderful world with new beauties, new peoples, new dangers. Journals and accounts of the voyages were eagerly read. Merchants scented profits, states-men saw the enemy's power hit in a sensitive spot.

For the one purpose as well as for the other concentration and co-operation soon proved indispensable. In lands where the Portuguese held most of the strategic points strongly occupied and where native society was constantly kept con-vulsed by wars and general insecurity, unbridled competition could not but lead to disaster. It was desired, moreover, to establish monopolies. The natives, especially in the Spice Islands, the Moluccas, were to be forced to trade with the Dutch to the exclusion of every other nation. Power was needed. In the young Republic, born out of opposition against an oppressive central authority, all private interests fought their own battles without caring much for unity or govern-ment, and circumstances were so favourable that this was on the whole the best way for the nation's vital forces to develop. The idea of a privileged Company was uncongenial therefore, and in spite of the energetic intervention of the States-General much persuasion was required before the various Companies could agree to combine. The United Dutch East India Com-pany, which was formed in 1602, is one of Oldenbarnevelt's greatest creations. The capital subscribed was very consider-able; the Company was given a monopoly of trade between the Cape of Good Hope and Cape Magelhaes; complete sovereign rights within the same area were delegated to her. Possessing vessels of war, and soon fortresses and troops, the Company, which disposed of a great freedom of movement while in the last resort remaining dependent on the States-General, was a formidable weapon in the struggle with Spain as well as a capable gatherer of wealth. Many small purses had contributed to the capital, but the shareholders had no real control over the directors. The constitution of the Company gave to the magistrates of the trading towns in which the various "Chambers" were situated a large say in the appointment of the latter. The Company thus became intimately connected with the "regent" oligarchy of the two maritime provinces, which in course of time owed to it an increase in both political power and wealth.

In the whole of this brilliant economic movement the share of the South Netherlandish exiles was most considerable. Without the capital of the Antwerpers who had come north after the fall of the town, without their commercial knowledge and relations, Holland, small and in some respects still backward area, could not possibly have risen to the opportunities that were offered her so suddenly. Under Leicester's government, as we saw, the Flemings and Brabanders had not yet quite "settled down," so that they formed an element of political unrest. Soon, however, most of them were infected with the fever of money-making which was getting a grip on Holland and Zealand, and they prospered too well to spend all their time looking back longingly to their own provinces. In all bold enterprises, requiring initiative and breadth of vision, the exiles did their bit. No man worked in closer contact with the States and Maurice for the expeditions round the north than Balthazar de Moucheron, an Antwerper of French origin, who after the siege (during which he had been one of the colonels of the citizenship) had settled at Middelburg; he also undertook expeditions to Guinea planned in a strikingly big fashion. Another enterprising Antwerp merchant was Isaac Lemaire, whose name survives, however, mainly on account of the conflict into which he got later on with the Company's monopoly. But countless are the smaller men of Flemish and Brabant origin who rose to fortune by trade at home or made their way in the Company's service abroad.

What a contrast is presented by the bright and colourful

life of the North, in which the emigrants played their parts with so much zest, and the dreary dullness of the land where the foreigner had succeeded in restoring his rule! If Holland and Zealand flourished, it was partly because they fed on the best vital forces of Flanders and Brabant. The war, which "noticeably improved" them, had truly "spoilt" the Southern provinces. Trade was at a standstill, the towns impoverished with countless houses empty, wide regions lay open to the States' cavalry, which now (like the Spanish had been wont to do some years previously in Gelderland and Friesland) from their bases at Breda, Ostend, and other places, laid Flanders and Brabant under contribution. Meanwhile the Spanish soldiery had not changed. They still were formidable to the enemy when they had a mind to fight, but too often they broke out into mutiny and made themselves formidable only to the obedient populations. In 1598 the Antwerpers were rudely reminded of the events of 1576. The garrison of the citadel mutinied and demanded payment of the citizens by firing cannon-shots.

Which made many people flee with their money and most valued possessions, being in great anxiety and at all hours of the day uncertain of their lives and goods. The Spaniards grew so bold that they considered it to be a great courtesy on their part when, instead of summoning the magistrates by means of canon-shots to come to them as they would call their lackeys, they wrote letters to these gentlemen: "A los de la casa de la Villa," that is to say, "to those of the town-hall," without giving them any title.

Small wonder that the Southerners longed fervently for the end of the war, and that, much more than did their more fortunate brethren in the North, they treasured in their hearts the memory of the lost unity of the Netherlands.

In 1598 the States-General were called together to Brussels in order to learn from the Archduke Albert that he was to marry Philip II's daughter Isabella, and that the King intended to cede to them, with the approval of his son and heir, the sovereignty over the Netherlands. Albert set out to fetch his bride, too late to find Philip alive. The old King, who had for forty years pursued the visions of Spanish world power

and of a Catholic Europe—indissolubly connected in his mind
—had died at the moment when his policy had definitely come
to grief. Just as in his father's life so in his, while a single
great aim is tenaciously kept in view, one scheme is generally
coming up before the other has been done with, until all
together threaten to go under in financial catastrophe. Yet he
left the tradition in its full strength to his heirs, and the transference of the Netherlands by no means meant that they would
no longer be expected to act as an advanced post in northern
Europe in the service of his double ideal.

It was only in outward appearance that Philip met the
Netherlands' desire for independence. He hoped, and so did
the South Netherlanders, that this would be enough to win over
the rebels. Richardot, the new President of the Privy Council,
a Burgundian like Granvelle, and the marquess of Havré, a
brother of Aerschot (who had died shortly before), used the
good offices of an emigrant Antwerper, Daniel van der Meulen,
in an attempt to make the North Netherlandish statesmen see
that it must now be possible to conclude peace. They too—
so they gave to understand—were heartily sick of the Spaniards;
a bare recognition of the Archdukes' right would be sufficient;
everything could remain as it was, the Nassaus and the States
in power, free exercise of religion. But as soon as Van der
Meulen, who visited Brussels with a passport, wanted to
know whether the Reformed would be allowed to return to
the South, he was met with evasive replies. What could be
the use of a reunion when in the two parts opposite principles
of government were to remain in force? Such an arrangement
could the less appeal to the States since they still felt far from
certain of their population, which would in the event of a
peace on those lines be exposed to influences from the re-
Catholicized South. But the principal objection was that the
independence of the Archdukes was a mere sham, and that,
no matter what Richardot and Havré said about the Spaniards,
the States understood perfectly well that the Southern Netherlands remained on the leash of Spain. Indeed, all precautions
had been taken that they should never fall to another dynasty.
In case Albert and Isabella came to die without issue, the

country would revert to Spain; the Spanish troops remained in the principal fortresses; for the carrying-on of war the new state was, as much as the former dependency had been, dependent on the subsidies, and therefore on the behests, of Spain.

How was it possible to think that the free States-General would let themselves be deceived by that appearance? It was merely inviting an utterly useless humiliation when, at the solemn assembly of the States-General at Brussels to welcome the new sovereign, benches were placed for deputies from the seven Northern as well as for those from the other provinces. And when they remained empty, the Archduke still could not leave it at that. He addressed to his unwilling subjects a letter not less mild than the one to which his brother Ernest had received so crushing a reply. At the same time the Brussels States-General, too, wrote to those at The Hague. The reply, given almost a year later, in March 1599, pitilessly exposed the weak spot in the position of the Southerners. The insufferable excesses committed, since the receipt of their letter, by the Spanish soldiery at Antwerp, thus wrote the Northern States-General, had caused them to hope that "their Reverences, Excellencies, and Worships," the States-General of the South, recognizing the single aim of the Northerners,

to wit, that we might one day see the Netherlands as a whole truly liberated from the Spaniards and their adherents, your and our sworn enemies, would have declared yourselves against the aforesaid horrible practices. But since we observe ever more clearly that the Spaniards and their adherents possess among your Reverences, Excellencies, and Worships so much power that they can prevent this happening, we, after thanking you for your good favour and affection and commending ourselves to you in right friendly fashion, do not know what to reply except that we firmly believe your Reverences, Excellencies, and Worships to be as well aware of the means and ways needed for your and our common liberation as we are ourselves. Meanwhile we beg your Reverences, Excellencies, and Worships to hold it for an incontrovertible truth that the Spaniards and their adherents cannot be got out of the Netherlands by means of any negotiation or treaty, but only by force of arms.

The letter ended with an assurance that in case of the Southern

States "taking up arms with us against the common enemy," they would be left free to settle religion and administration in accordance with their own views. The exhortation to revolt found no echo in the disheartened and enfeebled South. So desperate was the situation, however, that the Archdukes—in 1599 Albert had brought Isabella home to Brussels—were compelled to swallow the insult contained in the Hague States' reply, and in 1600 once more invoked the help of an assembly of the States-General in order to lure the Northerners into negotiations. In the ensuing discussion between the new sovereigns and the deputies of their faithful provinces it became clear at once how well the position had been understood at The Hague. The Brussels States attempted to arm themselves with a little independence in view of the forthcoming negotiations: they desired to be authorized to conclude with the Northern States a peace or a truce. It deserves attention that the Walloon provinces opposed this pacifist policy, which was promoted by Flanders, Brabant, and Upper Gelderland; the Walloons suffered less directly from the war, but at the same time the idea of Netherlands unity appealed to them less strongly. In any case there was not the slightest possibility of the Brussels States being left to act thus untutored. When the Archdukes refused to let the decision pass out of their hands, the States had to be content with the more modest task—but which in view of the temper in the North was bound to fail—of opening a conversation in order to consult with their sovereigns about the reply. So they drew up a letter (and asked obediently for the Archdukes' approval of it), in which they said no more than that they hoped it would be possible to find a way out of the labyrinth of war, if only they could come together "in talk and negotiation." As it was known by previous experience that the Northern States refused to accept from the Southern letters composed in French, the letter, which had been drafted in that language for the benefit of the Walloons and the Archducal Court, was translated into Dutch.

The reply, no less than that of 1599, went straight to the heart of the difficulty, which the helpless deputies of the South had on the contrary done their utmost to cover up. The Hague States showed not the least eagerness to meet any delegates of the other side, and observed:

To the great regret of all patriots we learn from a reliable source that the coming of your delegates would be directed under the authority of the Archdukes, and that a promise has been given to do nothing that might be prejudicial to their authority. From which it is concluded that this commission of yours (as tending towards the promotion of such illegitimate and harmful authority) utterly conflicts with the prosperity of the Netherlands.

Before a reply could be sent from Brussels to enable the appointed negotiators to undertake the useless journey—the Archdukes overlooking the fresh insult—an attempt of a quite different nature to restore peace and unity was undertaken by the North.

Oldenbarnevelt and the Northern States had, it will be easily understood, concluded from their correspondence with those of the South that the Archdukes' authority must be tottering. That consideration was a factor towards the decision they took to send Maurice with his army on a bold enterprise into Flanders. As the Spanish army was once again paralysed by a serious mutiny, they could wish for no better opportunity. The principal aim of the expedition was to be the capture of the privateering ports, Nieuwpoort and Dunkirk, but it was hoped at the same time that the appearance of the States' army would rouse the people of Flanders and that the position of Yper, Ghent, and Brugge would become untenable, if not at once, then after the occupation of the coast-line. Unfortunately Maurice held a different view. The plan seemed to him unsound, and he prepared for it reluctantly.

Relations between Maurice and the States, which unswervingly followed the lead of Oldenbarnevelt, were in many respects difficult. They were the sovereign, theirs was the responsibility for the conduct of the war, for which, moreover, they had to find the money—a heavy task in spite of the prosperity of the country. Yet Maurice was more—and he knew it—than simply a soldier in their service. He was the son of the great William of Orange, who was to have been the sovereign.

His campaigns had brought to him an enormous personal popularity. He lived in princely style, his income from war contributions and privateering being very large. In the army camp he was surrounded by hundreds of French and German noblemen who, attracted by his fame, came to learn the art of war under him. In that circle the supreme authority of the burgher States was looked upon as a freak. Undoubtedly he himself often chafed at his position, but actually it was in consultation with the States that he drew up all his plans of campaign, and he recognized their right to give orders to him, which, in fact, they did not hesitate to do when necessary. On a later occasion, for instance, being engaged in a deliberation with the States-General and Council of State about a certain projected enterprise, he described it as "not feasible and too hazardous," but he adds:

Unless the worshipful States were pleased to order them [meaning himself and William Louis] to act otherwise, in which case they, as being the servants of the worshipful States, will be found willing to conduct themselves accordingly with all possible zeal, industry, and duty.

Differences of opinion nearly always turned on this, that Maurice was thought too cautious by the States, or that he blamed them for recklessly staking their army and his reputation. The expedition into Flanders of 1600 fortified each side in its judgment of the other. To me, however, it seems undeniable—and there lies the importance of the event in this history—that Maurice failed to give its due to the last chance of breaking through the fatal equilibrium in which the split of the Netherlands was beginning to be stabilized.

It is certain that the States had underestimated the dangers. In spite of the flying leaflets announcing the coming of Maurice's army to deliver them from the Spanish yoke, the population of Flanders did not stir when the Northerners marched southward, almost touching Brugge. The full assembly of the States-General had gone to Ostend in order to be able to confer with Maurice. Already he had passed that town, when most unexpectedly the Archduke appeared with a con-

siderable army. Isabella herself had succeeded in persuading
the Spanish mutineers at Diest to return to their duty. Near
Nieuwpoort Maurice found himself cut off from his base at
Ostend, and had to give battle in order to avoid a disaster.
He gave battle on the beach and won a complete victory.
Instead of making use of it, however, he soon broke up the
siege of Nieuwpoort, undertaken after the battle at the insistence of the States, and embarked with his troops at Ostend
to be carried back to the Scheldt.

The States had departed before him. Oldenbarnevelt and
a number of deputies (three emigrant Brabanders among them)
had gone to Bergen-op-Zoom, where they met the envoys of
the Brussels States: the Count of Bassigny (Brabant), Colonel
Bentinck Lord of Bicht (Upper Quarter of Gelderland), and
Codt (pensionary of Yper). The chasm separating the position
and ideas of the Northerners from those of the Southerners
was revealed without delay. Oldenbarnevelt, as if continuing
the correspondence in which the parties had been engaged,
remarked that the Southern negotiators apparently lacked
powers to conclude anything without the Archdukes, so that
negotiating with the former really amounted to negotiating
with the latter, and ultimately with Spain, since the Archdukes
were inseparable from Spain. Codt, who had been among
Hembyze's prisoners at Ghent in October 1577, replied un-
compromisingly:

that the aforesaid States [at Brussels], being subject to their natural
princes, could not withdraw their allegiance and dutiful obedience
from them.

There was the rub. At Bergen-op-Zoom sovereigns faced
subjects. No matter how urgently Oldenbarnevelt exhorted
the Southerners to turn Maurice's victory to their advantage
and to rise, the reply was that the removal of the Spaniards

could be effected in a better and more Christian way by a good peace
than by violence, by which we should plunge this unfortunate country
into a new war.

This left, indeed, no more to be said on either side, and
although the majority of the Brussels States-General on re-

ceiving the report of their deputies wished to write to The Hague once more, the Archduke now intervened and made an end of the negotiations—if negotiations can be called what from the side of the Northerners had been no more than exhortations to rise.

The Netherlands historian may hesitate whether to criticize the Brabant and Flemish deputies for their submissiveness or to blame the Hollanders for having been too inflexible. However much he may deplore the confirmation which the split of the Netherlands received from an impact like that of Bergen-op-Zoom, he will have to admit that neither side could have acted differently. Consciousness of common nationhood was certainly not lacking in that tragic meeting. Oldenbarnevelt was continuing the tradition of William the Silent when, leaving aside the religious differences, he called upon all Netherlanders to join in the fight against Spain. But the fact was that he and the Northerners stood there as free republicans, accustomed to administer their own affairs and to give orders to their princely army-chiefs. And although silence was kept about religion, none the less did they stand there as Reformed, whose position in their own country still seemed to require active enmity against Spain.

The Southerners, on the other hand, were no more than the representatives of a defeated people, impoverished and exhausted. Twice had the South risked a revolt, both times it had been struck down. It had lost its economic prosperity, and its bravest and most enterprising men, who were now steeling the strength of the North. It is not to be wondered at that the idea of a new revolt could not inspire the Brussels States. The spring had been broken. Besides, their impotence was not merely moral, it was physical.

The States of Brabant, Flanders, etc., mastered by castles and garrisons, had no other means for promoting the peace than their humble remonstrances, setting out how needful peace was to them, wretchedly lamenting about the war and the unpaid soldiery.

Thus writes the chronicler Van Meteren, with respect to the situation of a few years later, and Buzanval, the French

Ambassador in The Hague, in this same year 1600 deprecates the possibilities of a revolt in the South, recalling

the gripping bit by which they are held.

There was one thing more. It was all very well for the Northerners to make solemn promises that in case of a successful rising in the South they would leave religion and government as they were. But experience had shown that revolt inevitably threw up a new leading class to be the bearer of Protestantism. The members of the States of Brabant, Flanders, Upper Quarter of Gelderland, clergy, nobility, magistrates, felt that their personal positions were at stake. Just as nearly thirty years earlier the magistrates of Amsterdam, just as less than ten years before the magistrates of Groningen, they felt that they would be unable to maintain themselves without Catholicism. That being so, they had to take the Archdukes, and even the Spaniards, into the bargain.

And yet they imagined that they could still carry on the old policy of opposition. Being good Netherlanders they were offended by the servile ceremonial at court, in accordance with which Richardot addressed the Archdukes kneeling. They desired to supervise the Spanish troops and to have a share in the administration of the subsidies, which they were indeed still obstinately refusing. Then to their consternation Richardot came to dismiss them in the name of his masters, telling them at the same time that the subsidies asked for would be looked upon by the Government as having obtained their consent. In their conflicts with the true wielders of power in their own country as well as with the true States-General in the North, the Brussels States appeared to be no more than a shadow-show. They vanished uttering idle protests, and thirty years were to elapse before, in even more depressing circumstances, they were again called together—so that they might go through the same hollow performance once more.

The Southern Netherlands were no longer the masters of their souls. No share was left to the people in the direction of the country's higher interests, nor could it be otherwise since this direction was still determined by Spain. The privileged classes had to console themselves with the miserable local self-government saved from the wreck, but a class of national statesmen, reared in an atmosphere of active and enlightened interest in national policy, such as existed in the North, was beyond the reach of the enslaved Netherlands.

Battle was joined once more between the Northern States-General and the Archdukes, who indeed stood for Spain. It has been briefly noticed above that the respective forces kept each other balanced on land. Philip III's zeal for the war equalled that of his father, but Spain was too severely exhausted to be able to profit by the isolation into which the Republic was falling. It was considered necessary, first of all, to get hold of Ostend. Maurice's invasion of Flanders had shown up the dangers inherent in the continued occupation of that place by the Northerners. The States of Flanders raised special subsidies in order to be rid of that post from whence a wide circle of their country could be laid under contribution. But as the defending troops could be continually supplied, strengthened, and replaced, owing to the free communication by sea with the North, the siege, to the astonishment of Europe, was dragged out for three years and swallowed treasures of blood and money. While the enemy was being kept riveted to that place, Maurice took Grave and Rheinberg (the latter town had changed hands once more since he ejected the Spanish garrison in 1597), and just before the end Aardenburg and Sluis. By the capture of these two places south of the Scheldt the menace to Zealand was eliminated, the approaches to Antwerp were more strongly guarded, and new *points d'appui* were gained, not less useful than Ostend itself, for laying the Flemish country-side under contribution.

The man to whom in 1604 the blackened ruins that had been Ostend were surrendered was Ambrosio Spinola, of Genoa, who had come, with his brother Federigo, to place his fortune and his talents at the service of Spain and of the Catholic Church. Federigo, who some years earlier had conducted his own Mediterranean galleys to Sluis, had already been killed when Ambrosio was entrusted with the direction of the siege and showed himself to be a born general. In 1605

Philip III compelled the Archduke to leave the command-in-chief to Spinola. At the same time the Genoese upstart, created Marquess and Knight of the Fleece, was designated to be the King's Governor in the Netherlands in case the sickly Albert came to die. The childless Archdukes were overshadowed by the brilliant stranger who enjoyed the confidence of Spain. Hardly the semblance of independence was left.

In the two years following upon the conquest of Ostend, when, moreover, the international situation had grown even more unfavourable for the North owing to the peace concluded between Spain and England after Elizabeth's death, Spinola led his army against the eastern frontier of the Republic. He proved to be a formidable adversary. Maurice followed his movements carefully all the time, secured the Ysel against an attack with masterly tactics, but avoided any direct engagement. In 1606 Spinola, after having recaptured Grol, marched away to take Rheinberg once more. In his absence Maurice lost no time in laying siege to Grol, but when Spinola, even though his army was weakened by yet another mutiny and his troops thoroughly fatigued, returned to drive him away, he broke up at once without giving battle. This made a painful impression in the Republic. The year ended with Oldenzaal and Grol in Spanish hands.

On both sides meanwhile the feeling was growing in intensity that no decision could be come to in this way. The net result of nine summer campaigns (1598–1606) was a few towns gained and a few towns lost. Nothing was altered in the large lines of the situation. The statesmen of the Republic felt concern about the state of the finances. Much more depressing, however, was the condition of the subjected Netherlands, and the Archdukes were longing for the end of a war which seemed to hold out no prospects. Spain, too, was panting for breath. The penury of the public exchequer became unbearable. The young navy of the States—it was in 1607 that Heemskerk's fleet carried out its famous coup off Gibraltar—gave rise to fears for the safety of the Spanish Plate Fleets from America. Spinola himself was discouraged and wished for peace in order to get back the large sums of money he had advanced to Spain.

e. CONCLUSION OF THE TWELVE YEARS' TRUCE

The first moves were made as early as 1606. The States replied that no negotiations were possible so long as the other side continued to maintain any claims conflicting with the resolution of abjuration of 1581 and with the established right of the Netherlands, which had been recognized as a free state by the greatest kingdoms. So the Archdukes signed a statement in which they expressed their readiness to negotiate with the United Netherlands

in the capacity of, and as taking them for, free lands, provinces, and towns, against which they claim nothing.

On that basis an armistice was at once concluded in April 1607 on conditions wholly favourable to the North. It still cost some trouble to obtain the assent of Spain, and so it was not until February 1608 that peace negotiations could begin at The Hague. There was now no longer even a pretence that it was the representatives of the South Netherlands people who came to meet the Hague States-General. The preliminary exploration of the ground had been made for the Brussels Government by Dutch-speaking Netherlanders, of whom the Brabander Father Neyen became the best known, and he continued to play a very secondary part in the latter stages. But throughout, everything was done in the name of the Archdukes and of Spain. During the negotiations proper Spinola and Richardot were at the head of a delegation representing Philip III as well as Albert and Isabella. It was agreed fairly easily, although the Archdukes had hoped to get back the fragments of Flanders and Brabant occupied by the States by exchanging them for Oldenzaal and Grol, that the territorial separation would be effected on the principle of *uti possidetis*. The demand which resulted in a deadlock was one in which only Spanish interests were concerned, although Richardot had to stand by it. It was the demand that the North Netherlanders should abandon the navigation to the Indies. There also was a serious dispute over the position of Catholics in the Republic. Philip III (and in this no doubt the Archdukes were whole-heartedly with him) felt that it was due to his honour to obtain freedom of worship for his co-religionists; the States, however, declined all interference with their domestic arrangements. Yet the really unsurmountable obstacle was the question of the Indian trade, and in September the negotiators left The Hague. France and England, however, who had played the part of mediators throughout, now intervened somewhat more emphatically. Now that peace appeared to be unattainable, they put pressure on the States to consent to a truce for a number of years.

Public opinion in the Republic was violently agitated. There was a war party, which had from the first followed the negotiations with vociferous suspiciousness, launching bitter attacks and insinuations against Oldenbarnevelt, whom everyone knew to be the moving spirit. A stream of pamphlets burst forth. From the pulpit there resounded denunciations of the bad patriots. To many zealots any treaty with Spain appeared to be a betrayal of the cause of the revolt. It cannot indeed be denied that a truce or a peace, concluded while the Spaniards still kept their grip on the Southern Netherlands, signified an acquiescence in the partial failure of the national programme. But was it possible for the Republic, especially now that France and England were threatening their displeasure, to bear the financial burden of a continuation of the war, let alone to drive the Spaniards out of the Southern Netherlands? Maurice's last campaigns were hardly of a nature to inspire any such hopes.

Yet Maurice, after having privately worked against Oldenbarnevelt's policy for some time, in September 1608 openly came forward as leader of the war party. The letter which he sent out to the States of those provinces of which he was Stadtholder deserves our attention. Uttering a warning against the deceitfulness of the Spaniards, he merely pleaded for the necessity of an absolute recognition on their part of the independence of the United Provinces—that is to say, he declared against the compromise of a truce. It would, in his opinion, result in an ambiguous situation, in a "reunion" full of dangers. That is all he had to say on the question of Nether-

lands unity. The hope that Flanders and Brabant could still
be liberated, and especially that they could still be united on
the only terms acceptable to the war party, namely, through
Protestantization—that hope had become faint indeed after the
disappointment of the Flanders expedition and the negotiations
of Bergen-op-Zoom.

The objections to the truce came mainly from those who
in the spirit were living in an earlier period, when the party
of resistance, strongly impregnated with Calvinist zeal, still
had to found the state. Those men had difficulty in adapting
themselves to the new situation in which the state existed and
in which the need was for normal conditions. Maurice still
felt that his own position and the entire constitution of the
state were the products of the war, and were dependent upon
it for their consolidation. In the letter mentioned above he
gave as a principal reason why it was impossible to do without Spain's absolute recognition of Northern Netherlands
independence, the following:

in order to make it plain to our own citizens that they must not
expect another sun to rise, which, failing that recognition, they will
be told will happen.

Van Meteren is even more explicit when he writes that fears
were entertained especially on account of

those of Gelderland, Overysel, and Groningen, who had come to arms
under compulsion; in which provinces the nobility has the most
votes, and these, having their possessions in the country-side, would
keep out of the danger [of a renewal of the war] and seek the support
of the most powerful.

Maurice's attitude in this affair brought him the acclamations
of the very groups against which in the days of Leicester he
had let himself be used, and which were now overjoyed to
see him make a stand against their old enemy Oldenbarnevelt.
Only it should not be thought that what this party wanted
was a restoration of the Netherlands community which the
war had torn asunder. No doubt the Flemings and Brabanders,
in so far as they belonged to the Reformed Church, still constituted a chief support of the ministers who were now again

fulminating against the States. In their new surroundings they still hung together as a distinct group, with which orthodoxy and an irreconcilable hatred of Spain had become traditional. At the same time, however, most of them were now too well off in Holland and Zealand to worry seriously about returning to the South, even though their acquiescence was mingled with that wistfulness which is suppressed but not concealed in some beautiful lines of Van Mander. After having recalled the church spire of his native village in Flanders, the poet says:

> But this is done. I now will deceive myself
> And consider all that country covered with salt sea.
> To have exchanged it for this is now no sorrow to me.

Van Mander, it should be added, was not a Calvinist, but a Baptist. All that the bitter-enders were able to do, at any rate, was to make even more irretrievable the moral separation which had already entered upon the heels of the political events. If need be they would admit the accomplished fact of the re-Catholicization of the South, but in their eagerness to complete the Protestantization of the North they looked upon the resumption of normal relations as so much the more objectionable.

Inevitably material interests were mixed up with these considerations of a higher nature. Powerful groups saw their advantage in a continuation of the war. In the first place the military; next the privateers, in whose activities the Zealand trading world was deeply concerned; also the war contractors of all descriptions. Finally, there were those who had for a considerable time already been preparing for the foundation of a West Indies Company, a project directed against Spain's own colonial territory in America, and which Oldenbarnevelt therefore, as soon as the negotiations were opened, strove to suppress. The Antwerper Usselinx was the fervent propagandist of that scheme. In his imagination he saw prosperous settlements, which would transplant to America Netherlands nationality and Reformed religion, thus providing the mother country with vigorous assistance as well as with valuable

I

markets. Unfortunately the theory of colonization, such as Usselinx developed it in masterly pamphlets, never appealed to the rulers of the North Netherlands state, and the Amsterdamers who made use of his services certainly were more interested in privateering raids at the expense of the Spanish colonies than in the founding of settlements of their own race. In any case the project was inconsistent with either peace or truce, and it had therefore to give way before the need of rest which actuated Oldenbarnevelt's policy, and which, indeed, was so generally felt that the opposition to the negotiations proved to be a good deal less firm that it was violent. Even before the end of the year 1608 Maurice, Zealand, and Amsterdam accepted the inevitable, and in March 1609, after further conversations at Antwerp, a truce was concluded for a period of twelve years.

It was for the Seven Provinces an astonishing victory. On practically every point that had been under discussion the Archdukes and Spain gave way. The recognition of independence with which the negotiations had opened (and which, even though on account of the word *as* it could not be called absolute, actually left little to be desired) was repeated. Trade with the Indies was not explicitly prohibited. The Catholics in the North obtained no protection, except, by a separate agreement, those in the districts torn from Brabant, which the States-General kept. The Scheldt was not explicitly thrown open for navigation to and from Antwerp. To the Southern Netherlands the treaty gave nothing but twelve years of rest. How much more did it give to the Northern provinces!

There the Netherlands race had acquired a territory—unfortunately no more than half of that on which it had a claim in nature—where, under its own political direction, it could form its own civilization. The Republic had succeeded in maintaining its independence, in the course of a generation of war, against the most powerful monarchy of the world. More, that empire had almost bled to death from the wound it had received in the Netherlands. The self-confidence of the North Netherlands people was heightened, and indeed the other European Powers, too, were impressed, when they saw proud Spain in so much need of a breathing-space as to submit to the humiliations of the Treaty of Truce. The territory of the States—the entire history of the last thirty-seven years went to prove it and is itself explained by the fact—was strongly situated. The eastern frontier was now lightly encroached upon once more, and in any case was not yet based very firmly upon the great rivers—the Rhine being in States' possession only up to Schenkenschans, the Maas only up to Grave. But apart from that, the natural strategic lines of defence had not only been attained but had been confirmed by the occupation of posts beyond. The States had even continued the movement of expansion of the Burgundian-Habsburg rulers, and had pushed on outside the seventeen provinces. Rheinberg had not ultimately remained in their possession, but, making use of the dissensions between the town of Emden and the pro-Spanish Count, they had in 1595 occupied several places in East Friesland. This looked like the beginning of an annexation, and in any case directed the political life of that country towards The Hague for a long time to come. Everywhere the Netherlands remaining under Spain had been pushed back from the water, except for the seacoast, which from Heist to Grevelingen had now been freed from States' occupation. But this flat and straight Flemish coast had never been the true entrance to the country. That was the Scheldt, which on both sides was held by the States—albeit with the English for the time being at Flushing—and in spite of a general guarantee of free intercourse between North and South in the Treaty of Truce, the States, and especially the States of Zealand, took advantage of their position to force any ships on their way from or to Antwerp to break cargo. Antwerp remained a big dead town. It was now mainly the motive of commercial competition that inspired the Scheldt policy of the Hollanders and Zealanders, but the original motive had been a different one and it still counted: Antwerp could not be left free to become a busy port again, where a native merchant fleet might be developed, as long as it was not what nature had meant it to be, a Netherlands town, but on the contrary was a weapon in Spanish hands.

Next to the geographical configuration of their country, it was to their superiority at sea and on the rivers that the Northerners owed their independence. Under the provisions the Truce, which left to the States the most part of the river-courses in the Netherlands as well as all the estuaries and sea arms, and which, moreover, did not prevent their navigation to the Indies, that superiority could be fully developed—and always with the help of the trading resources in men and capital that had been wilfully expelled from the South. In the next generation or two the Republic was thus to rise to undreamt-of heights of prosperity and power, but it must be added that the international constellation created, during most of that time, exceptionally favourable circumstances.

Yet these could not but be temporary. As soon as they began to fail the Republic, it became apparent that she, with all her advantages of situation and of trade, was a small-sized state, very small indeed in the midst of the Great Powers of Europe. North Netherlands historians have often praised the fate by which the forces of the whole of the Netherlands people were drawn together on that small territory north of the rivers, since as a consequence this narrow strip of land became the scene of an incomparable splendour of political, economic, and intellectual life. This view betrays a sad lack of imagination. Those whom it satisfies must turn a blind eye on the political, economic, and intellectual misery which that concentration was to bring to the southern half of the Netherlands people. We shall in our last chapter see something of the contrast that was provided during the last decades of our period by the buoyant intellectual activity in the North and the desolation in the South. It would be difficult indeed to look upon that unnatural spectacle and rejoice.

It is true that at the time the North seemed so much the darling of fortune that not even the emigrant Flemings and Brabanders could fully realize that the split was a disaster to the Netherlands people as a whole. As a matter of fact the consequences to the South were without comparison heavier. Brabant and Flanders, only a generation earlier the heart of the Netherlands people, the rich source out of which had been drawn so many of the best forces now helping to build up the young state in the North, were lying overpowered and disheartened, under the cloak of a national Government subjected more helplessly than ever to a foreign ruler and destined only to serve his policy. No doubt the Catholic spirit, which owed to the conqueror its triumphant return, again possessed spiritual creativeness now that it had been rejuvenated by the Counter-Reformation. As soon as the worst war misery had subsided, during the Truce, a cultural life of marked character grew up in the South, Antwerp and Leuven being the centres. But circumstances were really too unpropitious. The deadness of economic life, the lack of independence paralysing political life, the renewed conjunction with the Walloon provinces under a foreign court, the gallicized nobility possessing greater influence than ever, and this at a time when the war and the difference of religion were raising obstacles in the intellectual intercourse with the suddenly emancipated North—all these factors could not but weigh heavily, to the detriment of the entire Dutch-speaking community, on the civilization of Dutch-speaking Flanders and Brabant.

In addition to this the unnatural restriction of its territory involved dangers for the North and its state and society. Exhaustion soon followed upon the overstrain of "the golden age"; that splendour was short-lived. Speaking politically, the weakness of the Southern Netherlands was very far from being an unmixed benefit to the Dutch Republic. That unhappy country was but a fragment of the Burgundian state which fate had overtaken in its rise, a fragment with indefensible frontiers, which, as it were, offered a standing invitation to invaders. Had the Archdukes been able to pursue a truly South Netherlandish policy, they would have sought the friendship of the North in order to be covered on one side at least. Since they were but the agents of Spain, the war with the Republic was resumed after the Truce, and the menace of France, reinvigorated under Richelieu, held therefore the greater danger. Long before the peace of Munster, the northward expansion of France at the expense of the Southern Netherlands began to rouse uneasiness at The Hague.

No more proof can be required that the split of the Netherlands had not merely weakened the powers of resistance of
the Southern provinces, but that it had compromised the safety
of the whole of the Netherlands race, which in the Middle
Ages already had found in Flanders a bulwark against the
French advance.

After the account given in the last three chapters it is unnecessary to subject to a set criticism the view, which has long
been current, and according to which the split was determined
by some inherent divergence within the Netherlands people.
A Protestant North (not without numerous Catholics however)
and a Catholic South were not predetermined by the natures
of the populations. Those two great cultural currents of
Catholicism and Protestantism originally mingled their courses
in both North and South. It was only the outcome of strife,
of war with the foreign ruler, which brought about that fatal
redistribution of forces which was to estrange the two regions
for so long. That outcome was not determined by any greater
courage possessed by the North, or even by Holland and
Zealand alone (for the conventional view conveniently over-
looks the fact that the Eastern provinces had to be reconquered
for the Republic by force). That outcome was determined by
the great rivers. Brabant and Flanders lay open for the enemy,
and soon therefore their Protestants went to strengthen those
in the impregnable river area. Gelderland, Overysel, and
Groningen, much less affected by Protestantism than Flanders
and Brabant, could not be held for the Catholic Church because
the swords of Parma and of Spinola lost their striking-force
when stretched precariously beyond the rivers.

North Netherlands historians have been slow to see these
matters in their true colours, because the dazzling brilliance
of the Dutch seventeenth century prevented them, as it had
prevented contemporaries, from discerning failure in the course
of events. National and Protestant self-consciousness, moreover, seemed to require the carrying through of a contrast as
against "Belgians" and Catholics. Certain Belgian historians,
on their side, wanting to give a respectable historical background to present-day Belgium, which they look upon as the

natural state organism for both Walloons and Flemings, cannot but welcome the emergence of the Southern Netherlands, which I pictured as an indefensible and subjected fragment, but in which present-day Belgium can for the first time be unmistakably recognized. To them this must be an inevitable development—nay, a fulfilment.

We need not occupy ourselves with views which are so clearly artificial and inspired by later political prejudice. The split was a disaster brought upon the Netherlands race by foreign domination. Time was to show what misfortunes lay hidden in the situation that resulted from it.

REVOLUTIONS IN NETHERLANDS CIVILIZATION

About the middle of the sixteenth century one revolution was, as has been described above, well under way. The Renaissance had made its entry from more southerly regions. Painters and architects were eager to carry out the precepts of Italy. In literature the new spirit as yet manifested itself mainly in feeble imitations, although we saw the first signs of a better understanding of the true meaning of the Renaissance in the opposition to the bourgeois and moralizing prosiness of the Rhetoricians and in the attempts of some daring spirits to stand on their own feet. But this great change was not to be left to run its course undisturbed and in accordance with its own laws. From the start two other revolutions interfered with it: firstly, the Reformation; and secondly, the political troubles, which about the middle of the period under review led to a forcible shifting of the cultural centre within the Dutch-speaking Netherlands.

As far as the Reformation is concerned, it is true that the first thing to be noticed is the length of time during which it continued side by side with the Renaissancist intellectual movement without making much impression on it. The two great movements were in many respects intrinsically antagonistic. The Renaissance was fundamentally worldly. Full of admiration for the old pagan civilization, it accepted life and nature, and its joyful cult was devoted to beauty. Often beauty was conceived in an exuberantly sensuous manner, and the worshippers revelled in a fullness and richness of expression which seem to us excessive. The life of that generation was in all its manifestations permeated by this spirit, and the surprising thing to us is the absence of any clear consciousness of the contrast between it and the moral tendency of Protestantism. The gorgeous displays of the Rhetoricians, for which on great social occasions poets and painters lent their services, bore the same character whether they were intended to celebrate the entries, into Brussels or Antwerp or The Hague, of Orange, Anjou, Leicester, or of Matthew, Ernest, Albert, and Isabella. These were the externals of Renaissance civilization which could most readily be brought to the attention of the masses. Behind them there was a keen and courageous intellectual activity; individuality, arising eagerly, asserted itself. These intellectual tendencies were doubtless closely allied with the forces that were breaking up Catholic unity, but no sooner had the new Church been organized than it attempted to ban within narrow limits the searching spirit to which in part it owed its existence. And even more definitely did that Church range itself against the sensual inclinations of the Renaissance. In Calvinism was reborn the ideal of primitive Christianity, according to which truth, having been revealed, could do without the free development of human reason, and nature and the world were of the devil.

But as has been suggested, that conflict did not come to light at once. In the minds of many men of that period the principles of the Renaissance and of the Reformation lived peacefully together. As long as the Reformation appeared to be primarily a movement of opposition against the tyranny of Spain and Rome, we are struck by the vigour with which the forces of the mind continued to strive after freedom and beauty; and this in spite of the rival claims made on spiritual and intellectual energy by rebellion and war, and by vehement theological disputes. But as soon as the Reformation had apparently triumphed, those who most truly embodied the new ecclesiastical conception, the ministers of the Word, entered upon a systematic struggle with the forces of the time and attempted to fetter society and civilization afresh. Then it became clear at once that the intellectual movement, however completely it had seemed to be under the influence of the Reformation, followed the impulse of its own principles. The roots of the Netherlandish civilization which was now beginning to blossom north of the rivers extended not only outside the region to which Parma's armies restricted its growth, but also outside the religion which was aspiring after dominion in the young Republic. Liberty was dearer to the hearts of poets and thinkers than orthodoxy, and neither they nor the artists could regard the world, man, and nature as mere corruption outside God.

Considered by themselves, the ministers of religion present an important and highly characteristic appearance in the Netherlandish cultural movement of the second half of the sixteenth century. In the cult of Catholicism the sermon had never held a very conspicuous place, even though, for instance, the Dominicans had always made much of it, and the Modern Devotion had frequently made direct appeals in the popular language to the hearts and minds of the faithful. In the Reformed cult the sermon, along with psalm-singing, counted for everything. It was Dathenus, the Flemish minister, whose translation opened up the world of the psalms to the Netherlands people. Meanwhile the preachers up and down the country expounded to the congregations that Biblical view of life which taught the Reformed to look upon themselves as the chosen people, as the New Israel. This concept became a source of confidence and courage to them, and on it they built up their strong and narrow national sentiment. The influence which was thus exercised by the Reformed ministry cannot easily be over-estimated, but as soon as we direct our attention more particularly to literature, art, and scholarship, we are struck by the paucity of strict Calvinists among the leaders in those spheres.

This latter development can be traced to its natural conclusion only in the Northern Netherlands, although the origins, as we know, are to be found in the South no less. Parma's conquest for a while concentrated all living cultural forces on the northern section of the Dutch linguistic area, preparing at the same time for the civilization of the South a future on the basis of the Counter-Reformation. There is no organic connection at all between his interference and Netherlands intellectual life; it was extraneous and by its nature physical and accidental. Yet it created insurmountable barriers in what ought to have been a continuous development, and we cannot but accept in our survey of the civilization of the period the division which is marked by them.

a. BEFORE THE SPLIT

During the first decades of Philip II's reign, Netherlands unity manifested itself in the sphere of intellectual life no less freely than in the political agitation which swept all the provinces along with it. As of old, it was in Flanders and Brabant that the heart-beat was strongest; yet its rhythm made itself felt ever more insistently in the North, especially in Holland.

In painting, little that was new appeared in the years before the great parting, except that Breughel, whom I mentioned above, came to his full development only then. But Breughel was a figure apart from the fashion of the time, which was to be a slave to Italianism and classicism for many years to come. Coxie and Frans Floris were still regarded as the great men. Good work was done in portraiture by Frans Pourbus and Adriaan Key, who both lived at Antwerp. But far superior to them was a master who, in a way very different from that of Breughel, remained somewhat outside the general movement of Netherlandish art—namely, the Utrechter Antonie Mor, one of the greatest portrait-painters that the country has ever produced. There is in his work a subtlety and a distinction which are entirely foreign to the bourgeois society of the Netherlands and which obviously owe much to Italian schooling, and yet Mor cannot be described as Italianate. He came to be the painter of the aristocracy, and the Dutch-speaking area soon grew too small for him. Even Antwerp could not retain him for long. He worked a great deal at the King's Court in Spain; even to-day his name is generally given in a Spanish form (Antonio Moro). Philip himself, Alva and Granvelle sat to him.

In architecture attempts were still being made to reconcile the rules taken over from Italy with the native traditions. A purely classicist current maintained itself, of which the little town hall at The Hague, built in 1565, is an example. But side by side with this a more playful and whimsical style was developed, which left greater room to the display of native character. The most famous building of the period was the town hall of Antwerp, built in 1564 by Cornelis de Vriendt, a brother of the painter Frans Floris; and although the ordering was rather severe, so that the whole building makes a somewhat chilly impression, it yet contains decorative detail which, though really incongruous, was to have a great future in the Netherlands. The influence which spread from the Antwerp town hall was considerable; yet if the bold decorative effects which broke through the severe classicist style were soon to be adopted all over the country, this was largely due to the inexhaustible inventiveness of the designer, Hans Vredeman de Vries. Born in the North—de Vries means the Frisian, and, in fact, Vredeman's father was a German mercenary soldier who came to Friesland with Albert of Saxony and settled there—Vredeman de Vries worked mostly in the South, in Antwerp and Brussels, until Parma's conquest drove him to Germany. There, too, his influence made itself felt, and from there we shall see it, saturated with the traditions of those parts, penetrate during our second period into the Northern Netherlands. Vredeman's work consisted mainly of collections of designs, displaying an inexhaustible fertility in variations of those cartouches and grotesques which went right against the purely classicist taste of the early Renaissance in the Netherlands and replaced its cheerful and delicate chasteness with a certain heavy luxurious exuberance. Yet at the same time he carried on the line of Coecke and proclaimed the rules of Vitruvius. The Hospital of St. John at Hoorn (1563), in which classicist window pediments are placed in a brick façade with a pointed and stepped gable, and statuary and cartouche work on the steps, is a good example of the hybrid building which sometimes resulted. Vredeman himself never attained to a profound harmonizing of the various elements, but he nevertheless did great service in preparing the way for the really brilliant, if brief, period of Netherlandish architecture the beginnings of which we shall notice in our last paragraph.

In literature, too, the noteworthy events during the sixties and seventies took place in the South. It was not a time of great achievement in this sphere. But from the point of view of later developments it was undeniably most important that attempts were made to give Dutch verse mastery over the new

Renaissance forms—real mastery, moreover, which would not rest content with the superficial imitation in which the Rhetoricians took pleasure. These attempts were made by some South Netherlandish poets, especially De Heere, of Ghent, and Van der Noot, of Antwerp. They scarcely produced beautiful poetry, and moreover the results of their pioneer labour were largely lost in the convulsion caused by rebellion and reconquest. Before we glance at their work, which was solely intended to serve literature, and which will always appeal to those who come to the past with minds set on literary discovery, some attention must be given to the numerous writings to which the troubles themselves gave rise. Sometimes the writers, with no conscious literary intention, yet by true passion and profound humanity, achieved literature.

I am inclined to mention in this connection Marnix van St. Aldegonde and even Dirk Volkertszoon Coornhert. Both the Brabant nobleman and the Haarlem engraver and notary public were certainly writers of exceptional gifts, both attended most carefully to problems of style—both, for instance, purged their language of the foreign words in which the Rhetoricians indulged and which sound so hateful to modern Dutch ears; but to both public affairs and the questions which agitated the people were the principal incitement to writing. Marnix was inspired by his hatred of popery and zeal for the Reformation; Coornhert by his aversion from all coercion of conscience, including that applied by the Reformed, and by his yearning after rational philosophical convictions in the midst of the theological disputes that raged all round him. Coornhert, born in 1522, and so older than any of the other writers here mentioned, did not reach his full development until the second period discussed in this chapter. Marnix, too, who was born in 1538, completed his translation of the psalms only during the retirement following upon the cutting short of his political career after the surrender of Antwerp; but his *Beehive of the Holy Roman Church* appeared as early as 1570. In this virulent pamphlet Dutch prose was for the first time employed for the purpose of bitter satire, and this by a man who was at home in French and classic literature. It goes without saying that not even the truest passion or the profoundest humanity will always enable writers to express themselves in literature. If an example were needed, Dathenus' translation of the psalms —made in 1566, not after the original, but after Marot—would suffice. No more deplorable hack work can be imagined, and it says little for the literary discrimination in Reformed circles that this translation was not only adopted by the new Church, but actually retained for two centuries despite the claims of several better versions.

Many Beggar songs are little better, yet taken as a whole these productions of mostly anonymous poets constitute a collection for which Dutch literature has reason to be grateful. Now hopeful, then despondent, stately or vehement, expressing scorn or hatred, sorrow or confidence, these songs preserve the memory of an arresting period of Netherlands history with a freshness unequalled by chronicles or documents. The North, which alone won independence during that period, has as it were appropriated that treasure, of which the *Wilhelmus* song is the most precious jewel. Yet Flemings and Brabanders had their share in making the songs no less than in doing the deeds which gave rise to them, and the *Wilhelmus* itself is almost certainly the work of a Brabander, possibly of Marnix.

Many of these songs were made by Rhetoricians who were swept beyond the narrowness of rhetorical convention by the compelling reality of their theme. But at the same time that convention was still diligently pursued in the Chambers, numbers of which continued to flourish in spite of the suspicion with which they were regarded by the Government. They took themselves with profound seriousness, these Rhetoricians, and if they were to be believed, the collection of moralities published after the Antwerp Land Jubilee of 1561 proved that, compared with former times,

wits in these Netherlands are brighter, all arts plied with greater skill; many are the poets, and the lovers of literature without number; so that one might truly say that Mount Parnassus now rises up in our midst and *Castalides Nimphae* have chosen this country as their dwelling-place.

The brightest of all these bright wits was in the judgment of the "lovers of literature," or rather of Rhetoric, Jan Baptista Houwaert. Homer, Virgil, Ovid, Petrarch—no venerated name sounded too great to be applied to Houwaert. In sober truth he was a rhymer of the usual pattern, who tried in vain to invigorate his spineless verse and to add lustre and an appearance of modernity to his conventional thought by a liberal use of classicist allusions and foreign words. By his very addiction to foreign words he proved himself to be a poet of the old stamp. A Brusseler of good family, the owner of a country house in the Sonien Forest, Houwaert, like so many others, was in 1568 imprisoned in the Treurenborch by the Blood Council and cruelly maltreated. In those days he inclined to the heresy then current. In 1577 we saw him act as organizer of the festivities on the occasion of the Prince of Orange's entry into Brussels. But later on, in 1594, he acted in the same capacity when the Archduke Ernest made his entry. At that time he was a councillor in the Brabant Chamber of Accounts and obedient to both Roman Church and Spanish Government.

North Netherlandish historians have sometimes applied scornful conclusions drawn from Houwaert's career to the character of the South Netherlandish people as a whole. They forget that, had political disasters overtaken the North, his type, which is of all nations, would inevitably have made its appearance there too. How many exiles could be quoted, on the other hand, to prove that Flanders and Brabant were not the homes of time-servers only, but of characters of a more stubborn type! This much may be said, however, that the political vicissitudes of Flanders and Brabant had a depressing effect on the tone of the intellectual life in those provinces. It was not Catholicism, or the Counter-Reformation either, it was the defeat and the restored authority of the foreigner: men had to bow down or be broken.

The lives of the two poets to whom I alluded when mentioning the development of Dutch prosody contain further striking illustrations of this fact. For although the inspiration of those men was essentially literary, this does not mean that they could keep aloof from the great religious and political revolution of their time, or that the conditions of their whole being were not, partly at least, shaped thereby.

Lucas de Heere was a painter of Ghent (1534–84), who, in a volume published in 1565, *The Garden and Orchard of Poetry*, had been the first to try the strict iambic metre, and who wrote odes, epigrams, and even sonnets. Soon afterwards he had to flee to England on account of his religious convictions. Having returned after the Pacification he accepted an official position in his native town, to die soon after the recapture by Parma during a second exile. Different, but hardly more enviable, was the fate of Jonkheer Jan van der Noot, "patricius of Antwerp" (1538–95). In 1566 and 1567 Van der Noot had been conspicuous among the most zealous Calvinists; during his exile—also in England—he manifested as bitter a hatred of Catholicism as did Marnix himself. But exile and poverty broke his conviction though not his pride, or at least his pretensions: on his return after the Pacification he conducted himself as a Catholic once more; and after Parma's reconquest of Antwerp, which he applauded, his Catholicism became positively fervent. Meanwhile he begged the administrations under successive regimes for support in his need, and occasionally received a small sum, both on account of his rank and because of

his great industry in imitating the French poets.

Van der Noot was a more important poet than De Heere. He too experimented and played with the new forms, and he did so with less visible effort, with greater mastery. The replacement of the old free verse by the iambic metre which, as it was put, involved "counting the feet," had a deeper significance than might be thought at first sight. It was one more sign of the desire of that generation for order and discipline in the conduct of their mental affairs, it was a means of expressing their joyful sense of having gained a firmer control over themselves and over life than was possessed by their predecessors. In this way it was a European phenomenon.

But in these Dutch poets the dependence on the French is marked indeed. Van der Noot not only repeatedly imitated

Ronsard, his ambition was to do for Dutch literature what the *Pléiade*—for he had moved on beyond Marot—had done for French literature. It was through them that he came to Petrarch. It was with their eyes that he read the classics. Their sense of the high value of the poet's office, their proud consciousness of speaking for the ages—in a man who had not really anything to say, all this became a hollow pose. A delicate sense of verse, that undoubtedly Van der Noot possessed, but what he lacked (possibly the time, too stern for poetry, destroyed it in him) was character. In his volumes *Theatre* and *The Thicket* of about 1568, in his great work of 1579, the *Olympias*, Van der Noot won new beauties for the Dutch language such as were not dreamt of by his friend Houwaert. Unlike the Brussels councillor, he never, for all his imitation of the French poets, indulged in the abuse of Romance word forms. But the fame of this other Homer, Virgil, and Petrarch (the comparisons in this case are his own) penetrated but little beyond a small group of adulators, so that with the catastrophe which soon came to upset the intellectual life of Antwerp his work sank into deep oblivion.

In science and scholarship, too, the South maintained down to that catastrophe its supremacy among the provinces of Dutch speech. In those spheres the middle of the sixteenth century was a rich and vital time. The scientific sense of the men of the Renaissance, their appreciation of facts and their courage in facing logical consequences undeterred by respect for tradition or fear of authority, were no longer manifested only in the literary criticism of the classical authors, in which the humanists had exercised those qualities. In art a similar attitude of mind had long won triumphs. Now men came in the same way to the study of nature and of the world around them. Netherlanders took a brisk part in that activity. For many years there lived at Mechlin, his native town, the physician, Rembert Dodoens (born in 1517), who, in 1554, published at Antwerp a work on botany in the popular language (*Het Cruyd Boeck*), which helped to lay the foundation for the scientific treatment of that subject. He lived to see several later editions through the press, mostly in Latin; his own name he latinized into Dodonaeus. At an advanced age he went to Vienna to take up the post of Court physician to the Emperor, and towards the end of his life he answered a call from the University of Leyden. A man of even greater significance was Mercator (Gerard de Cremer), who was born at Rupelmonde in 1512, learned the geography of Aprianus of Ingolstadt from the Frisian Gemma at Leuven, and at a very early age founded in the last-named town an institute for cartography and geometrical instruments. Having been troubled by the Inquisition in 1544, Mercator spent the remainder of his life at Duisberg under the protection of the Duke of Cleve. His maps and atlases excelled in the careful incorporation of all the knowedge about distant and nearby countries then available, but, moreover, he introduced new methods which helped the science of geography to make further progress. At Antwerp lived his colleague Abraham Ortels, a little younger than he (Ortelius, 1527-98), and a less original mind, but whose *Theatrum Orbis Terrarum*, a large world atlas, achieved an enormous success (1570; Dutch edition, 1571). It was published in all languages and a popularized version in Dutch by Pieter Heyns of Antwerp became almost equally famous. Ortelius was a man of means with many scientific interests, who was in correspondence with a large number of scholars in the Netherlands and abroad. His cabinet of "medals" became one of the curiosities which visitors to Antwerp must see. The antiquarian and engraver, Hubert Goltzius (born at Venlo in 1526, generally living at Brugge), had assisted him in forming the collection.

A man who did more even to make a centre of learning of the great town was Christophe Plantin, a Frenchman (born in 1524) who founded a printing business at Antwerp about the middle of the century which was destined to become world-famous. He established his reputation by the publication, with papal sanction and royal support, of a Bible in the original languages together with the Latin translation. It was a work in many volumes, on which huge sums were spent, and a number of scholars were engaged on it for years. The financial success of the firm rested on the monopoly which Plantin obtained, in all the Spanish lands, of liturgical books printed in accordance with the precepts of Trent. But this royal and Catholic publisher belonged in secret, as did Ortelius also, to a heretical sect, "the Family of Love." He had no difficulty in adapting himself to the changes occurring at Antwerp in his lifetime. After 1576 he became printer to the States-General and to the town, in 1583 even to the University of Leyden; and yet after 1585 he returned to Antwerp to spend his last days in the strictly Catholic atmosphere of the subjected town. His son-in-law Moretus (Moerentorff), who was to continue it after his death, had by that time acquired a large share in the direction of the firm. But Plantin had rendered his greatest services to learning before 1585. It was he who published the later editions of Dodoens, as of Ortelius, Guicciardini's description of the Netherlands, and the works of Hubert Goltzius. Furthermore his fund contained Hebrew dictionaries, collections of laws and ordinances, and the works of the great Latinist, Justus Lipsius (1547–1606). Lipsius was a Brabander, who left Leuven when it was threatened in 1577 by the Spanish troops, to go and add lustre to the young University of Leyden. Disturbed by the disputations with which theologizing Holland resounded, he was to return later on, in 1591, to Leuven, which had then found security under Parma. Since 1558 Plantin employed as corrector Cornelis van Kiel (Kilianus, 1528–1607), who issued in 1574 his famous Dutch dictionary, to the third impression of which he gave in 1599 the title of *Etymologicon Theutonicae Linguae.*

In these two men, Lipsius and Kilianus, the renowned professor and the simple amateur, may be seen the representatives of two currents in the Netherlands Renaissance which, sprung from the same source and frequently mingling their courses, are yet clearly to be distinguished, and of which one was in the long run to have a much more fertilizing effect on Netherlands civilization than the other.

Justus Lipsius was a high priest of that cult of the ancient civilization out of which the renovation of intellectual life had largely arisen. At this juncture, it found equally zealous worshippers, but—more than had been the case some generations earlier—they worshipped for devotion's own sake. It is true we saw Maurice and William Louis studying Caesar for lessons in military tactics, and Vitruvius proclaimed as a guide for architects. Yet the great humanists themselves rarely made so immediate a connection with practical life, they did not grapple so powerfully with the ideas of their contemporaries as their predecessors, such as Wessel Gansfort or Erasmus, had done. A man like Lipsius certainly got involved in the theological strife of his time—more so than was agreeable to him—but it was simply as a Latinist, as a master of conjectural criticism, as the editor of Tacitus and Seneca, that he was venerated. We find it hard to understand the almost superstitious respect with which a great classicist was surrounded; the figure which a Lipsius cut in the world leaves us puzzled. We must remember that the hopeful, vigorous, and vital Renaissance was stiffening —without the contemporaries being conscious of any change— into a mere subjection to pure Latinity. A crowd of scholars shut themselves up in an ideal world, the world of the classics; the education of the rising generation amounted to an introduction into that magic circle. The joy of discovery, which had found vent in heightened intellectual energy and love of adventure, was beginning to settle down, and a hard and fast convention was being forged, which would soon prove as cumbersome to the national movement of civilization as the first contact with the classics had been invigorating and inspiring.

There were also, however, those who applied the lessons of the ancients with a little more independence and tried to use the new methods of research and the new spirit of interpretation for the building up of the national tradition. That was done partly by means of Latin, for most humanists were unconscious of the conflict here indicated. They did not see that the exclusive use of Latin must harm the popular language and the national civilization. An example is the Hollander Adrianus Junius (1511–75), a man of an older generation than Lipsius, who praised him on account of his learning as a second Erasmus. Junius—a Haarlem physician, whose real name was De Jonghe—began a great work, entitled *Batavia*, in which he proposed to treat the oldest history of his province, of Holland.

This was, of course, an enterprise in the true spirit of the Renaissance: historical interest was stimulated, if only by the example of the classic historians, to imitate whom people turned to their own past. At first there were few signs of a really new attitude of mind. Little more criticism was applied than had been done by the medieval chroniclers, whose work was used as almost the only source. It also proved beyond the powers of vision of these writers to look across the boundaries of their own province and view the Netherlands as a whole. The name of Johannes Goropius Becanus, of Antwerp (Jan van Gorp van Hilvarenbeek; as it chanced, another physician), is still remembered for the solemn argument set out in his *Origines Antverpianae* (published by Plantin in 1569) to prove that the oldest language, from which all others are derived, is Dutch.

Interest in the popular language manifested itself in more fruitful fashion than this. It has been shown how, since the protest raised by Jan van der Werve of Ghent (which was mentioned in the introductory chapter), the best poets banned foreign words—a reform of the literary language which demanded thought as well as enthusiasm. Van de Werve's work had been continued by several others. Coornhert, for instance, sounded the alarm against the foreign intruders in 1561. Moreover, spelling rules as well as etymologies were proposed. As early as 1550 a *Nederlandsche Spellynghe* had been published at Ghent, by Joas Lambrecht; in 1576 Anton Tsestich published an *Orthographia Linguae Belgicae* (that is, of the Dutch language) at Leuven; in 1581 Pontus de Heuiter, of Delft, issued a *Nederduitsche Orthographie* with Plantin at Leyden. The mother tongue was beginning to be regarded as a worthy object of study. The importance of Kilianus lies in the fact that he more than anybody was the founder of the true scientific study of the Dutch language. He dabbled in rules and precepts less than most of his contemporaries, and apart from etymologies, which were no better than was usual at the time, his work consisted of collecting, classifying, and interpreting, all done with great care and acumen.

The scientific and scholarly movement described above was

mainly carried on in the South. Even though Lipsius returned to Leuven, and Kilianus never stirred from Antwerp, we shall see in the next paragraph that it was mainly continued in the North, partly by refugees from the South. Already in the seventies the insecurity prevailing in Brabant and Flanders interfered with the careers of scholars as well as artists and men of letters—we have come across several instances in the preceding pages. At the same time the foundation of the University of Leyden—a sign of the enhanced importance and self-confidence which resulted from Holland's separate rebellion —meant the creation of a new centre for the movement of learning in the Netherlands. With the definitive subjection of the South and the exile of so many of the most vigorous-minded Brabanders and Flemings, there ensued a veritable revolution in the respective positions of North and South, as far as their contributions to the common stock of Netherlands civilization were concerned. Nay more, the unity of that civilization itself was endangered, and a duality was introduced which was, however, too directly in conflict with Netherlands history as it had been shaping before these catastrophic events ever to be carried through to its logical conclusion.

b. AFTER THE SPLIT

In Flanders and Brabant during the eighties, as a result first of the war, then of the conquest and the emigration, all cultural activity was paralysed. Holland, on the other hand, the stronghold of the truncated Netherlands community which was still maintaining its independence under Protestant leadership, was already offering a sufficient measure of that order and security without which civilization cannot flourish. There was more than order and security; there was a brisk economic movement which, as sketched above, created prosperity in the midst of war. It was especially Amsterdam that inherited the position of Antwerp as a trading centre, but at the same time great new enterprises, partly planned by South Netherlanders, brought the rising town, and indeed the whole of Holland, into direct contact with the colonial world, increasing the intensity of intellectual, together with that of economic, life. The textile manufacturers, employers and workmen, who had left the South, settled mostly at Haarlem and Leyden, where they greatly increased the population and the trade. And while Brussels had been the capital under the alien regime of Burgundians and Habsburgs, The Hague had now become the centre of a domestic political system, essentially Netherlandish, even though the Court added a foreign note to it—not so much through the Stadtholder, who never married, and who in the summer was generally away in the field, as through his stepmother, William the Silent's widow, Louise de Coligny. In any case Holland had suddenly become fertile soil for all the activities of civilization.

By no means all the abundant growth that was soon now to be observed there presented a character distinct from what had gone before, either by specifically North Netherlandish or Protestant features. In many ways it was the continuation —certainly in rather different circumstances, in a still more preponderantly urban and middle-class society, which for that reason alone was more exclusively Dutch—of the common Netherlandish cultural tradition, strongly influenced by the Romance South, which until then had found a more favourable soil in Flanders and Brabant. Catholic inspirations and associations could not have been suddenly cut out of that tradition without killing it, and although Protestant conceptions and Protestant conditions of life at once made their influence felt, Protestantism, let alone strict Calvinism, was far from dominating cultural life in the North during these decades. And not only did building proceed on the old, "general Netherlandish" foundations, but among the builders we shall come across innumerable Flemish and Brabant immigrants. As a class these men, as we know, were generally the strictest Calvinists, and they had a profound influence on the development of the Dutch Reformed Church in that sense. But when one tries to estimate their influence outside ecclesiastical history, how varied do their contributions and stimuli appear to have been! Sixteenth-century Holland was, compared with Flanders and Brabant, a small town community; there were certainly few aristocrats among the immigrants; yet they introduced a larger, and a more ostentatious, mode of life. Hollanders of the old stamp frequently grumbled against, or mocked at, these characteristics of the refugees. Yet undoubtedly the latter helped to brighten up "the dull Hollanders"—the old Brabant nickname for their northern neighbours. In any case the Brabant invasion helped to bring about that quickening of the rhythm of life, that bursting of old bounds, and that colourful variety, which were to count for so much in the rich charm of the civilization of Holland in the seventeenth century.

More than any other intellectual or spiritual activities, painting and architecture demand settled social conditions. In Flanders and Brabant, for twenty years exposed to the excesses of Beggars and Malcontents, of Spanish, German, and Walloon mercenaries, the old centres were rudely uprooted, and in the order, such as after a while it was, restored by Parma, the former prosperity was still too much lacking for these centres to spring into being again very readily. Nevertheless Antwerp, which had indeed been gradually monopolizing all such activities during the preceding period, remained, in spite of the paralysis of its trade due to the closure of the Scheldt, a large town with a great deal of old-established wealth; and here Parma's conquest, which meant the triumph of the Catholic Church, opened another period of brilliant prosperity for painting. The Calvinist interregnum had robbed the painters of Church patronage. Now, on the contrary, religious pieces of all descriptions were in great demand for the restoration of the sacked and emptied churches: the studios were soon active as they had not been for long. In the work then done, the spirit of Frans Floris still set the fashion. Italianate and academic as it is, it has not much to attract us to-day. Mindful of the great time which was soon to begin for the Antwerp school of painting under the leadership of Rubens, the modern art lover will watch especially for signs of the baroque breaking through the stiff forms of the ageing Renaissance. We know that soon the fervent, though externalized, religious life of the Counter-Reformation will produce its own style. About this time, young Rubens was already at work in his native

town, before his departure to Italy in 1600; his masters were
Tobias Verhaecht, Adam van Noort, and Vaenius. Is it possible
to find in the paintings of those older men any rays of light
announcing the rising sun? The work of Otto Vaenius, despite
his deficient sense of colour, yields most to this questioning.
Interesting from this point of view are also two other contemporary painters, the brothers Francken: especially Hieronymus
Francken, who in 1589 painted the martyrdom of St. Crispin
and St. Crispinian for the cathedral of Our Lady at Antwerp;
this is a picture with the true baroque vehemence of expression.
(The centre piece is now in the Antwerp Museum.)

Otto Vaenius, or Van Veen (1556–1629), Parma's court painter,
deserves a moment of our attention. He came of a good Leyden
family. His father had been burgomaster before 1572, but had
gone into exile when the Beggars arrived. (This is by no means
the only instance of a migration in the opposite direction from
that of the Protestant Flemings and Brabanders who settled
down in the North.) No painting was—under the double
influence of the Counter-Reformation and of Italy—more
completely divorced from realism, more conventionally idealistic
and grouped in a more theatrical way, in short none was more
what would later be regarded as typically "Flemish" and "un-
Hollandish" than the work of this exile from Leyden, who had
received his first lessons in his native town.

During this period there was little inclination to build in
the South, but in the North architects found plenty of work
before the end of the sixteenth century. Towns were expanded,
well-to-do merchants wanted houses in accordance with their
wealth, new municipal buildings were required, weigh-houses,
shooting galleries for bowmen's companies (*doelens*), town
halls. Two style currents continued side by side. In so far as
a separate Flemish element had existed in each, this was now
completely absorbed into the Northern tradition; first by
means of imitation, as in the Flushing town hall (since demolished), for which that of Antwerp had served as a model;
or in the house called "De Steenrots" at Middelburg (1590),
which is reminiscent of the classicist style fashionable at
Antwerp or Brugge for buildings of that kind: and secondly,

by means of the original work of masters born or schooled in the South, who were driven North by the troubles. For example, the son of Hans Vredeman de Vries, Paul, born at Antwerp, was now working at Amsterdam in his father's style. A really great figure among these refugees was Lieven de Key, of Ghent (1560–1627), who became town architect of Haarlem. He used both manners of building between which the time hesitated. If the weigh-house at Haarlem was classicist, the meat hall, in which the interplay of brick and stone creates an incomparable effect, is a triumphant instance of that peculiarly Netherlandish Renaissance style, which had come into being before the great political change, but which could attain its full development only in the circumstances of the liberated North. For us, at any rate, it is hard not to regard that style as the true expression of the time. How eminently suited are its brave and cheerful forms to the mood of the prosperous burghers who were emerging from the struggle as the real victors. Nevertheless, as has been hinted above, there were, at the same time, strong German influences at work on this style. It is uncertain how large a share De Key had in the planning of the famous Leyden town hall (built in 1598, recently destroyed by fire), but probably the principal man engaged in the actual building of it was an "Easterner"—that is to say, a North German—Luder van Bentheim, who had done most of his work at Bremen. To this, no doubt, Van Mander alluded in his *Schilderboeck* (about which more will be said later on) when he wrote:

It is a pity that a new, foul, modern manner of building after the German fashion has once more come into use; we shall be hard put to it to get rid of it, but in Italy it will never be adopted.

For he, like many others who wanted to be considered connoisseurs, continued to regard the classicist style, such as Pieter Coecke had expounded it after Serlio, as simply "the right manner of building." In spite of this condemnation by the orthodox, colourful and gaily decorated buildings continued to spring up in every town, and another great master of the Dutch Renaissance style rose to fame, namely Hendrik de Keyser, of Utrecht (1565–1621), who became town architect of Amsterdam. Before the Twelve Years' Truce he built—or at least began—the South Church, the East India House, the Exchange (demolished in 1838), all at Amsterdam. His work has a gracefulness of its own. He made freer use of Italian architectural forms than did De Key, so that in the next period, when public taste turned more in that direction, he was better able to maintain his prestige.

It is a surprising thing that painting in the North survived not only the passing unrest of the seventies, but the permanent loss of Church patronage. It shows how firm a tradition had already grown up in Holland and Utrecht no less than in Flanders and Brabant. Not only were there well-established studios and schools, but the public, the middle-class as well as the aristocracy, had learned to love pictures and wanted them to decorate their interiors. A good deal of work was done even for export, for instance, to the Frankfort Fair. In Haarlem, Leyden, Utrecht, Amsterdam, the old groups of painters managed to maintain themselves and work could even be found for the numerous newcomers from the Southern provinces; soon other towns, Dordt, Delft, The Hague, became important centres. In all this activity the old Holland traditions were inextricably intermingled with those of the South Netherlandish schools; in any case, of course, all had sprung from the same source and had always greatly influenced each other. Lines in which the Flemings used to excel now found their best continuation in the Holland school; as, for instance, lands capepainting. Here Gillis van Coninxloo (1544–1607), who moved from Antwerp to Amsterdam, constituted a link; later, his Kortryk pupil, Roeland Savery, who settled down at Utrecht, continued the chain; but Breughel's work, which became known through engravings, also exercised influence. A genre which had early found a favourable soil in Holland was further developed as if in preparation for triumphs still to come, namely the group portrait, in which members of municipal committees or of civic guard companies sat together. Good work was done in this line by Cornelis Ketel of Gouda, Aert Pieterszoon, the son of Pieter Aertszoon, and Cornelis van Haarlem. The last-named, as a rule, revelled in large theatrical compositions and Michelangelesque nudes, but it is pleasant to see him once in a while forgetting this romantic showiness when painting the portraits of soberly attired Haarlem burghers. Another national trait was the penchant for the illustration of scenes from domestic life; before Aertszoon had made it into an accepted genre which Breughel soon carried to undreamt-of heights, the primitives had shown an inclination for it even in their religious art; and now we have, for instance, David Vinckeboons, a native of Mechlin (1576–1629), who worked at Amsterdam. In the Antwerp school those tendencies were certainly by no means lost, yet neither the spirit of society, through Spanish rule and Counter-Reformation in open communication with the Romance world, nor the patronage of Church and aristocracy, was favourable to their development. Conditions in the North, on the contrary, as it were, invited the painters to cultivate a loving pride in everyday environment. In the South everything pressed towards narrowing down art to one attitude of mind. The North inherited the Netherlands traditions in the full wealth of their variety.

For that Italian-classicist style which triumphed at Antwerp was by no means abandoned in Holland and Utrecht. It still ruled in several studios, and the power of literary fashion caused the most cultured art lovers to regard it as the true and only style. I mentioned Cornelis Corneliszoon van Haarlem (1562–1638) as a representative figure. Another one was Hendrik Goltzius (1558–1616), a member of the same Venlo family to which the antiquarian Hubert Goltzius belonged. He too worked at Haarlem, where he had learned engraving from Coornhert.

Goltzius, home from Italy, had so firmly impressed on his memory the beautiful Italian paintings that he still saw them as in a mirror whenever he wished to and wherever he found himself. Now he enjoyed the angel grace of Raphael, then the natural fleshes of Correggio, or again the surging heights and receding depths of Titian, the fine silks or other well-painted materials of Veronese; beside all this the native painters seemed disappointing and less perfect to him.

So does Karel van Mander sketch the true "Romanist." He,

the Fleming (1548–1606), also settled at Haarlem, felt no less veneration for the Italians and the classics than did his friend Goltzius, but in his *Schilderboeck* (Book of Painters; 1604) he nevertheless described, proudly and lovingly, the lives and works of "the native painters"—naturally he did not discriminate between Northern and Southern Netherlandish. The very fact of his undertaking this task (conceived after Vasari) proves the emergence of an entirely new conception, namely, of art as a highly important matter, which adds to the honour of a people. The book itself brims over with pleasant anecdotes and with particulars about the painters' work and methods. It is most enlightening about the ambitions and opinions of the artists of the time. They and their patrons, the *liefhebbers* (art lovers) with their "cabinets," live on in Van Mander's pages.

A book like this extended the boundaries of Dutch literature, which had been perilously narrowed down during the alien rule of the Burgundian-Habsburg dynasty, when history and politics had been more and more reserved for treatment in French. The Renaissance, as we know, in spite of the overwhelming admiration for the classics and the Italians which it enjoined, had quickened the interest in national intellectual possessions. But it is obvious that the political and economic circumstances in which the North now found itself must no less powerfully promote the spirit of independence and of enterprise in intellectual matters. How immediately these circumstances influenced literature can be seen from the accounts of voyages to which expeditions to the Indies and America gave rise, and from the chronicles, which were not slow in appearing, of the great events through which the country was passing.

It is true that the literary value of most of the voyages is nil, although Gerrit de Veer's account of Heemskerck's and Barentsz's expedition round the North, to give only one instance of the more successful few, will always charm by its straightforward and sincerely human tone. But it was a thing of importance in itself that this wonderful new world and the epic of its exploration and conquest were described in Dutch, however unskilled the writers were in the use of the pen. As a matter of fact the work with which this new kind of literature opens, Jan Huygen van Linschoten's description of the Portuguese empire in the Indies, is a masterpiece of observation and insight, which still has considerable historical value.

As to the chronicles, under the pressure of the stirring times they were at one blow cut free both from the petty local and from the un-Dutch and dynastic tradition. Pieter Bor, of Utrecht (1559–1635), Emanuel van Meteren, of Antwerp (he lived in London; 1535–1612), and Everhard van Reyd, of Deventer (1550–1602), constitute a remarkable trio. The first part of Bor's work appeared in 1595, of Van Meteren's in 1599; both spent the remainder of their lives in writing sequels of it. Van Reyd's book was not printed until years after his death. Bor is the matter-of-fact registrar and collector; although not infrequently (the reader has met with some instances above) by a simple remark or some description very much to the point he throws light which the modern researcher has looked for in vain among the documents. Van Meteren, who was a cousin of Ortelius, and in touch with the whole of that cultured circle, strove to write something like a connected story and was more alive than Bor to problems of causation; he was particularly interested in economic conditions. Van Reyd was councillor to Stadtholder William Louis and relates vividly all that comes within his particular circle of vision. Of the three, he is the most individual writer.

Many scribblers [as he puts it himself] seek the glory of being called impartial. Yet the pen can ill be so governed that inclination do not sometimes appear. Therefore do I boldly declare that with my counsel and actions I have always supported the party of religion and liberty, but with my pen only that of truth, hiding neither the virtues of enemies nor the shortcomings of friends.

How confidently this writer speaks his mind in the mother tongue on a problem which the preceding generation would hardly have presumed to tackle but in Latin! And, indeed, there was now a public consisting not of international scholars, or of French-cultured noblemen and royal officials, nor exclusively of the writer's own townsfolk: an historian of the formidable events of the immediate past could count on the attention of citizens and citizen magistrates in all the provinces of the Union.

But not in this direct way only did circumstances affect Dutch civilization. Far more important in its consequences was the awakening of national confidence. Deeply stirred by the great trials they had gone through, men felt that the nation was called to a brilliant future. In all spheres of the mind this mood had a stimulating effect. The determination grew that all should be opened to a people which had gloriously defied the mightiest monarchy of the earth. Many of the best minds realised that the national language must be the key.

The exhortations of Van de Werve, the complaints of Coornhert, had certainly found some response. But when Hendrik Laurenszoon Spieghel of Amsterdam in 1584 published his *Dialogue of Dutch Literature*—Coornhert had been delighted to write a preface—a whole generation was ready to receive the message and to act upon it. The influence of that essay was immediate and profound. The language was stripped of the abuse of foreign words as of a parasitic growth and after the operation appeared in pristine purity. It is true that the watchword was not accepted so readily for non-literary purposes; in town halls, States assemblies, merchants' offices, a much less pure language remained in use. A standard had nevertheless been set up which was never again to be lost. Nor was this reform limited to the Northern Netherlands. There was very little literary activity in the South during this unhappy period, but as soon as circumstances permitted a revival of literary interest it appeared that writers in re-catholicized Flanders and Brabant had adopted the same conventions as their brothers in the North. In fact, the movement had been begun before the split, and by Southern writers; and, moreover, the prestige of the poets of Holland soon came to stand high in the subjected provinces.

For, as a matter of fact, much more was done in the North than to cultivate respect for the language and to purify it from "bastard words." This was but one condition for literary achievement. The important thing was that the achievement itself followed. It had been centuries since the Netherlands produced such a group of striking personalities who used Dutch as their medium of expression. Take only Marnix, Coornhert, Van Mander, and Spieghel.

Marnix, the temperamental Calvinist nobleman, had retired to his country seat at West Souburg in Zealand after the disastrous end to his active career; there he spent his time translating the Bible, writing political and theological essays, and, above all, a masterly version of the Psalms, in which he sought a durable form for that confidence befitting a chosen people, however severely tried, which had proved too hard for him in reality. Van Mander, the artist, lover of life, not content with painting and with describing the painters, chased beauty in poetry as well; his *Scriptural Songs* long remained popular with his co-religionists (the Baptists), but he himself could not rest satisfied with them, because, as he put it, "he could not take pleasure any longer in our common old lame manner of writing verse"; he was nearly fifty before he reached a "true understanding of the French metre" and was able to write real Renaissance poetry. Coornhert, the wisdom-loving engraver, notary public, and politician, of Haarlem, indefatigable defender of liberty, undaunted fighter against Catholic and Protestant intolerance, found time in the midst of so much strife and polemical activity for other work even than the building up of a pure Dutch language, freed from the conventions of the Rhetoricians; his great achievement was a book published in 1586, *The Art of Well-living*, an untheological, Christian-stoical system of morality, in which, in the teeth of the Protestant doctrine of man's corruption, he maintained the attainability of virtue; this earnest and bigly-planned book, utterly different from the religious writings of preachers and mystics, was another *novum*, by which the area of Dutch prose was expanded. Spieghel, the Amsterdam merchant who, far from allowing himself to be worried out of the Catholic Church, declined public office as a protest against the breach of faith involved in the tearing up of the Satisfactions, yet recognized in his country's independence

the condition for the independence of his intellectual development; averse from incongruous decoration, be it French or
classical, a stern servant of truth, he made a sober appearance;
in his principal work, *Hertspieghel* (The Mirror of the Heart),
he confessed in verse of most individual tone and imagination
to a conception of life closely akin to that which his elder
friend Coornhert had expounded in prose.

A quartette, these two South Netherlanders and these two
Hollanders, of which any literature might be proud. Of the
four, Marnix was the most isolated; his relations were mainly
with the scholars, the theologians, and the statesmen. Van
Mander was surrounded by a group who made their bow in
a volume, *De Nederduytsche Helicon*, which was published in
1610, a few years after their leader's death. They were mostly
refugees. In Haarlem, Leyden, and Amsterdam, the Flemings
and Brabanders had founded their own Chambers of Rhetoric,
while entertaining close relations with the native poets; in
De Nederduytsche Helicon, for instance, are published poems
of Scriverius and Douza (both of whom we shall meet later on).
It must be admitted that most of the refugees were rhymers
of the old stamp. Spieghel's group were men of a different
calibre. He, too, was a member of a Chamber of Rhetoric, for
which, in fact, his *Dialogue* of 1584 had been written. The
"Chamber of the Eglantine," with the motto, "Flowering in
Love," was generally called the "Old Chamber," in contra-
distinction to the "Chamber of the White Lavender," which
was the chamber of the refugee Brabanders at Amsterdam.
A number of men from the "regent" circles of Amsterdam
belonged to the Old Chamber, which moreover disposed of
more talent than did its Brabant sister institution. Fellow
member with Spieghel was his friend Roemer Visscher, also
a merchant and a Catholic, whose epigrams achieved great
popularity. But Spieghel was the master mind, strong in his
clear conception of the unity of life, the whole of which he
wanted literature to master. It was this that gave him his
influence over the younger men, and it was to the younger men
that the Chamber "Flowering in Love" was to owe its fame
in Dutch literature. Even before the end of our period, the

K

poetry of Pieter Corneliszoon Hooft (1581–1647), the son of burgomaster Cornelis Pieterszoon Hooft, himself a member, roused the delight of lovers of literature. Never before had Dutch verse attained to that full Italian beauty. Gerbrand Adriaenszoon Breero (1585–1619) and Samuel Coster (1579–1655) were soon to raise the Amsterdam stage to an unparalleled position in the literary and intellectual life of the Netherlands. Meanwhile the greatest of all those figures who were going to illustrate the next period belonged to the Brabant Chamber, namely Joost van den Vondel, of Antwerp (1587–1676); but his poetical development, too, was to owe a very great deal to the circle of "the Eglantine."

With what keen understanding Spieghel and his friends tried to promote the construction of a sound and many-sided Dutch civilization appears from the request which in 1585, the year after the *Dialogue*, they addressed to the University of Leyden, begging that the courses might be given in the mother tongue,

so that we Hollanders might at last enjoy learning in our own speech, which we must now with great labour cull from unknown tongues.

But there was, unfortunately, no chance of that request being acceded to. The Latin tradition was too powerful and it had made of Leyden a stronghold for itself. Yet even here something was achieved. No man was ever a more enthusiastic advocate of the use of Dutch for scientific purposes than Simon Stevin (1548–1620), a refugee (although a Catholic) from Brugge, who in the eighties worked and taught at the University of Leyden. His works, written in Dutch, on mathematics and mechanics, prepared the way for important developments, especially of the latter science. Their immediate practical value too was considerable, and Maurice caused Stevin to be appointed (in spite of his religion) to the post of Engineer and Quartermaster with the States army. When in 1600 the Prince founded a school for engineers at the University of Leyden, it was Stevin who drafted the statutes, in which it was laid down that the medium of instruction should be the mother tongue.

But as a whole the University and the scholars who formed

part of it remained unalterably addicted to Latin, and that is one of the principal reasons why that little world so often makes the impression of a colony leading its own life fenced off from the rest of Dutch society. The use of Latin erected a partition between scholarship and the nation. On the other hand it enabled the Leyden professoriate to attract foreigners into their lecture rooms and to admit them within their own circle, while they could freely carry on intellectual intercourse with their equals over the whole of Europe.

But the intellectuals of those days gave hardly a thought to that language problem. It was possible to share the new feeling of nationality and at the same time to be a confirmed writer of Latin. For men of that way of thinking the glory of a great scholar—and nothing could impart such glory to a scholar as service to the mystery of Latinity—was reflected quite automatically on to the entire nation. Douza, who was a curator of the University, and himself a humanist who combined an intense national sentiment with his enthusiasm for antiquity, declared that his work in keeping out the Spaniard during the siege did not constitute so great a service to the country as his success in bringing Lipsius to Leyden. And when Lipsius absconded after a stay of thirteen years, it was thought a complete compensation for the disaster when the great Frenchman, Scaliger, was prevailed upon to leave his disturbed country (this was in 1593, before Henry IV restored order), and to come to Leyden. The negotiations that took place over that appointment, in which Prince Maurice and King Henry intervened, the conditions that were offered, and according to which the famous scholar would not even be obliged to lecture, the splendid reception at Leyden when at last he appeared with a suite of noblemen—all that makes one realize the respect that was felt for the study of the classics. The succession of Lipsius and Scaliger was continued after the latter's death in 1609 by his favourite pupil, Daniel Heinsius, of Ghent (1580–1655), and gave to the young university uncommon prestige in the international world of scholars. There were, indeed, several men who did excellent work in other subjects. It has been mentioned above that Dodoens—

Dodonaeus—came to Leyden when quite an old man, and after his death in 1589 botany was taught by Clusius. Snellius was a famous mathematician, although later on to be excelled by his son; Bonaventura Vulcanius, a good Greek scholar. In 1586 Raphelengius was appointed professor of Hebrew; he was a son-in-law of Plantin, who had left to him, who belonged to the Reformed Church, his Leyden printing firm when he returned to Antwerp; Raphelengius studied the Koran in Arabic.

If I stressed the fact that Latin was the language used at Leyden and that the outlook there was in many ways cosmopolitan rather than national, I do not for a moment mean to suggest that the existence of so brilliant a centre of learning was of no account for Dutch intellectual life generally. It would be difficult to trace the effect in all its ramifications, but without the shadow of a doubt the treasures of knowledge and of ideas gathered at Leyden enriched the national civilization. Moreover, after having noticed that the scholars in a sense kept themselves apart, one must not overlook the numerous relations which nevertheless existed between them and Dutch society in general and the exponents of the new cultural aspirations in particular.

The thing that involved them in the life of the nation more than anything else was their position in the great European struggle between Protestantism and Catholicism. Leyden was an advanced post of Protestantism not in Holland alone but in the world. It is true that in the early years the theological faculty had to contend with greater difficulties than any of the others. The need for ministers was urgently felt, but the office was of little account socially, and not until a system of scholarships had been instituted could the training of Reformed preachers be taken seriously in hand. A college was founded for theological students, but its history was marked at first by stormy incidents, which throw a lurid light on the rowdyism of youth, and even Calvinist youth, in those days. But when these gales had been weathered the faculty encountered even heavier seas. One might say, however, that it was the dissensions among the Reformed which brought the University and the nation into the closest contact.

The disputes within the Church, of which we have heard something above, never quite died down, and when in 1602, beside the strictly Calvinistic professor Gomarus, of Brugge, the Hollander Arminius was appointed to the second chair of theology, strife flared up almost at once, and the training for the ministry came to be the very object of contention. Years before, certain sermons which Arminius had delivered at Amsterdam on the subject of grace and election had caused a considerable stir. His appointment to a chair at Leyden carried into the very heart of the Reformed system in Holland opposition to the extreme doctrine of the corruption of man and the setting apart as the elect of the small group who regarded the State as having been made for their sake alone. Gomarus and his supporters soon raised the cry of popery, and in fact it was the essentially Catholic tradition of Erasmus that Arminius continued, even though there was no thought of a reconciliation with Rome. The Truce had not long been concluded before this theological quarrel developed into a great political conflict which shook the very foundations of the Republic.

Until that crisis at any rate, which was to give to the orthodox party a firmer control over the University, more latitude was allowed in the matter of religion at Leyden than in most other Universities in Europe. The town Government and the States of Holland, on whose authority the curators acted, lived up to their libertinist principles. After the very first years no religious test was demanded of either professors or students; as far as the latter were concerned, that remained the position even after the synod of Dordt in 1619. This liberty unmistakably benefited the University. Lipsius, for instance, in all the thirteen years that he spent at Leyden, never once partook of the Reformed Communion, and was able afterwards to maintain that he had never receded from his Catholic convictions. Yet the case of Lipsius shows that there were inevitably limits to this liberty.

Lipsius was not by nature a fighter. In a disturbed and cruel age, tranquillity was what he wanted. At first he believed he had found it at Leyden and was full of praise for the tolerance prevailing there. But he soon began to fear the ministers and their tyrannical proclivities. To his Libertinist friends, Van Hout and Douza, a strict upholding of the rights of the secular power seemed to be the only safeguard against this danger, and now Lipsius himself expounded this point of view in such a way that his book (*Politica*) caused another Libertinist, the passionate Coornhert, to take up arms against him, protesting that Lipsius wanted to reintroduce the killing of heretics. The great Latinist was profoundly disturbed by that attack, the more so as it was couched in the popular language, which seemed to him derogatory to his dignity as well as fraught with danger. It made him reflect that the tranquillity he coveted so heartily was, after all, to be found only in a Catholic country, under the double authority of Pope and King, and soon he was back at Leuven, which was now again enjoying security behind the shield of Parma. To a man who felt no spiritual affinity with the Reformation, Leyden, in spite of liberty, could scarcely be a home. Nor can such a man have been readily accessible to the influence of that new feeling of nationality based on the Northern Netherlands which might have prevented Lipsius from calling the Hollanders rebels and from paying such unrestrained homage to the Habsburgs as he did after his transition.

Non-Catholic scholars, whether Libertinist or orthodox, were for all their Latinist cosmopolitanism unable to escape that influence altogether. They showed the effects of it in many ways, both by their connections and their own works. The strongest link between the academic world and those poets in Dutch who were most deliberately building up a national civilization was formed by Douza and Jan van Hout, those doughty comrades in literature and arms. Curator and secretary to the curatorium of the University, they were at the same time in constant intercourse with the poets of their own town and of Haarlem and Amsterdam. Both also wrote Dutch verse, but perhaps the most fruitful work that they did for Dutch civilization was their scientific study of the older national history; Scriverius, of Haarlem (Pieter Schryver, 1576–1660), who later on moved to Leyden, shares this honour with them. Inasmuch as they limited their attention to their own province, they continued the Batavian tradition of Junius. But the method of research was carried by them far beyond Junius's limits. With a detachment without precedent they assailed the tradition of the chronicles at whose meaningless lies they scoffed mercilessly. They went to the original charters. In 1591 even, Douza, in conjunction with Spieghel, whose interest extended to these matters too, published the medieval chronicle in Dutch verse by Melis Stoke, which had been so completely forgotten that on the appearance of the book the clever ones suspected a hoax; the author's name was unearthed only much later by Scriverius. The publication of this chronicle was an event also for the study of the medieval Dutch language. Douza wrote a preface for it in Dutch verse. (He generally wrote in Latin; Scriverius, however, very frequently in Dutch.)

Scriverius was a convinced advocate of the use of the mother language for the higher functions of intellectual life. In the universal estimation he never did greater service to that cause than when he persuaded Daniel Heinsius, a few years after our period (in 1615), to publish his Dutch poems. Heinsius, of course, primarily served the Latin muse. Ever since the beginning of the sixteenth century the Netherlandish humanists had been active in that service. The results, however, in general amounted to no more than an utterly lifeless stylistic exercise. Latin was no longer handled so freely as in the Middle Ages (the same is true for prose); Latin poetry therefore was all imitation and erudition. Many who had read his poems in manuscript knew that the famous Heinsius sometimes deigned to rhyme in Dutch. What a triumph that he should not think it beneath him to let these poems be publicly printed! There is little real poetry to be found in the *Nederduytsche Poemata*. Interesting, apart from the fact of its publication under so illustrious a Latinist name, is the tone of vigorous patriotic pride sounded, for instance, in a poem celebrating Heemskerck's heroic death off Gibraltar in 1607. Heinsius—born as has been said at Ghent—was so much aware of his origin in the lost provinces as to write:

Wherever you (Spain) are not, there is our fatherland

Yet he confidently claimed his share in the glory of the Republic, and when he boldly asserts that "we were born to be free," he identifies himself with the successful Netherlanders of the North. Heinsius' mood was typical of the generation that had grown up with the war of independence. Another young man who served Latin and patriotism with equal conviction was Hugo de Groot (Grotius, 1583–1646), of Delft; he had been as great a success at Leyden as Heinsius himself, but was soon called away to enter upon a "regent's" career. This Hollander already identified without a qualm the *Respublica Batava* with the fatherland. In a poem addressed to Douza (and written before the latter's death in 1604) he abjured classical history (which he had served by editing some texts) and vowed himself to the study of the *fasti* of his native country. But he did so in Latin, and indeed it was but seldom that Grotius was to use Dutch in the whole course of his life.

It is hardly surprising that the Catholic Brabander, Lipsius, could not accept the patriotic ideal of the Reformed Fleming and the Libertinist Hollander. It would not be fanciful to represent him as having remained faithful, in the face of the triumphant dualism that was going to divide the Netherlands for so long, to the older sixteenth-century national sentiment, which embraced all the provinces. When he made his choice in 1591, the prospect in front of the rebellion was still far from hopeful, and he might reasonably expect the power of Spain to heal the fissures in the Netherlands. Even when shortly afterwards Parma's chances of conquest came to nothing, he still prophesied that a truce would cause grave religious quarrels to break out in the Republic—had he not seen at Leyden how the heretics hated each other!—that the new state would collapse and the Archdukes be enabled to extend their authority over the whole country. But those expectations were confounded. For the time being duality was confirmed in the Netherlands. And in the South, whither his fears had driven (and certainly his heart drawn) him, Lipsius found a society weighed down, not only by adversity in war and economic distress, but also by alien rule and a religious coercion infinitely worse than that which he had seen threatening in the North. A society which might afford tranquillity to the scholar, but in which for the builder of a healthy national civilization—a part, it is true, for which Lipsius never felt any ambition —circumstances were sadly unpropitious.

SOURCES OF THE QUOTATIONS

PAGE

38. See Henne, *Règne de Charles V aux Pays-Bas*, VIII.
44. After p. 154 of the contemporary French translation.
54. Quoted in Roersch, *L'humanisme belge*.
57. *Refereinen*, 154.
60. Burgon, *Life and Times of Sir Thomas Gresham*, I, 175.
78. Quoted by Fruin, *Verspreide Geschriften*, I, from *Vita Viglii*.
80. Lasco, *Opera*, II, 349, note 2.
81. Quoted in Van Schelven, *Nederduitsche Vluchtelingenkerken*, 112.
83. *Bibliotheca Reformatoria Neerlandica*, VIII, 374.
84. *Kroniek van G. van Haecht*, edited by Van Roosbroeck, 66.
91. *O.c.*, 72.
93. Marcus van Vaernewijk, *Van die beroerlijcke tijden van Ghent*.
94. Quoted by Knappert, *Opkomst van het Protestantisme*, 241.
99. The latest edition of collected Beggar Songs is by E. Kuyper.
102-3. Quoted after Fruin, *Verspreide Geschriften*, II, 89, and Rachfahl, *Wilhelm von Oranien*, III, 142.
113. Quoted after Fruin, *Verspreide Geschriften*, II, 172.
115. Conyers Read, *Walsingham*, I, 154 (Walsingham to Leicester).
118. *Archives de la Maison d'Orange-Nassau*, III, 512, and IV, 4.
119-20. *O.c.*, IV, 29; letter from Count Neuenahr (Nieuwenaer).
122. Pieter Bor, *Nederlandtsche Oorloghen*, I, 269.
123. J. van Vloten, *Nederland's Volksopstand tegen Spanje*, volume on 1572-1573, p. xliv.
127. Bor, I, 275.
128. Bor, I, 266 ff.
130A. Kluit, *Hollandsche Staatsregering*, I, 378; letter from the Prince to the town of Gouda.
130B. Bakhuizen van den Brink, *Cartons tot de geschiedenis van den Nederlandschen vrijheidsoorlog*, II, 202.
130C. *O.c.*, 205.
132. Bor, I, 302 ff.
134A & B. Bor, I, 327.
137. *Oude verhalen van het beleg van Leiden*, edited by Fruin.
147. *Resolutiën der Staten-Generaal*, edited by N. Japikse in "Rijks Geschiedkundige Publicatiën," I, 8.
152A & B. Bondam, *Verzameling van onuitgegeevene stukken*, I, 283.
152C. De Jonge, *De Unie van Brussel*, II, 17.
153. Quoted after Blok, *Geschiedenis van het Nederlandsche Volk*, II, 131; the original in the *Correspondance de Philippe II*.
155. Bondam, *o.c.*, III, 55.
159. Bondam, *o.c.*, IV, 282.
162A & B. Hessels, *Archivum Ecclesiae Londino-Batavae*, 626.

PAGE

165. De Schrevel, *Troubles religieux en Flandre* (edited for the Société d'Emulation de Bruges), II, p. xviii.

167. Van de Spieghel, *Bundel van onuitgegeevene stukken (voornaamelijk Unie van Utrecht)*, I, 34.

168A & B. Account of the Diet held at Arnhem, published in *Bijdragen voor Vaderlandsche Geschiedenis*, I, 126.

169. *O.c.*, 328.

171. Bor, II, 164.

172A. In a poem entitled "Nieuwjaar, 1678."

172B. Report of Van Leyden, burgomaster of Utrecht, published by Blok in the *Bijdragen en Mededeelingen van het Historisch Genootschap te Utrecht*, 1919.

178. In a pamphlet entitled *Bedencke van der Nederlanden noodt ende hulpe*.

182. *Politieke Balladen*, edited for the "Vlaanische Bibliophielen," II, VII, 293.

185. Q. Janssen, *Kerkhervorming in Vlaanderen*, II, 209.

188A & B. Everhart van Reyd, *Voornaemste Geschiedenissen in de Nederlanden*, 39, 41.

190A. P. Verheyden, *Antwerpsch Letterkundig Leven*, 13.

190B. Janssen, *o.c.*, II, 275.

193. *Archives de la Maison d'O.-N.*, VIII, 133.

195. Printed in Bor, III, 28 sqq.

199. *Calendar of Foreign State Papers*, 1584–1585, 622; Le Sieur to Walsingham.

205. Thus Vrancken in the discourse mentioned above, p. 198 (Bor III, 33).

209. Joris de Bye, in a memorandum printed *Bijdragen en Mededeelingen van het Historisch Genootschap*, 1888, p. 424.

212A & B. *Calendar of Foreign State Papers*, 1586, 63.

213. After the Dutch translation given by Bor.

220. Published by Haak, in *Bijdragen voor Vaderlandsche Geschiedenis*, 1920, 23.

223. Van Meteren, *Belgische ofte Nederl. Historie van onsen tijden*.

229. Ypey en Dermout, *Geschiedenis der Nederlandsch Hervormde Kerk*, II, 108.

230A, B, C, D, & E. The report was published in the *Bijdragen en Mededeelingen van het Historisch Genootschap*, 1884.

233. *Memoriën en Adviezen van C. P. Hooft*, edited for the Historisch Genootschap, 1871.

234. Elias, *Schetsen van het Nederlandsche Zeewezen*, I, 71.

239. Van Meteren, *o.c.*

241. Gachard, *Etats-Généraux de 1600*, p. cxlii.

243. *O.c.*, 764.

PAGE

244. Van der Kemp, *Leven van Maurits*, II, 460.

245A & B. *Gachard*, *o.c.*, 780.

246. Van Meteren, *o.c.*

247. Extracts from his correspondence were published in the *Codex Diplomaticus* of the Historisch Genootschap.

252A. Published in Bor.

252B. Van Meteren, *o.c.*

NOTE ON SOURCES AND SECONDARY WORKS

The mass of published material available for the study of the Netherlands revolt is enormous. Dutch and Belgian historians have filled a library with their volumes and series containing the correspondence of Philip II, Margaret of Parma, Granvelle, William the Silent, Leicester, and Oldenbarnevelt, or illustrating the activities of the States-General (both of that of 1576,which was continued in the North, and of the loyal assembly called together in the South in 1600), the formation of the Union of Utrecht, the beginnings of the Reformation in the whole of the Netherlands, the religious troubles in Flanders, the relations of the insurgents with Anjou and with England. In addition there are numberless *mémoires*, especially on the royalist side and for the first years of the rebellion, and the invaluable Dutch chronicles have their counterpart in excellent Spanish descriptions of the war.

In the preceding list of references for the quotations in the text the titles of several of the most important of these collections of sources as well as of some secondary works will be found, but that list was not intended to give a complete or well-balanced survey of either category. To append a fuller bibliography would be beyond the scope of this work. The studious reader may be referred to the *Bibliographie de l'histoire de Belgique*, by H. Pirenne, third edition, 1931, which covers the whole of the Netherlands down to 1598, and which is especially useful for the sources. The reader in search of a guide to the modern literature on the subject would be well advised to begin with the chapter bibliographies in Gosse's and Japikse's *Handboek tot de Staatkundige Geschiedenis van Nederland*, second edition, 1927.

The lack of modern contributions in English has been noticed in the Preface. Much excellent work was done by Dutch nineteenth-century historians, like Bakhuizen van den Brink, Fruin (especially

Fruin[1]), Van Vloten, P. L. Muller, Bussemaker. All these writers, it is true, viewed the events from a strictly Protestant and North Netherlandish standpoint. Unconsciously they projected the "Belgium" which seemed so alien to them in their own day back into the sixteenth century, when it was, in fact, still far to seek. The mental attitude of Belgian historians was the complement to that of their Northern neighbours. M. Pirenne gives in the third and fourth volumes of his *Histoire de Belgique* a striking and brilliant version of the story, but he ignores practically the work of his Dutch predecessors while proceeding, like them, on the tacit assumption that the severance of Flanders and Brabant from the rest of the Dutch-speaking area was a perfectly natural consummation. The period still repays original research, and the years since the war have witnessed the appearance of a number of interesting monographs both in Holland and Belgium; Flemish historians are more and more frequently using Dutch for their publications.

[1] A minor work of Fruin, which is a good specimen of his method, is now available in a translation by Elizabeth Trevelyan: *The Siege and Relief of Leyden in 1574.*

INDEX

A

Aerschot, *see* Croy

Aerssens, Cornelis —, 1543–1627, of Antwerp, secretary of Brussels, greffier of the States-General Aug. 1584 124

Aertsen, Pieter —, 1508–75, of Amsterdam, painter 64, 279

Albert, Archduke of Austria, joint sovereign of the Netherlands with his wife Isabella 1598–1621 225, 227, 228, 232, 239–251, 254, 257, 261, 292

Albert, Duke of Saxony, commander for Maximilian 33, 264

Alberti, Leon Battista —, 48

Alva, Ferdinand Alvarez de Toledo, Duke of —, 1508–83, Governor of the Netherlands 1567–73 74, 98, 100–110, 112, 115–117, 119, 123, 124, 126, 128, 130, 133, 136, 156, 191, 223, 228, 231

Ammonius, Laevinus — (Lieven van der Maude), Carthusian monk at Ghent 54

Anjou, François de Valois, Duke of —, 1556–84, accepted as sovereign by the States-General 1581 164, 181–190, 192, 195, 196, 203, 261

Aremberg, *see* Ligne

Arminius (Hermans), Jacobus —, 1560–1609, of Oudewater, Holland, professor of theology at Leyden 1603 289

Asseliers, Jan van —, 1520–84, brother-in-law of Wesembeke, secretary of Antwerp, greffier of the States-General 1577 184

B

Bakkerzeele, *see* Casembroot

Barentsz, Willem —, of Terschelling, navigator, died on voyage home from Nova Zembla 1597 281

Bassigny, the Lord of —, Brabant nobleman employed by the Southern States-General in the negotiation of Bergen-op-Zoom 245

Beauvoir, Philippe de Lannoy, Lord of —, died 1574, commander of Walloon troops 98, 107

Becanus, Johannes Goropius — (Jan van Gorp van Hilvarenbeek), of Antwerp, physician and historian 273

Bellay, Joachim du —, French author 47

Benninghe, Sicke —, Groningen chronicler 63

Bentinck van Bicht, nobleman of the Upper Quarter of Gelderland, employed by the Southern States-General in the negotiations of Bergen-op-Zoom 245

Bergen, *see* Glymes

Bergh, Willem Count van den —, 1538–86, Gelderland nobleman, married in 1556 Maria of Nassau, sister of William the Silent, Stadtholder of Gelderland for the States-General 1582, deposed 1583 85, 104, 116, 119, 120, 191

Berlaymont, Charles Count of —, 1510–78, of Namur, Knight of the Fleece, President of the Council of Finance 1559 70, 87, 101, 103, 109, 146, 148, 154

Berlaymont, Gilles de —, Baron of Hierges, eldest son of the former, killed before Maastricht 1579, Knight of the Fleece, Stadtholder of Friesland, Overysel, and Gelderland 1572, of Holland, Zealand, and Utrecht 1574. [The statement in the text, p. 148, that he was appointed to the latter position on the capture of Bossu should be amended: he succeeded Noircarmes as Bossu's *locum tenens*.] 107, 142, 148, 153, 154, 166

Bertulphus, H. —, of Lede in Flanders, secretary to Erasmus 1522–24 55

Blois van Neerijen, Flemish nobleman, signatory of the Compromis 1566 86

Blois van Treslong, Willem van —, 1530–94, nobleman with estates in Holland and Flanders, Sea Beggar, Admiral of Zealand 1576 116, 122, 127, 198

Bloyere, Hendrik de —, Brussels popular leader in 1576, burgomaster 1581 146

Boisot, Charles de —, of Brussels, employed in the negotiations of Breda, 1575, killed before Zierikzee later in the same year 141, 142

Boisot, Louis de —, of Brussels, admiral of Zealand 1573, of Holland 1574, killed before Zierikzee 1576 124, 135, 137, 141, 142

Bombergen, Antoine van —, of Antwerp 97

Bor, Pieter —, 1559–1635, of Utrecht, notary public and historian 282

Borchgrave, Daniel de —, 1550–90, of Ghent, uncle of Daniel Heinsius, secretary of Leicester's Council of State 210, 215

Borluut, Joost —, of a famous Ghent family, pensionary of Ghent in 1567, died 1597 103

Bossu, see Hennin

Bournonville, Oudart de —, Baron of Capres, etc., 1533–85, commander of Walloon troops 107

Bray (or Brès), Guy de —, of Tournai, Reformed minister 82, 93, 98, 138

Brederode, Hendrik Count of —, 1531–68, Holland nobleman 85–89, 91, 92, 96–100, 104

Breero, Gerbrand Adriaenszoon —, 1585–1619, of Amsterdam, poet and playwright 286

Breughel, Pieter —, 1525–69, Brabander, painter 49, 50, 64, 263

Brimeu, Charles de —, Count of Meghen, died 1572, Knight of the Fleece and Councillor of State 1555, Stadtholder of Gelderland 1559, of Friesland, Groningen, and Overysel 1568 76, 77, 79, 87, 91, 98, 101, 154

Bronkhorst, Dirk van —, governor of Leyden for Orange, died during the siege, 1574 137

Busleyden, Hieronymus van —, 1470–1517, jurist, member of the Great Council at Mechlin 53

Buys, Paulus —, 1531–94, pensionary of Leyden, Councillor of State under Leicester 94, 111, 212

Buzanval, Paul Choart Lord of —, French envoy with the States-General 246

Bijns, Anna —, died 1540, of Antwerp, school-mistress and poetess 46, 57

C

Cabeliau, Jacob —, Lord of Mulhem, of Ghent, Sea Beggar chief, governor of Alkmaar in 1573 134

Caesar 272

Calvin, Jean —, 79–82, 140

Cammen, Jan van der —, pensionary of Mechlin 103

Cant, Reinier —, 1537–95, of Amsterdam, member of the magistracy after the "alteration" 1578, member of the Committee of the Closer Union 1579 171

Carolingians 26, 27

Casembroot, Jan van —, Lord of Bakkerzeele, of Bruges, councillor of Egmont, executed 1568

Casembroot, Nicolaes (?), burgomaster of Bruges in 1584 191

Charlemagne 27

Charles the Bold, Duke of Burgundy, ruled 1467–77 29–33, 65, 69

Charles V, ruled the Netherlands 1515-55 23, 34-40, 55, 59, 60, 69, 71, 76

Charles of Egmont, Duke of Gelderland, ruled 1508-43 36, 61, 63

Charles IX of France, ruled 1560-74 114, 115, 117

Chimay, see Croy

Clercq, Gilles le —, of Tournai, jurist, secretary to the Synod of the Walloon consistories 83, 85

Clusius, professor of botany at Leyden 288

Codt, Hendrik de —, 1529-1606, pensionary of Ypres 1571, delegate at the States-General 1598, 1600, employed in the negotiations at Bergen-op-Zoom 245

Coecke, Pieter —, 1502-1550, of Alost, artist and writer on architecture 48, 264, 278

Coligny, Gaspard de —, Admiral of France, murdered 1572 111, 114, 117

Coligny, Louise de —, daughter of the last-named, married to Orange 1583 275

Condé, Louis Prince of —, assassinated 1570 111

Coninxloo, Gillis van —, 1544-1607, of Antwerp, painter at Amsterdam 279

Coolhaes, Caspar —, of Köln, 1536-1615, dissident minister at Leyden 206

Coornhert, Dirk Volkertszoon—, 1522-90, of Haarlem, secretary to the town, to the States of Holland 1572, notary public, engraver, author 103, 129, 178, 206, 265, 280, 283-285, 290

Cornelis Corneliszoon van Haarlem, 1562-1638, painter 279, 280

Correggio 280

Coster, Samuel —, 1579-1655, of Amsterdam, physician and poet 286

Coxie, Michiel —, painter at Mechlin 49, 263

Crecques, see Croy

Cremer, see Mercator

Croy, Charles de —, Prince of Chimay, 1560-1612, son and successor of Aerschot, Stadtholder of Flanders for the States-General 1582 76, 191, 192

Croy, Charles-Philippe de —, Marquess of Havré, 1549-1613, brother of Aerschot, Councillor of State 1577 240

Croy, Eustache de —, Lord of Crecques, commander of Walloon troops 107

Croy, Jean de —, Count du Roeulx, Stadtholder of Flanders for the States-General 1576 107, 148

Croy, Philippe de —, Duke of Aerschot, 1526-95, Knight of the Fleece, Councillor of State, etc. 76, 77, 87, 97, 101, 107, 146-148, 154, 156-158, 173, 175, 190, 224, 240

Culemborch, Floris van Pallandt, Count of —, Gelderland nobleman 85, 89, 90, 104

Cuyck, Jonkheer Jan van—, Lord of Erpt, 1532-1613, of Heusden, agent of Orange with the Sea Beggars 122

D

Dathenus, Petrus— (Pieter Daets or Daten), 1531-88, of Kassel in Flanders, Reformed minister 91 163-165, 172, 262, 266

Delenus, Petrus — (Pieter van Delen), 1510-63, of Alkmaar, minister of the Dutch church in London 80

Dodoens, Rembert — (Dodonaeus), 1517-89, of Mechlin, physician and botanist 269, 271, 287

Does, Jonkheer Jacob van der —, 1500-77, of Leyden, member of the States of Holland 137

Does, Jonkheer Jan van der —, Douza, of Noordwyk near Leyden, nobleman and scholar 137, 287, 290-292

Dolhain, or Ollehain, Adriaen van
St. Winoks Bergen, Lord of —,
commander of the Sea Beggars
1569, killed before Mons 1572 114

Duifhuis, Huibert —, independent
minister at Utrecht 210

E

Eggius, Elbertus —, Catholic priest
228

Egmont, Lamoral Count of —,
1522-68, Knight of the Fleece
1546, military commander, Stadtholder of Flanders and Councillor
of State 1559 75, 76, 78, 84-90,
94, 95, 98, 101, 103, 106

Egmont, Sabina of Bavaria, Countess of —, 76, 101

Elizabeth, Queen of England 115,
116, 164, 182, 183, 196-198, 203,
212, 214, 217, 218, 225, 226

Entes (or Entens), Jonkheer Barthold —, Lord of Mentheda,
1539-80, Groningen nobleman,
Sea Beggar 126, 177

Erasmus, Desiderius —, 1466-1536,
of Rotterdam, scholar 51-56, 64,
78, 140, 205, 272, 289

Ernest, Archduke of Austria, Governor of the Netherlands 1594-95
223, 224, 226, 241, 261

Escovedo, secretary of Don John,
murdered 1578 160

Eynde, Jacob van den —, Advocate
of the States of Holland 103

Eyck, Jan van —, 1385-1441, of
Maaseik (Dutch-speaking part
of the Bishopric of Liège),
painter 47

F

Fabritius, De Smet, Carmelite of
Bruges, burnt 1564 83

Ferdinand of Arragon 34

Floris, Frans — de Vriendt, 1517-70,
of Antwerp, painter 49, 263, 264,
276

Floris, Cornelis — de Vriendt,
1518-75, brother of the last-
named, architect and sculptor
263

Francis I of France, ruled 1515-47
35, 36, 40

Frederick, Don F. de Toledo, son
of Alva 119, 120, 132, 133

Fuentes, Pedro Enriquez de Aze-
vedo, Count of —, brother-in-law
of Alva, Governor of the Netherlands 1595 223-225

G

Gansfort, Wessel —, 1419-89, of
Groningen, religious writer 51,
52, 272

Geldorp, Hendrik — (Geldorpius),
1522-85, Brabander, exiled from
the Netherlands 1558, rector at
Duisburg 113, 114

Gianibelli, Italian engineer at Antwerp 198

Glymes, Jean de—, Marquess of
Bergen (op Zoom), 1529-67,
Knight of the Fleece, Councillor
of State, Stadtholder of Hainaut
and Cambrésis 76, 79, 90, 101,
103

Glymes, Jacques de —, died 1612,
Bailiff of Nivelles and the Walloon district of Brabant 146

Gnapheus, Guilielmus — (Willem
de Volder), 1493-1568, Hollander,
religious writer, emigrated 1528
55

Goltzius, Hendrik —, 1558-1616,
of Venlo, painter at Haarlem
280, 281

Goltzius, Hubert —, 1526-?, of
Venlo, archæologist at Bruges
270, 271, 280

Gomarus, Franciscus —, 1563-1641
of Bruges, Reformed minister,
professor of theology at Leyden
1594 289

Gossart van Mabuse (of Maubeuge),
painter at Antwerp 49, 65

Grange, Pérégrin de la —, Reformed minister, of Lille, hanged at Valenciennes 1567 93, 98

Granvelle, Antoine Perrenot, Lord of —, 1517–86, of Besançon, Franche-Comté, Bishop of Arras 1543, President of the Netherlands Council of State 1559, Archbishop of Mechlin 1560, Cardinal 1561, recalled 1563 69–71, 75, 154, 240

Grapheus, Alexander— (De Schryver), 1519–73, secretary of Antwerp 55

Groote, Geert —, 1340–84, of Deventer, religious leader 28, 51, 52

Grotius, Hugo de Groot, 1581–1645, of Delft, scholar and "regent" 292

Guicciardini, Luigi —, 44, 271

Guise, Henry Duke of —, assassinated 1588 218

H

Haemstede, A. C. van —, 1525–63, of Zierikzee, Reformed minister at Antwerp 81, 83

Hames, Nicolas de —, bastard, Herald of the Order of the Fleece 1561–67, killed 1568 85, 86, 107

Haussy, see Hennin

Havré, see Croy

Heemskerck, Jacob van —, 1569–1607, of Amsterdam, navigator and admiral, killed off Gibraltar 1607 235, 236, 249, 281

Heere, Lucas de —, 1534–84, of Ghent, painter and poet 265, 267

Heinsius, Daniel —, 1580–1655, of Ghent, Latinist and poet 287, 291, 292

Hembyze, Jan van —, 1513–84, burgomaster of Ghent 157, 158, 161, 164, 172, 192, 245

Hennin, Jacques de —, Lord of Haussy, or Auxy, younger brother of the following 148

Hennin, Maximilien de —, Count of Bossu, or Boussu, 1542–79, of Hainaut, Stadtholder of Holland, Zealand, and Utrecht to replace Orange 1567, captured on the Zuiderzee 1573, commander for the States-General 1577 124–126, 133, 135, 148, 151, 165

Henry II of France, ruled 1547–59 70, 76, 77, 219

Henry III of France, ruled 1574–89 182, 188, 195, 196, 218

Henry IV of France, ruled 1589–1610 218, 219, 223–226, 287

Heuiter, Pontus de —, of Delft, philologist 273

Heyns, Pieter —, 1537–98, of Antwerp, publicist 270

Heze, Guillaume de Hornes, Lord of —, executed 1580, commander of a regiment for the States-General 1576 164, 173

Hierges, see Berlaymont

Hohenlohe, Philip Count of —, 1550–1606, commander for the Closer Union 1579, married a daughter of William the Silent 1595 170, 177, 188, 197, 198, 213, 215, 219

Homer 267, 269

Hooft, C. P. —, 1547–1626, burgomaster of Amsterdam 233, 286

Hooft, Pieter Corneliszoon —, 1581–1647, son of the former, poet 286

Hoogstraten, see Lalaing

Hoorne, see Montmorency

Hout, Jan van —, 1542–1609, of Leyden, secretary of the town, scholar and poet 137, 140, 206, 207, 290

Houtman, Cornelis—, †1599, of Gouda, merchant and navigator 236, 237

Houwaert, Jan Baptista —, 1533–99, of Brussels, rhetorician 156, 267, 269

I

Ibarra, Esteban de —, Councillor of State 1594 223

Isabella of Castile 34

Isabella Clara Eugenia, Infanta —, 1566–1633, daughter of Philip II, joint sovereign of the Netherlands with her husband 1598–1621, Governess 1621–33 218, 223, 227, 232, 239, 240, 242, 243, 245, 247–251, 254, 257, 261, 292

J

John, see Nassau

John Casimir, 1543–92, Elector Palatine 164, 165, 181

John, Don J. of Austria, 1547–78, Governor of the Netherlands 1576–78 146, 148, 150–156, 158–160, 165, 166, 169, 173, 189, 203

Junius, Adrianus — (De Jonghe), 1511–75, of Haarlem, physician and historian 272, 291

Junius, Franciscus — (du Jon), Frenchman, Reformed minister at Antwerp 1565 83

Junius, Dr. Johannes Junius de Jonghe, of Halle near Brussels, employed in the negotiations of Breda 1575 141

K

Ketel, Cornelis —, 1548–1616, of Gouda, painter 279

Key, Adriaan —, active 1560–90 at Antwerp, painter 263

Key, Lieven de —, 1560–1627, of Ghent, town architect of Haarlem 278, 279

Keyser, Hendrik de —, 1565–1621, of Utrecht, town architect of Amsterdam 278

Kilianus, Cornelis van Kiel, corrector at Plantin's, philologist 271, 273, 274

Koninck, De —, see Regius

L

Lalaing, Antoine de —, Count of Hoogstraten, about 1535–68, Knight of the Fleece, Councillor of State 76, 101, 104, 107, 166

Lalaing, Emmanuel-Philibert de —, Baron of Montigny, 1557–90, commander of Walloon troops for the States-General 1577 164, 173, 176

Lalaing, Georges de —, Count Rennenberg, died 1581, brother of Hoogstraten, Stadtholder of Friesland, Groningen, Drente, and Overysel for the States-General, 1578 166, 170, 176, 177, 181

Lalaing, Philippe Count of —, half-brother of Emmanuel-Philibert Baron of Montigny, Great-Bailiff of Hainaut 151, 164, 176

Lambrecht, Joas —, of Ghent, philologist 273

Lasco, Johannes à —, Polish Reformer at Emden 80

Leefdael, Flemish nobleman 86

Leicester, Robert Dudley, Earl of —, 1531–1588, 196, 201, 203, 209–217, 238, 252, 261

Lemaire, Isaac —, of Antwerp, merchant at Middelburg 238

Leoninus, Elbertus —, Albert de Leeuw, 1520–98, of Zaltbommel (Gelderland), professor at Louvain, Chancellor of Gelderland 1581 184, 191

Leyden, Lucas van —, 1494–1533, painter at Leyden 49

Lier, Van —, deputy on the States-General for Gelderland 1577 159, 167

Liesvelt, Dirk van —, 1521–1601, of Brussels, jurist, Councillor of State under Matthew 158

Ligne, Jean de —, Count of Aremberg (in Luxemburg; it came to him through his marriage with Marguérite de la Marck), 1525–1568, Stadtholder of Friesland, Overysel, and Groningen 1548,

Ligne (*continued*)
Knight of the Fleece, killed at Heiligerlee 76, 77, 98, 101, 105, 106

Linschoten, Jan Huyghen van —, 1563–1611, of Haarlem, traveller and writer 236, 282

Lipsius, Justus —, 1547–1606, of Overyssche, Brabant, Latinist, professor at Louvain and Leyden 271, 272, 274, 287, 289, 290, 292, 293

Louis, *see* Nassau

Louis XI of France, ruled 1461–83 30

Louis XIV of France, ruled 1643–1715 23, 25, 175

Luder van Bentheim, architect 278

Lumey, *see* de la Marck

Luther, Martin —, 53, 54

M

Maerlant, Jacob van —, thirteenth century, Fleming, poet 28, 65

Mander, Karel van —, 1548–1606, of Meulebeke, Flanders, painter and writer at Haarlem 49, 253, 278, 280, 281

Mansfeldt, Peter Ernst Count of —, 1517–1604, Saxon, Knight of the Fleece 1545, Councillor of State 1565, Governor-General 1593 76, 94, 98, 101, 154, 223

Marck, Guillaume Count de la —, Baron of Lumey, 1542–78, Liège nobleman, Prince of the Empire, with estates also in Holland 116, 126–129, 132, 134

Margaret of Austria, Duchess of Parma, 1522–86, natural daughter of Charles V, Governess of the Netherlands 1559–67 70, 75, 78, 79, 87–92, 94–96, 98, 100, 101, 154

Maria Duchess of Burgundy, daughter of Charles the Bold, ruled 1477–82 30, 32

Maria of Austria, Dowager Queen of Hungary, sister of Charles V, Governess of the Netherlands 1530–55 38

Marnix, Jean de —, Lord of Tholouse (in Franche-Comté), 1537–67, of Brussels (the family originated from Savoy), killed at Oosterweel 85–87, 97, 98

Marnix, Philippe de —, Lord of St. Aldegonde (in Hainaut), 1540–98, of Brussels, Councillor to the Prince of Orange 1569, burgomaster of Antwerp 1583–85, Dutch and French publicist, Dutch poet 85, 86, 93, 111, 126, 130, 132, 134, 141, 154, 155, 158, 197–200, 265, 266, 284, 285

Marot, Clément —, 1497–1544, French poet 266, 269

Mary Queen of England 80

Matsys, Quinten —, 1466–1530, of Louvain, painter at Antwerp 48

Matthew, Archduke of Austria, 1557–1619, Governor of the Netherlands commissioned by the States-General 1578–81 (Emperor in 1612) 156, 158, 160, 163, 173, 181, 183, 223, 261

Matthijsen, Jan —, of Haarlem, Anabaptist leader 57

Maude, Lieven van der —, *see* Ammonius

Maurice, Elector of Saxony 76

Maurice, *see* Nassau

Maximilian, Archduke of Austria, Regent of the Netherlands for his son Philip the Fair 1482–94, for his grandson Charles V 1506–15 30, 32–34, 36, 69, 95

Meetkerke, Adolf van —, 1528–91, of Brugge, Councillor of State under Leicester 184, 194, 209, 210, 213–215, 217

Meghen, *see* Brimeu

Memlinc, Hans —, 1430–94, of Mainz, painter at Brugge 47

Mercator, Gerard de Cremer 1512-94, of Rupelmonde, Flanders, geographer 270

Merode, Bernard de —, 1525–89 or '91, of Liège, governor for Orange of Mechlin in 1572   119

Merovingians 27

Meteren, Emanuel van —, 1535–1612, of Antwerp, merchant and consul of the Netherlands merchants in London, historian 246, 252, 282

Meulen, Daniel van der —, of Antwerp, merchant and refugee, employed in negotiations 1598   240

Micronius, of Ghent, minister of the Netherlands church in London 80, 81

Moded, Herman — (Moded is a Hebrew rendering of his real surname Strycker), died 1603, of Zwolle, Reformed minister 91

Mondragon, Spanish commander 123, 142, 145

Montigny, see Lalaing and Montmorency

Montmorency, Florent de —, Baron of Montigny, 1527–70, younger brother of the following, Knight of the Fleece and Stadtholder of Tournai 1559, executed in Spain 75, 90, 101

Montmorency, Philippe de —, Count of Hoorne, 1518–68, Knight of the Fleece, Admiral-General, executed at Brussels 75, 76, 78, 100, 101, 103, 106

Mor, Antonie — (Antonio Moro), 1512–77, of Utrecht, painter 263

Moucheron, Balthazar de —, 1552–1609, of Antwerp (of French origin), merchant at Antwerp and in Zealand 238

Muis, Father —   129

N

Nassau, John Count of —, 1535–1606, brother of William the Silent, Stadtholder of Gelderland 1578–80 118, 165–171, 176, 177, 182, 191, 197

Nassau, Louis Count of —, 1538–74, brother of William the Silent, killed at Mook 85, 86, 92, 104–107, 112, 114–117, 135

Nassau, Maurice Count of —, 1567–1625, second son of William the Silent, Stadtholder of Holland and Zealand 1585, of Utrecht, Overysel, and Gelderland 1590, called Prince of Orange, although he inherited the principality only on the death of his elder brother in 1618   194, 208, 213–216, 219–222, 224–226, 231, 233, 236, 238, 243–245, 248, 249, 251, 252, 254, 275, 286, 287

Nassau, William Count of —, known as the Silent, 1533–84, inherited principality of Orange and Netherlands estates and position 1544, Councillor of State and Knight of the Fleece 1555, Stadtholder of Holland, Zealand, and Utrecht 1559, deposed by the King 1567, restored by the States of Holland and Zealand 1572, of Utrecht 1577, Ruward of Brabant 1577, assassinated at Delft 60, 75–78, 85–87, 89, 90, 92, 94–102, 104–135, 137, 139–141, 143, 146–167, 169, 171–173, 176–178, 181–185, 189–195, 197–200, 204, 205, 218, 246, 261, 267, 275

Nassau, William Louis Count of —, 1560–1620, eldest son of John (see above), Stadtholder of Friesland 1584, of Groningen and Drente 1594   177, 213, 215, 216, 219, 222, 228, 229, 244, 282

Neyen, Father Jan —, 1560–1612, of Antwerp, Franciscan, employed in the negotiations for the Truce 1607–9   250

Nieuwenaer, Adolf Count of N. and Meurs (Nyenar or Neuenahr, and Mörs), died 1589, Stadtholder of Utrecht, Overysel, and Gelderland for the States-General   197, 210, 216

Noircarmes, Philippe de St. Alde-gonde, Lord of —, died 1574, Captain-General and Great Bailiff of Hainaut, Stadtholder of Holland, Zealand, and Utrecht to take the place of Bossu during the latter's captivity, Knight of the Fleece 97, 98, 103, 109

Noort, Adam van —, 1562–1641, painter at Antwerp 277

Noot, Jonkheer Jan van der —, 1538–95, of Antwerp, poet 265, 268, 269

O

Oldenbarnevelt, Johan van —, 1547–1619, of Amersfoort, pensionary of Rotterdam, Advocate of the States of Holland 1586 198, 212, 213, 215–217, 219, 224, 237, 243, 245, 246, 251–254

Ortelius—Abraham Ortels, 1527–1598, of Antwerp, geographer 270, 271, 282

Ovid 267

P

Parma, Alexander Farnese Duke of —, 1555–92, son of Margaret of P., Governor of the Netherlands 1578–92 85, 169, 172, 173, 175–178, 181, 183, 188, 189, 191, 192, 194, 196–203, 208, 211, 217–223, 261, 276, 277, 290, 292

Patinir (or Patenier), Joachim —, about 1475–1524, of Dinant, painter at Antwerp 65

Petrarch 267, 269

Philip the Good, Duke of Burgundy, ruled 1421–67 29, 31, 69

Philip the Fair, ruled 1493–1506 34, 76

Philip II, ruled 1555–98 23, 38, 59, 60, from 69 on, passim

Philip III, ruled 1598–1621 248–250

Pieterszoon, Aert —, son of Pieter Aertszoon, 1550–1612, of Amsterdam, painter 279

Plancius, Petrus —, 1552–1622, of Bailleul in French Flanders, Reformed minister at Amsterdam, geographer 236

Plantin, Christophe —, 1524–1597, Frenchman, printer and publisher at Antwerp and Leyden 270, 271, 273, 288

Pourbus, Frans —, 1545–81, of Brugge, painter at Antwerp 263

Prouninck, Jonkheer Gerard —, died 1610, of Den Bosch, exiled from that town 1579, burgomaster of Utrecht 1586–88 210, 211, 215, 217

R

Raphelengius —, professor of Hebrew at Leyden in 1586 288

Rassenghien, Maximilien Vilain, Lord of —, Stadtholder of Walloon Flanders 1567 97

Regius—Jacob de Koninck, 1545–1601, of Courtrai, Reformed minister in London, 1578–84 at Ghent 162

Reingout, Jacob —, of Brugge 211

Rennenberg, see Lalaing

Requesens, Don Luis de —, died 1576, Governor of the Netherlands 1573–76 136, 140–142, 144, 153

Reyd, Everhard van —, 1550–1602, of Deventer, councillor to William Louis, historian 282

Richardot, Jean —, 1540–1609, of Franche-Comté, President of the Privy Council at Brussels 1597 240, 247, 250

Rio, del —, Spaniard, member of Alva's Blood Council 102

Ripperda, Jonkheer Wigbold van —, executed 1573, of Winsum, Groningen, Beggar governor of Haarlem 132, 133

Robles, Gaspard de —, about 1530–85, of Spanish origin, military commander, Stadtholder of Friesland 1573–77   107

Roda, de —, Spaniard, member of the Council of State 1576   145–147, 150

Roels, pensionary of Leuven 1576   146

Roeulx, du, see Croy

Ronsard, Pierre de —, 1524–85, French poet   269

Rubens, Pieter Paulus —, 1577–1640, of Antwerp, painter   276

Rudolph, Emperor 1576–1612   223

Ruusbroec, Johannes van —, 1294–1381, Brabander, mystic   28, 51

Ruychaver, Sea Beggar   134

Rijcke, Roeland de —, pensionary of Leuven 1567   103

Ryhove, François van der Kethulle, Lord of —, 1531–85, Great Bailiff of Ghent   157, 158, 161, 164, 165

S

Saravia, Adrien —, 1530–1612, of Artois, professor of theology at Leyden 1581–87   214

Savery, Roeland —, of Courtrai, painter at Utrecht   279

Scaliger, Frenchman, Latinist, professor at Leyden 1593–1609   287

Schenck, Maarten —, Van Nydechem (or Nideggen), 1550–89, Upper Gelderland nobleman, commander under Parma   177

Scorel, Jan van —, 1495–1562, of Schoorl in North Holland, painter at Utrecht   49

Scriverius, Pieter Schrijver, 1576–1660, of Haarlem, historian   290, 291

Seneca   272

Serlio   48, 278

Simons, Menno —, 1492–1559, of Witmarsum, Friesland, Anabaptist teacher   58, 62

St. Gertrude, Jan van der Linden, Abbot of St. G. near Louvain   146, 175

Smet, de —, see Fabritius

Snellius, Rudolphus —, 1546–1613, of Oudewater, professor of mathematics at Leyden 1581   288

Snellius, Willebrord —, son of the last-named, 1580–1626, succeeded his father 1613   288

Sonoy, Jonkheer Diederik —, 1529–1597, of Calcar, Cleve, married to a Holland heiress, governor of the Northern Quarter of Holland for Orange 1572, deposed 1588   125, 129, 133, 134, 141, 166, 171, 177, 214, 215

Spieghel, Hendrik Laurenszoon —, 1549–1612, of Amsterdam, merchant and poet   172, 283–286, 291

Spinola, Ambrosio —, 1569–1630, of Genoa, Knight of the Fleece, Commander of the Spanish forces in the Netherlands 1605   248–250, 258

Spinola, Federigo —, 1571–1603, brother of the former   248

Stanley, Sir William —, 1548–1630, English professional soldier, governor of Deventer 1586   201, 213

Stevin, Simon —, 1548–1620, of Bruges, Quartermaster-General of the States army, mathematician   286

Straelen, Antonie van —, 1521–68, burgomaster of Antwerp, executed at Vilvoorde (not at Brussels as stated in the text)   92, 101, 103, 106

Straeten, Van der —, Brussels lawyer   155

Swieten, Van —, Holland nobleman   125, 127

T

Tacitus   272

Taffin, Jacques —, 1530–1582, of Tournai, councillor of the Prince of Orange   162

Teylingen, Floris van —, 1510–85, burgomaster of Alkmaar 134

Thil, Van —, burgomaster of Zutfen 1577 151, 152

Thin, Floris —, died 1590, pensionary of the town of Utrecht 1568, Advocate of the States of the province 1577 169, 211

Titian 280

Treslong, *see* Blois van Treslong

Tseraerts, Jerome —, Brabant nobleman, governor of Flushing for Orange 1572 122, 123

Tsestich, Anton —, of Louvain, philologist 273

Tympel, Olivier van den —, Lord of Corbeeck, 1540–1603, Brabander, governor of Brussels for the States-General, 1579–85 199

U

Usselinx, Willem —, 1567–1647, of Antwerp, business man and publicist 253, 254

Utenhove, Jan —, of Ghent, elder of the Netherlands church in London 80, 81

V

Vaenius, Otto —, Van Veen, 1556–1629, of Leyden, Parma's court painter 277

Vargas, de —, Spaniard, member of Alva's Blood Council 102

Vasari 281

Veer, Gerrit de —, sailor and author 281

Verdugo, Spanish commander 181, 188

Vergil 267, 269

Verhaecht, Tobias —, painter at Antwerp 277

Veronese, Paolo —, 280

Viglius ab Aytta Svichemius (Wigle van Aytta van Swichem), 1507–77, of Wirdum near Leeuwarden,

Viglius—(*continued*)
Friesland, jurist, President of the Council of Justice 1549, Chancellor of the Order of the Fleece 70, 75, 78, 101–103, 146

Villers or Villiers, Pierre Loiseleur de —, 1530–90, of Lille, court preacher to the Prince of Orange 1575 162

Vinckeboons, David —, 1576–1629, of Mechlin, painter at Amsterdam 280

Visscher, Roemer —, 1547–1620, of Amsterdam, merchant and poet 285

Vitruvius 48, 264

Vondel, Joost van den —, 1587–1676, of Antwerp, poet at Amsterdam 286

Vorroux, pensionary of the States of Namur 103

Vosmeer, Sasbout —, 1548–1614, of Delft, Apostolic Vicar in the Northern Netherlands 1592, Archbishop *in partibus infidelium* 1602, exiled from the Republic in the same year and since resident at Cologne 227, 228

Vrancken (or Vranck), François —, 1555–1617, pensionary of Gouda 195, 197, 213

Vriendt, Cornelis de —, *see* Floris

Vries, Hans Vredeman de —, of Friesland, sculptor and designer 264, 278

Vries, Paul Vredeman de —, born at Antwerp, artist and designer at Amsterdam 278

Vulcanius, Bonaventura —, professor of Greek at Leyden 288

W

Wasteel, Pieter —, pensionary of Mechlin 103

Werff, Pieter Adriaenszoon van der —, 1529–1603, one of the burgomasters of Leyden during the siege 137

Werve, Jan van de —, of Antwerp, nobleman, lawyer, and writer   47, 273, 283

Wesembeke, Jacob van —, 1524–74, pensionary of Antwerp 1556–67, councillor to the Prince of Orange 1570   92, 111, 112

Wilkes, Sir Thomas —, 1545–98, Englishman, member of the Netherlands Council of State 1586–87   213

William the Silent, *see* Nassau

William Louis, *see* Nassau

Y

Yorke, Rowland —, died 1588, English professional soldier, in charge of the entrenchment opposite Zutfen 1586   201, 213

Printed in Great Britain
by Lowe & Brydone (Printers) Ltd.
London, N.W.10